THE RELUCTANT TUSCAN

THE RELUCTANT TUSCAN

by Phil Doran

Published in Great Britain in 2005 by
Virgin Books
Thames Wharf Studios
Rainville Road
London W6 9HA

First published by Gotham Books,
a division of the Penguin Group (USA) Inc.
375 Hudson Street, New York, New York 10014, USA
First printing April 2005

ISBN 0 7535 1015 4

Typeset by Phoenix Photosetting, Chatham, Kent
Printed and bound by Clays Ltd, Bungay, Suffolk

CONTENTS

To Betty, who gave me
the greatest gift of all

ACKNOWLEDGMENTS

My heartfelt thanks to Lauren Marino, Hilary Terrell, Betsy Amster and Barbara DeMarco-Barrett for editing, facilitating, agenting and mentoring this book.

Grazie mille.

1. IL PICCOLO RUSTICO

I had a machete in my hand and I was thinking about using it on Henry David Thoreau. You know, that guy they made you read in school who popularised the notion that we should find solace in nature. Maybe I was doing this all wrong, but I had been hacking my way through nature all morning and all I had to show for it were blisters, sweat and a shooting pain up my arm. I didn't think I was having a heart attack, but if I were, it would have been more amusing than dealing with a hill covered in underbrush so thick it made this little corner of Tuscany look like a Brazilian rain forest.

Of course the land was only part of the problem, because at the top of this hill sat a 300-year-old stone farmhouse we had just bought. Perhaps house was too grand a word to describe this crumbling heap of rubble. In fact, the dwelling was so insignificant, it didn't even have an address. Folks around here simply jerked their thumbs in its direction and referred to it as *il piccolo rustico*. An apt description, because it was certainly rustic and definitely small. Just the perfect size for its current occupants, the scorpions and the spiders.

I gathered up my tools and began the long trudge uphill. When I had started, the morning sun was slanting low through the olive trees, casting gnarled shadows across the hill. But as the day grew warm, a low, silvery-white haze descended over the countryside. The Tuscans call this *il sfumato*, which comes from the Italian word for smoke. And as my wife, Nancy, pointed out to me at the Uffizi Gallery, artists as far back as the Renaissance have been suffusing their canvases with its pearly glow.

I gazed out, realising how integral *il sfumato* had become to my very perception of Tuscany. It made me feel as if I was looking at life through a fine linen bandage that blurred the edges, softened the colours, and cloaked the undercurrents of intrigue that threatened to engulf us.

My feet crunched on a floor of pyracantha berries and I stooped to pick a weed. I stuck it between my teeth in a jaunty Huck Finn pose that greatly belied how I felt. We had invested most of our savings in this house, but in our attempts to make it livable we had managed to alienate our neighbours, infuriate the local government and generally outrage the normally serene citizens of this fair land.

So much fuss over such a crummy little house. Stone walls splitting apart where ancient mortar had decayed into dust. Wood beams so riddled with wormholes, they looked like they had been peppered with birdshot. A wide crack running up one of the exterior walls had caused part of the roof to cave in and stove over. There was no electricity, water or gas, and only the vaguest rumour of a septic tank buried somewhere. Even if everything ran smoothly, we could finance a lunar probe for what it was going to cost to restore this place.

I stopped to breathe in a dizzying mixture of rotting humus and wild jasmine and thought about the chain of events that had brought me here, and how this run-down, neglected little house in Tuscany had become a metaphor for my life. Call it a late-life crisis, but in my mid-fifties I had turned my back on my career and on a way of life that had sustained me for the previous three decades. In the process of forging a life here, I struggled to rediscover myself, my wife and our life together.

And like many improbable adventures, it all began with a phone call.

'Guess what?'

'You're pregnant.'

'I bought a house,' Nancy said.

'You what?' I gripped the receiver in astonishment. 'Where?'

'Here. In Italy.'

I rolled my eyes and whimpered.

'I think we could really be happy here.'

'I'm happy here,' I said. 'And how could you buy a house without me even seeing it?'

'I had to move fast. But you'll see it now. How soon can you get here?'

'I'm going to fly all the way from L.A. just because –'

'Yeah, come on, get over here.'

'I'm still working on this goddamn script,' I mumbled as I peeled the foil off a roll of Tums with my teeth. 'And then pilot season starts in a couple of –'

'*Dai!*' she said, which is how Italians say, 'Come on.' She'd been working there so long, she had started to think in their language. 'Just come take a look. If you don't like it we can always.' She ended her sentence there.

'Always what?'

'Forget it, you're going to love it.'

She launched into all the reasons why I was going to love it, and my eyes glazed over. I found myself watching the sun drop behind the Santa Monica Mountains. I've always wondered about people who could stare endlessly at sunsets and roaring fireplaces. For me, they were pointless because you knew that both were going to end in cold and darkness.

'The house is over three hundred years old!' she said, as if that were a good thing. 'It sits on a hillful of olive trees with a magnificent view of the village of Cambione.'

'And that's something I want to look at?'

'The view is to die.'

'What about the house? Is that to die too?'

'I won't lie, it needs a little work.'

'What a surprise.'

'But the construction's pretty basic. Except for putting in the road.'

'You bought a house on a hill that doesn't have a road?'

'That's why we got it so cheap,' she said triumphantly.

'Let me see if I got this,' I said. 'In the long history of Tuscany, which has been occupied by the Etruscans, the Greeks, the Romans, the Visigoths, the French, the Spanish, the Austrians, the Nazis, and now the baby boomers, no one has ever thought to run a road up to this house?'

'We'll put one in.'

'We are talking about Italy, aren't we?'

'Yeah,' she said defensively.

'Do you see where I'm going with this?'

'Relax, honey. There's always a way.'

The sun had dropped behind the mountains and I sat in darkness.

2. CAMBIONE

Two weeks later I finished the script I'd been working on and sent it to my agent. Rather than stay in L.A. and brood about it and wait for his phone call, I boarded a plane for Italy to brood about a house I didn't want.

Dai, Nancy, what are you doing to us? Aren't we being crushed enough under this jackboot of a house in Brentwood? And now that I'm struggling to find work, why do we need this added pressure? God, this flight is long.

I felt the plane shudder and looked out the window. We were being buffeted by turbulence over the Alps, but while everyone else saw snowcapped peaks and cottony cumulus, I could only think of the clouds of plaster dust that seemed to follow Nancy wherever she went. My wife is a chronic nest builder with a strange compulsion to find places nobody wants and devote all her energy to making them beautiful. When she sees a house she wants to redo, she gets a look on her face like a fifteen-year-old boy on a topless beach.

When Nancy and I first started going out twenty years ago, she was working at Universal Studios as a set designer and moonlighting as an interior designer. This meant that she never met a room she didn't think she could improve. In fact, the night she walked into that party, I thought she was checking me out, while she claims she was thinking about opening up an interior wall and bullnosing all the wainscotting.

Before she turned up, it was a pretty boring party full of artsy types dressed in black arguing about things like The Future of Bio-morphic Abstractionism. I was in the kitchen watching the guacamole turn brown when I looked up and saw her in the doorway. She was slim and graceful and had a way of standing with one hip cocked like a dancer. She had thick blonde hair and

5

playful dark eyes that were almond shaped and made her look slightly Mediterranean. She was pretty and she had such a great smile, I was sure she was an actress, which was not necessarily a good thing because of the policy I had about not dating actresses or any other female impersonators. But when she came over with a corn chip in need of guacamole, we chatted and she told me about her work and how she loved the designing part but hated the bullshit. I told her I felt the same way about writing for TV, which is why I aspired to direct my own features. She had an ambition of her own, to work in Italy as a marble sculptor, which is what she had studied in art school. Little did I realise that night that she would live out her dream, while I was still waiting for mine.

The plane banked and the sun blazed through my window. I cupped a hand over my eyes and squinted out at a sky that was suddenly clear enough to see all the way up to the stratosphere. Below me lay the city of Pisa, all ochre walls and terra-cotta roofs fanning out like a mantilla around the cathedral in the Piazza del Duomo. The locals called this 'the Square of Miracles', and there is no greater miracle in all of Italy than Pisa's own symbol, the leaning tower. The plane began its descent into Galileo Airport, and I admired how this Romanesque torre, constructed with all the confidence of the High Middle Ages, leaned thirteen and half feet off the perpendicular, making it look both majestic and improbable at the same time.

Our plane landed and taxied to a stop. We then had the pleasure of sitting on the hot tarmac for 45 minutes while the Alitalia ground crew figured out how to open our door. This gave me ample time to recall how this whole chapter of our lives had begun.

About fifteen years earlier, I had been working on a TV show so beset with problems that between the network, the ratings and the star, we writers never went home. This plunged every writer's life into a shambles. But instead of screaming and calling a divorce lawyer like the other spouses, Nancy told me that she was going to Italy to carve marble. So she came to this part of Tuscany and bought a block of the white statuario that's mined from the nearby Carrara Mountains. With the help of the local *artigiani*, some of whose ancestors had been working the stone since the days of Michelangelo, she sculpted a statue that eventually wound up being shown in a museum in Florence.

This arrangement worked out well and it became a steady fixture of our lives. Nancy and I would figure out the busiest time of my production schedule and she'd plan her annual trip. Over the years, as she morphed into an Italian, she became gripped by the desire to find us a charming little stone farmhouse where we could one day retire.

The airplane door finally popped open, and my fellow passengers and I filed out. I claimed my suitcase and presented myself at passport control. When the official asked me the purpose of my visit, I had to fight the urge to tell him that I had come here to murder my wife. I cleared customs and wheeled my suitcase through the gate. Nancy rushed into my arms, and we kissed in the middle of the airport like people did back in the fifties in those movies with William Holden and Audrey Hepburn.

She guided me out to where she had parked in a taxi zone. As I stuffed my suitcase in the trunk, she asked me how I was doing. I told her I was fine because I didn't want to talk about how I was living on antacids, suffering anxiety attacks and migraines, and popping Trazadone when I couldn't sleep, which was often.

But she knew. She opened her arms and hugged me in a way that always calms me when I'm going through life like my hair's on fire. We held each other for a long time, prompting ill-tempered shouts from the taxi driver waiting for us to leave. Nancy broke off our embrace to holler back at him. I feared that the whole thing would spiral into an opera buffa as can only be performed by the Italians. Or at least one Italian and one Italian-speaking girl from Santa Monica.

But as we were getting into the car, I noticed that the taxi driver had stopped yelling and was now blowing kisses at Nancy and muttering, '*che bella*', his face contorted in pain as if her beauty had stung his eyes like smoke.

'No wonder you like it here,' I said as she started the car.

'I like it here because they know how to treat an artist.' She showed me a cheque.

'Oh, you finished. How'd it come out?'

'Vulgar bordering on the pornographic,' she said.

'I'm sure it's beautiful.'

'It would have been if he had let me sculpt her the way I wanted. But while I'm carving, he's screaming, "Make the tits bigger, make her waist smaller." I finally said to him, "Hey, you don't want a statue, you want a copy of Penthouse."'

We pulled out of the airport, and Nancy used her horn and her lungs to bully us through an onslaught of traffic that seemed to be moving in absolutely no relationship to traffic signals or stop signs.

'Is this the way to the hotel?'

'We're all meeting up at the house first.' Nancy whipped onto the Autostrada, executing a suicide squeeze into a lane of cars moving at a Grand Prix clip.

'Who's we all?' I said. Actually, I had to yell it over the sonic boom of the red Ferrari that roared past us, reminding me that I was now in Italy, where everybody has to drive at twice the speed of sound so they can get to a café and sit for three hours.

'We're meeting with Vincenzo, the *ingegnere*, Maurizio, the *geologo*, and Umberto, our *muratore* . . . that's stonemason to you, gringo.'

I clucked, calculating the cost of such an entourage.

'Actually, it's not going to be that bad. I paid most of their fees when the dollar was strong against the euro.'

'And what happens now that the dollar's weak?'

'*Boh*,' she said, which isn't exactly a word but more of a sound a Tuscan makes when he wants to say, 'Who the hell knows? Stop bothering me!'

Cutting off an Alfa full of fat people who responded with rude hand gestures, we exited the Autostrada and merged onto a narrow road choked with Fiats and Lancias creeping behind sputtering tractors and overloaded produce trucks. Occasionally an impatient driver drifted over the nonexistent yellow line to pass, only to be pushed back into his place, muttering and cursing, by the unbroken line of oncoming vehicles. Only the two-wheelers made progress, from the souped-up motorcycle with its space-suited driver to the Vespa carrying two middle-aged women in housecoats and aprons, chatting and laughing.

We inched past groves of fruit trees and sprouting fields of new spring wheat, eventually reaching a sign that welcomed us to the village of Cambione in Collina. Even though I'd been to this country before, here's how I had pictured an Italian village: a desolate piazza, sun-baked to a ghostly white and dominated by a crumbling but implacable cathedral. Mandolin music played in the background as unemployed men in dark suits smoked unfiltered cigarettes while their wives scrubbed laundry in the fountain with a soap stick.

But my first approach into Cambione changed all that, as farmland surrendered to a loose alignment of houses, gas stations, goat pens, factories, and produce markets jammed next to each other with absolutely no sense of congruity. There seemed to be no such thing as a purely residential street, or a commercial one for that matter. When you did find a stretch of houses, each was a different height and seemingly angled in its own peculiar direction, as centuries-old palazzi sat next door to squat, shoe-box-shaped dwellings that looked as though they had just been built for the Festival di Cement.

There was, indeed, a main piazza with a church, a faded war memorial, and a fountain. But far from being desolate, it reverberated with the chaos of people shouting, whistling, swearing and singing. Clumps of teenagers joked and jostled each other as mothers called out to their children from second-storey windows. Groups of men in shirtsleeves, all talking at once, debated the key issues of the day at such volume that the veins in their necks stuck out.

We circled the piazza so Nancy could point out the fish market where we would buy the freshest *branzino* and the kiosk where she had already talked to the woman about saving me the *Herald Tribune* each day. I thanked her, then winced as she whipped down a side street that, because there was no sidewalk, was essentially a blind corner.

Darting through a warren of one-way backstreets and alleys so narrow that I found myself gasping, we roared past an abandoned stone quarry and turned onto a freshly paved asphalt road that led us uphill.

'Hey, I thought you said there was no road.'

'Shhh,' she cackled.

'Lucy, what have you done?' I said in an exasperated Cuban accent.

'I told you there's always a way.' Nancy slammed on the brakes to avoid hitting an ancient Italian woman dressed in black down to her knuckles except for the large white handkerchief on her head.

'That's our neighbour, Annamaria,' Nancy said. 'She told me all about the history of our house.' Then, by way of introducing me, Nancy called out, '*Signora, voglio presentare il mio marito.*'

The old woman poked a leathery face into my window.

'*Buon giorno, signora. Piacere,*' I said, using up ten per cent of my Italian vocabulary.

'She told me that no one's lived in there for years,' Nancy said. 'The farmers used it to store equipment and keep their goats inside during the winter. But get this . . . during the war people called it the Bunker because the Germans set up a machine gun right in our kitchen!'

'Hmm.' I nodded, wondering how many Cambionians one could pick off from up here.

'She was just a little girl then, but she remembers,' Nancy said.

Annamaria's face contorted into a dark scowl and she flicked her thumbnail against her front tooth, a gesture, no doubt, she used with regularity on every passing busload of German tourists.

We got out of the car and walked the old lady to where her goat was grazing in some tall weeds. Between expressions of '*Arrivederla*' and '*Troppo gentile*' she told us that when we were ready to move in, she'd come over with bread and salt. Then, wetting the side of her thumb and making a cross on her forehead, she also promised to bring us the other necessity of life, a statue of Maria Santissima.

Walking uphill, we began to hear an overture for cement mixer and earthmover accompanying a powerful baritone oratorio. The voice belonged to Umberto, the *muratore*, a stout, ruggedly built man, shirtless in shorts, construction boots, and a battered straw cowboy hat – which made him look like a slightly paunchy member of The Village People.

I soon learned that Umberto Baccarelli had dedicated his life to single-handedly disproving the cliché that the average Italian labourer has the work ethic of a third-generation welfare recipient. He whirled around the construction site like a dervish on amphetamines, screaming at anybody who dared slacken his breakneck pace. As a result, the rebuilding of our retaining walls was being done with such fanatical urgency that if the Italians had behaved this way during World War II, Mussolini would have been sitting in the White House.

Umberto stopped flagellating his crew to explain in fractured English that Vincenzo, the engineer, was not coming because, frankly, he wasn't very good in the mornings, and that Maurizio, the geologist, had just not shown up, lacking even the decency to come up with a shoddy excuse like Vincenzo's. He took a last drag off his cigarette, tossed it over his shoulder, and volleyed the butt into a pile of gravel. Then while Umberto and Nancy launched into a lengthy conversation about some aspect of construction that I wouldn't have been able to follow even if it were in English, I wandered off to take a close-up look at my new house.

It was a small, two-storey affair that had fallen into such disrepair, it was closer to a ruin than a dwelling. Wood planks lay rotting in the uncut grass, and there was so much debris scattered around, it looked as if the remains of a shipwreck had washed ashore. I was shaking my head at this folly, when I found myself walking under a canopy made of cut branches that abutted the side of the house. Glancing up at the tangle of vines snaking around the trellis, I spotted a glorious cluster of cobalt-blue grapes as perfect as wax fruit and succulent enough to adorn the brow of Bacchus. I picked one and popped it in my mouth. The sweetness was so pure it staggered me. For a long time afterwards I could taste the sun on my tongue.

Oh, no. I had only been here a few hours, and Tuscany was already beginning to work its magic. Its insidious charm and inexhaustible natural beauty were seducing me, and if I wasn't careful, I was going to find myself feeling happy for absolutely no reason.

I shook aside such subversive thoughts and pushed open the splintery wooden door. I entered and was immediately struck by the coolness and quiet inside the half-metre-thick walls. The house was small, built to the measure of a man – essentially just a kitchen on the ground floor connected by a rickety ladder to a bedroom above.

As I batted away the cobwebs, my eyes were drawn to the hearth, which was nothing more than a knee-high platform for firewood. Over this, somebody had fashioned a mortared hood so misaligned, it had allowed a black finger of soot to miss the flue and meander up the wall, where it found refuge in the methodical blackening of the centre beam. I studied the thick accretion of inky residue and pondered the dramas that had played out inside these four walls.

The births, the deaths, the quarrels, the passions. And that was just the goats.

As for the human chronicle, I could not even fathom the complexities and the vagaries of a dozen generations playing out their tragedies and comedies upon this tiny stage. Of people living continuously inside a structure built when America was a colony. A house that had stood in silent witness to every famine, flood and forest fire to be hurled at it over the past three hundred years, its very survival a living testament to the sturdiness of its construction and the indestructibility of its *macigno* stone walls, a quartz-bearing limestone hard enough that craftsmen in the Middle Ages had used it for grindstones.

The door swung open and Nancy entered.

'I'm so pissed,' she said, too angry to stop walking even though she was halfway inside the room. 'You're not going to believe this.'

'The Germans are back with their machine gun?'

'Umberto's quitting.'

'Didn't he just start?'

'He got offered another job.'

'And it didn't occur to him to finish ours first?'

'He got offered another job so he couldn't finish ours.'

'Who would do such a thing?'

'Who? The Pingatores, that's who.'

'Wait, aren't those the people you bought this from?'

'*Bastardi!*'

'I'm sorry to be making a wrinkle in the fabric of your alternate universe, but I'm not following this.'

'Don't you get it? They want their house back.'

'Why did they sell it to us in the first place?'

'Because nobody else would buy it, because it didn't have a road.'

'Speaking of that, where did that road –?'

The door flew open with a bang, and a wild-looking woman with flyaway hair and the deranged look of a spree killer stood in our doorway.

'*Puttana*!!' she screamed, her eyes glaring a *malocchio* so fierce, it would calcify flesh. Nancy rose to protest, which only prompted the old woman to hurl curses and threats at us, building to a shriek of '*Porca miseria!*' and all punctuated with the slamming of the door.

'What was that?

'Vesuvia Pingatore.'

'Who?'

'Mario Pingatore's sister. She seems to think that whoever put in that road tore down some of her trees and generally desecrated the sacred grounds of her childhood.'

'Great, now we have a neighbour who hates us.'

'Actually, it's a little worse than that. See, the road was put in *abusivo*, which means illegally, which is done all the time and is perfectly fine as long as nobody kicks up a fuss.'

'Well, that looked like some big-time fuss-kicking to me.'

'Yeah, she just went to the Comune di Cambione and issued a *denuncia* against us.'

'That sounds serious. Are we in trouble?'

'*Boh*.'

3. STRANIERI IN PARADISE

It was getting dark, and since our new house had no heat, electricity or bathroom facilities other than an oleander bush, we drove down the hill and parked in Cambione's Piazza Maggiore. The restaurants had not yet opened for dinner, but we were just in time for the *passeggiata*. A common custom in most Mediterranean societies, it's the time of day when the citizens of the town parade up and down the main walking street. Young people are looking for romance, the middle-aged are trading gossip, and the elderly are just making sure they're all still alive for another day.

In the midst of such cordiality, I felt Nancy's shoulders tighten under my arm. The cause of her tension was the approach of Mario Pingatore. He was a small man with the underslung jaw of a Hapsburg, which he thrust forwards in the manner of one more at home in the sixteenth century than in the twenty-first. He was dressed in military-cut hunting tweeds with tall riding boots. He walked with his hands clasped behind his back as he sucked on a briar pipe that curled down his chin.

'What the hell is your sister doing?' Nancy said, without so much as a greeting.

'Bit of a sticky wicket, eh, what?' Mario prided himself on his English, which he seemed to have learned from watching British movies from the 1930s.

'Can't you talk to her?' Nancy cried.

'Afraid the old girl's got her mind made up,' Pingatore harrumphed as he banged the bowl of his pipe on his boot heel. 'What can I say, my dear, but stiff upper lip.'

Every time he spoke I expected Ronald Colman to walk in wearing an ascot.

'I had a deal with you,' Nancy pleaded.

'But you didn't have one with her, and she's *molto* flummoxed over this cock-up.'

Nancy was so *molto* flummoxed over this cock-up, words failed.

'By Jove, look at the time.' Mario glanced at his pocket watch. 'Ta.'

He sauntered off with a backhanded wave as Nancy turned her wrath on me.

'Why didn't you say something?'

'What was I supposed to say? "Cheerio, old swot, which way to the fox hunt?"'

The piazza was now empty. As if on signal everyone had retreated behind their massive, carved doors for elaborate multicoursed dinners. Having no massive carved doors to retreat behind, we supped at a small family-run *trattoria* on the square, where we ordered a traditional Tuscan dish, *pici a braciole*. This is a hand-rolled pasta about the thickness of a thin french fry, coated in olive oil and seasoned bread crumbs. When Nancy described it to me, it sounded dry and tasteless, but this simple peasant dish had a creamy, nutty texture that far transcended its humble ingredients.

My serving was enormous and, try as I might, I just couldn't finish. I signalled our waitress for a container, but she was preoccupied trying to balance several steaming bowls of pasta on her arm as her five-year-old son clutched her knees and urgently proclaimed, '*Mamma, ho bisogno di un bacio!*' which Nancy translated to mean, 'Mama, I need a kiss!'

'I don't understand why they don't have doggie bags,' I said as I followed Nancy into our hotel room.

'Italians don't believe in leftovers.' She sat on the bed and massaged her toes through her open sandals. 'Food should be fresh.'

I wheeled my suitcase across a wooden floor that creaked like the deck of an old sailing ship. 'So, what? Their dogs just starve to death?'

'Does it look like anybody's starving to death around here?'

I opened a hand-carved wardrobe to the whiff of mothballs and the jangling of wire coat hangers. I slid Nancy's clothes aside to make room for mine.

'I'm just saying I don't know why anybody would want to live in a country that doesn't have doggie bags.'

'That's right, I studied the entire globe to find the only place on earth where my husband could have an anxiety attack because for once in his life he left some food on his plate.'

I winced at the mention of anxiety attacks. Even though she'd said it as a joke, I flashed on my last meeting with a 26-year-old development executive at the WB network. I was right in the middle of my pitch, when the glands in the side of my neck grew warm and my left eye started to twitch.

I opened my suitcase and started to unpack. Outside a treeful of jays screamed at the noisy children playing stoop tag in the piazza even though it was nearly midnight.

'Lest you think I'm a complete philistine,' I said, 'I really do like Italy.'

'But you don't want to live here.' She pulled her dress off over her head and slipped into a T-shirt.

'It's just that it's so rural,' I said, following her into the bathroom. 'And you know how nature makes me nervous.'

She stood at the sink washing her face, spitting water out with each word. 'I think if you just gave it a chance . . .'

'Nancy, it's a mess. The house is a mess, the deal's a mess. I don't understand how you got us into this.'

'Well . . . it's kind of the way things are done around here,' she said with a helpless little shrug.

'Oh, come on. Any place else on earth, from a Turkish bazaar to a Filipino fish market, you see something you want, you agree on a price, end of story. What is it about Italy that we have to play all these games?'

She finished patting her face dry, heaved a loose-shouldered sigh, and began to pour out the details of how we had come to be enmeshed in this intractable web of Italianate perfidy. She began by reminding me how we had often discussed finding a little house here where we could one day retire. Apparently, I had forgotten all about it but she hadn't, having spent months looking before she stumbled upon *il piccolo rustico*. And the first time she saw it, she knew it was the place for us to spend our Golden Years, a term I incidentally hate because I consider my Golden Years the ages sixteen though seventeen and a half when I spent most of my time making out with Carol Ann Stivic in the backseat of my father's Buick.

At any rate, Nancy entered into negotiations with the owners, the Pingatore family, who owned all the property surrounding the house in question, giving them home field advantage. The family was a large multigenerational sprawl of relatives, in-laws, and assorted kith and kin scattered all over this area, but whose interests in this house were essentially represented by brother Mario, who did all the negotiating in his faux British accent, and sister Vesuvia, last seen hurling curses of eternal suffering and damnation upon all our deceased relatives and yet-unborn children.

The Pingatores were a troublesome brood. The fact that the house was for sale was the result of years of painful bickering over which one of them was actually going to own it. Unable to come up with a solution, Nonno (Grandpa) Pingatore had made a decision. The house would be sold and the entire family would split the profits.

Nancy caught wind of this, and even before the *vendesi* sign went up, she made an offer. Mario made a counteroffer that Nancy laughed at as being ridiculous for a house that had no road. After much bargaining and half a bottle of Chianti, all principals agreed that perhaps the price was fair, if the house had a road. A few days later a road magically appeared, and Nancy bought it. To anyone who asked, both parties insisted that it was the other side that had put it in.

The reason for such subterfuge was the impossibility of making any home improvements in a region where nearly every property of value had been classified either *agricola* or *storico*. These designations were zealously defended by the pro-Green party Comune, whose principles, by the way, I wholeheartedly support, unless, of course, they infringe upon my constitutional rights to air conditioning and one hundred and twenty-five channels of cable TV.

But this 'he said/she said' defence promptly crumbled when Vesuvia Pingatore denounced us and caused the Comune di Cambione to rise up in wrathful indignation.

'So what happens next?' I said, sliding into bed with her.

She thought a moment, puffing out her cheeks in concentration. 'Well, we can't do any work on the house while the *denuncia* is pending. And if the Comune upholds it, we'll have to pay a fine.'

'OK.'

'And they could possibly throw me in jail.'

'Oh, that's it! We're getting the hell –'

'We can't! If we leave, it'll look like we're guilty.'

'Which we . . .?'

'Aren't! I swear I did not put in that road.' Her face looked so innocent, it rivalled the Lorenzetti fresco of the Virgin in the vestibule of the local church.

We turned away from each other, lying as far apart as we could on that narrow bed. That night I dreamt of doors being axed open by a blood-crazed Vesuvia Pingatore, while Nancy had nightmares about the large Sicilian woman who wanted to become her jailhouse bone daddy.

The next morning we agreed that, at least for the moment, we needed to stay and demonstrate a show of innocence while we ascertained the depth of the *merda* we found ourselves in.

Nancy had finished her commission, which meant that the art dealer who had ordered it would no longer be paying for her hotel room. So on a bright but chilly morning we set off looking for a place to live. After visiting a couple of rental agents, we stopped at a sun-splashed *osteria*, where we took the nip out of the air with steaming bowls of *papa al pomodoro*, a thick-as-pudding soup of tomatoes, garlic, basil and yesterday's bread. The waiter drizzled a C of olive oil on the surface of my soup, and the combined aromas gave new meaning to the term comfort food. We washed down our *papa* with a lustrous Chianti from Montepulciano, and as good as the wine was, I think I almost preferred the little bottles of home-made apple juice they served us – juice that was almost thick enough to pass for apple sauce.

Lunch, which I have been known to inhale while pulling out of a Burger King drive-through lane, lasted two and half hours. My soul was at peace and my body serene, harbouring the perfect balance of espresso to perk me up and grappa to mellow me out. Needless to say, I had eaten everything put in front of me, eliminating any need for a doggie bag.

We dragged ourselves out of the restaurant, prompted by the yawning of the waiter, who clearly wanted his *pausa*, or afternoon nap. We followed the meanderings of a narrow creek until we came upon a quaint section of houses painted in deep shades of melon and tangerine. This little stretch of houses was so unselfconsciously charming, we felt as though we had wandered onto a movie set. We continued down the narrow cobbled street until we spotted a vacant stucco cottage painted the pastel pink of an Easter egg.

I was trying to peer inside when a wide, beefy guy with a red face and an overgrown crew cut appeared. This was Dino, who travelled everywhere with a mangy pack of dogs named Ninja, Luna, Torpedo, Cosimo, Scheherazade, Pipistrello, Puccini, and Tiberius. The dogs swarmed around him peeing, pooping, snarling and fornicating, while Dino, oblivious, went about his business.

'You own this house?' I asked, hoping he spoke English.

'You want maybe to buy?' Dino said, finally grabbing Cosimo by the scruff of the neck to stop him from tearing off Puccini's ear.

'Just renting.' I looked down to see Luna sniffing my leg.

'You English?'

'Americani,' Nancy said.

'I knew you were *stranieri*, but I figure you for English. They only rent.'

'We already bought.' Nancy pointed up the hill.

'Oh, you the lady with the road.' Dino stared at her like she was Ma Barker.

'Can we look inside?' Luna continued to sniff my leg, undisturbed that Torpedo had just mounted her.

'Yeah, yeah, no problem, is open.' Dino took some scraps of raw meat out of his pocket and tossed them on the ground. The dogs suddenly stopped their various activities and began fighting over it like, well, a pack of dogs.

'Only, I better call my cousin Spartaco to make sure he don't need it no more.' Dino pulled out his cellphone. The phone slipped out of his hand and clattered to the ground, only to be snatched up by Ninja, who ran off with it in his mouth. Dino set off in pursuit, hollering at the errant hound, but by now the dog was across the yard, digging a hole to bury his newfound treasure.

As this classic struggle between man and beast played out, Nancy and I wandered inside. The living room was as dark as a catacomb, owing to the Italian practice of keeping all the shutters tightly closed even on the sunniest of days. We found a lamp and turned it on. The bulb was as dim as a votive candle, and the darkness of the room easily swallowed up its feeble glow. I opened one of the shutters, and a slab of white sunlight illuminated an arrangement of dark, funereal furniture and a candelabra the Addams family would have loved.

Our eyes skittered around the room, finally resting on walls completely covered with pinups of naked women, alternating with images of Jesus Christ.

'Cousin Spartaco seems to be a rather conflicted chap,' I commented as we split apart and proceeded to explore.

After a few moments Nancy called out, 'What do you think?'

'Well, the kitchen's a muck hole, the bedroom reeks from mildew, and the bathroom –'

'Did you look back here? There's a pizza oven and a swimming pool!'

'We'll take it,' I said to Dino as he walked in, wiping dog spittle off his cellphone.

'You will love this house!' Dino said with an expansive wave. 'I was born here, you know. Mamma gave birth to me right here on this kitchen table.'

'How appetising,' I said.

Dino suddenly made a face and hastened to the window, where he closed the shutter I had just opened. 'Have to keep these always shut. Sunlight fades the furniture.'

'Well, we can't have that,' I said, feeling for the couch.

Nancy entered, blowing into her cupped hands. 'Kinda nippy in here, isn't it?'

'Not to worry, I put in this brand-a-new heating system. German, works perfect!'

Dino pointed to a control panel on the wall. With its imposing bank of lighted buttons, it would have looked more at home on the space shuttle than in a humble pink cottage in Tuscany.

'How do we turn it on?' Nancy asked.

'I don't know,' Dino said. 'But my son can work it.'

'Let's see if we can't figure it out.' I cocked my head to the side to study the array of lighted buttons.

'Honey,' Nancy said, as if she had caught me running with surgical scissors.

'Gimme a minute here.' I started pushing a series of buttons, at first methodically, and then at random. Lights on the control panel blinked and there was a faint electronic hum, but otherwise nothing happened. In fact, no combination of buttons, dials or gauges, no matter how I pushed, twisted or turned them, did anything even remotely connected with the manufacture or delivery of heat. But feeling I was on the right track, I kept pushing buttons now two and three at a time, until we heard a faint fizzle from down the basement and the one lamp that was burning went out.

'Ooops.'

'Damn circuit breaker,' Dino muttered as he steamed towards the door to the cellar. 'Of course, that's Italian.'

'How soon can your son get over here?' Nancy asked.

'Oooofff!' Dino replied, as he barked his shin on a coffin-shaped coffee table.

'We'd like to bring our stuff over this afternoon,' I said, 'if we can agree on a price.'

'I can't get ahold of Rudolfo till maybe Friday,' Dino said, rubbing his shin.

'Friday?' Nancy said through chattering teeth.

'He's up at his Buddhist retreat all week.'

'Tell you what,' I said. 'Throw in a cord of firewood and a couple of miner's helmets and we'll move right in.'

I was trying to lighten the moment, but Dino was not amused. He proceeded to share his bitter disappointment over a son who had turned away from the One True Church to become a Buddhist. The fact that Rudolfo was thirty-four years old, lived at home, and had no job or education didn't seem to bother him. But this Buddhist thing . . .

Dino broke down and wept, sobbing through his nose with big theatrical gasps like a clown in a Verdi opera. I was constantly unnerved by the penchant Italian men have for spontaneously bursting into tears. The last time I remember crying I was nine years old and Bud Thomas had just split my lip for calling his sister a skank. I didn't even know what a skank was. It was something I had heard on Mod Squad.

'Look, Dino,' Nancy said, as she rubbed his heaving shoulders, 'we need to check out of our hotel. How much do you want?'

'*Un milione tre,*' Dino said with sudden dry-eyed clarity, all thoughts of errant Buddhist sons forgotten.

I winced at the word million, but Nancy explained that many Italians still give you a price in lira. She then countered, saying that it was a little steep for a house that was cold and dark enough to grow mushrooms. We went back and forth, and after half a bottle of Chianti, we agreed on a price.

What seemed to cap the deal was Dino's unexpected offer to pay for all the phone charges. And considering how much long distance and Internet we used, that could be considerable. We shook hands, and I counted out cash in the darkness. Dino handed us the keys and left, banging into the table he was born on with a painful yet cheery 'Oooofff.'

But as were gloating over the deal, we discovered that the house had no phone, nor any outlets to plug one in.

'It'll be OK.' Nancy flashed her best Jiminy Cricket smile. 'We'll buy an Italian cellphone and use the Internet café in the piazza.'

'Yeah, it'll be fine,' I said, casting a wary eye at Scheherazade, who had suddenly appeared in our doorway with a dead bird in his mouth.

4. CASTAGNE

Whatever visions of sunny Italy you harbour, I humbly ask you to put them aside as I testify that in the days that followed, Nancy and I endured a bone-penetrating cold so relentless that no amount of wool socks, thermal blankets or space heaters could make a dent in it.

The house we rented from Dino was essentially an uninsulated stone box sitting on a concrete slab. Without central heating, the interior was a full fifteen degrees colder than it was outside. And even though it was the middle of May, it was plenty cold outside. I was uncomfortable but surviving, thanks to the ancestral layer of body fat gifted to me by my Ukrainian forebears. But Nancy was suffering. Growing up in southern California, her blood had turned to orange juice, and she was physically incapable of surviving cold weather unless she was on a ski trip.

The nights were the worst. I awoke once at three in the morning with leg cramps from knotting myself into a ball. I looked over to Nancy, who was lying on her back. She had completely covered herself in a dense layer of blankets. The only opening was a hole for her mouth, where puffs of vaporised breath were coming out making it look like I was sharing my bed with a steam engine.

I was hoping that she would grow disenchanted, and give up, and we could go back to L.A., sit in our hot tub, and defrost. So I rarely missed an opportunity to point out the difficulties of living in Italy, the insoluble problems with the Pingatores, and, of course, Dino's having suckered us into renting this igloo. The last I was careful to frame around my concern for her comfort, which would have scored me enough points to merit some serious lovemaking if it had only been warm enough to take off our clothes.

The morning after my leg cramps, Nancy and I were trying to eat breakfast with our mittens on when we heard two of Dino's dogs, Pipistrello and Tiberius, scratching at our door.

Nancy peered out the window. 'Dino's bringing us firewood.'

'Oh, good, we're rescued.'

'Be nice,' Nancy hissed at me as she scurried around the room, closing all the shutters we had opened. 'And don't say anything about the cold.'

'*Buon giorno, signore, signora*,' Dino called out. '*Permesso*.'

'*Salve*, Dino.' Nancy opened the door to Dino holding an armful of logs. 'Here, let me help you with that.'

'No, no, I got it.' Dino entered, followed by Scheherazade gifting us with another dead bird.

'Oh, Dino, how kind of you to bring us wood,' I said with such Old World graciousness, Nancy glared at me for being an asshole.

'Is no problem.' Dino tossed a couple of logs into the fireplace, which startled the dogs into a frenzy of barking. 'I come by yesterday but you no home.'

'If we had a phone, you could have called first,' I shouted over the barking.

'*Stai zitta!*' Dino screamed at his dogs, urging them to shut up. 'I *molto* sorry for the phone. I talk to Telecom Italia, *che idioti*! They promise they install in two days but then they go on strike.'

'And how are we able to tell when they're on strike?' I asked as I picked up the dead bird Scheherazade had brought us and tossed it out the door.

'The thing is,' Nancy said in her gentlest tone, 'my husband's concerned that I'm not very comfortable in the cold, and –'

'Cold? *È maggio. Primavera.* Even in winter nobody uses heat.'

'Look, Nancy's prone to bronchitis,' I said, 'and this kind of damp cold –'

'*Ai*, you should have seen how it was during the war. I was just a baby. Nine months old. We hid up in the hills with the partisans when the Germans attack! My grandmother wrap me in leaves because we had no blankets and she carry me down the mountain with the Germans shooting at us from one side and the *Americani* dropping bombs on us from above!'

'My goodness,' Nancy said, cupping her hands over the coffeepot for warmth.

'And no food!' Dino squatted in front of the fireplace and struck a match to the kindling. 'Just how you say . . . *castagne*?'

'Chestnuts,' Nancy said.

'Yes, chest-a-nuts. And we had to fight the squirrels for them!'

'We can't go on like this,' I blurted. 'That fireplace is totally inadequate and unless we get some real heat –'

'That's what I'm here to tell you. Rudolfo come home tomorrow and he get your heater working.'

'Tomorrow?' I was, of course, sceptical.

'*Sì*, I invite you over to our house for dinner,' Dino said, shooing Cosimo away before the dog could pee on the firewood. 'I make a party for my son and you come and meet the whole family.'

'*Grazie*, Dino,' Nancy said.

'Yes, thanks for the invitation,' I said, 'but I don't see why you can't –'

'*O Dio, mia nonna!*' Dino suddenly remembered that he needed to put flowers on the grave of the grandmother who had carried him down the mountain wrapped in leaves. I fired off a look at Nancy that strongly suggested she say something either in English or Italian before he got out the door.

'Can we bring anything?' she called out as Dino departed in a cloud of dog dust.

'Can we bring anything?' I said, mocking her. 'You're such a wimp. If he pulled this in America, we'd throw him in jail for being a slumlord.'

'We're not in America,' she said. 'And you don't even try to understand how things work around here!'

'Oh, I'd love to understand how things work around here. But as hard as I try, I still can't figure out why every store and office in this country closes up for a four-hour lunch break in the middle of the afternoon. Why our *ingegnere* doesn't have an answering machine. Why two Italians'll block traffic by sitting in their cars in the middle of the road having a conversation. Why their houses have three different-sized electrical sockets and yet whenever I go to plug something in, it doesn't fit in any of them. Why every restaurant but McDonald's can't be open for dinner before eight o'clock at night. Why it's impossible to make an appointment with anybody, and when you finally get one, they're always late. And finally, how come when you question an Italian about any of these things they look at you like you're crazy?'

She laughed. Then she slumped down at the table and started to cry. I felt terrible. I reached out to touch her and she looked up at me with eyes radiant and tender. Blinking back the tears, she told me that moving to Italy, and even the house itself, was really about saving my life. She explained that she had bought the *rustico* with the sole idea of getting me out of Hollywood.

I knew she was worried, but I hadn't expected this. Despite my constant assurances that I was handling things, she felt that unless we got away from our life in L.A., I was going to stress myself into a stroke. Nancy's father had died when he was about my age. She was a teenager at the time, so she grew up painfully aware of how fragile life can be. And I'd certainly done my part to give her cause for concern.

Ever since I'd turned fifty and the television business suddenly saw me as a relic from another age, I had been flipping out in the most colourful ways. My mood volleyballed back and forth between sullen and contrite, interrupted only by episodes where I was irritable and downright argumentative. Problem was, I was so used to defining myself by my Big Job and my Big

Title that without it, I felt naked and empty. With no office to go to, my days became interminable. Minutes crept by like centuries. I tried to stay current by reading the trades, but that only led me to obsess over other people's success. I threw myself into writing spec scripts, but instead of concentrating on the work, I kept brooding about doing this for no money, only to have it judged by somebody half my age with a fraction of my experience.

My nights were consumed with flailing under the covers, ruminating over all the mistakes in my life, and replaying old conversations in my head. It was becoming increasingly difficult to get anybody on the phone, including my agent, and each small indignity only fuelled my bitterness and rage.

Nancy's instincts were correct. L.A. is such a company town, everything there reminded me that I was now on the outside looking in. I wanted to run away, perhaps out of humiliation. Live like a Bedouin and keep travelling wherever the winds blew. Never settle down again – certainly not in a place as backward as Italy, where, when it's three o'clock in New York, it's AD 1537 in Florence.

But mostly I wanted to keep working at the only life I'd ever known. Hang tough and ride out this nightmare. After all, I had come to Hollywood with no connections or friends in the business and through hard work, hustle, and sheer dumb luck, I had made myself into an established sitcom writer-producer. And, hey, if I could do it once, I could do it again. I just needed to come up with that one golden idea that would rocket me back to the top. So I kept writing and bugging people for meetings as I watched our house in Brentwood eat through our savings like fire ants in a candy store.

I refused to sell it, though. That house was more than just our dwelling. Its four bedrooms, seven television sets and sprawling view of the Santa Monica Mountains were a temple to my success. To sell it would be to admit that I had lost confidence in myself. Besides, what would I be leaving it for? To become an olive wrangler in a house Ted Kaczynski wouldn't live in?

Maybe someday I'd be ready to retire. But not now. And certainly not in that sinkhole she'd gotten us into.

I knew I'd get nowhere arguing with her. I needed to come at it from a different angle. Perhaps I should tell her that if she really wanted to live in Italy that bad, we should get out from under this disaster. Then maybe we could go find a place together, the operative word being maybe.

I was staring at the back of her head as she stood at the sink. As I watched her rinse off the breakfast dishes, I reminded myself that Nancy seemed to like fixing up these places more than she liked living in them.

Of course! She was like me ... she needed a project. If we could somehow resolve this *denuncia* issue, and Nancy was able to gingerbread this place, I was sure we could get our money out. Maybe even make a few bucks. After all, everybody wants a house in Tuscany. Everybody but me, it seemed.

'I think you got the wrong idea about how I feel,' I said.

'Wonder how I got that?' She turned to me and blew a strand of hair off her face.

'Truth is, despite all my whining, there's something about Tuscany I really love.'

'Other than the food?'

'I don't know, I think this place is starting to get to me. Like, I was walking around our land the other day and it was so aromatic, I could just about smell the colours green in a million shades and hues.'

'Are you pulling my noodle in some weird passive-aggressive way?'

'I'm just saying that maybe you're right. Maybe getting away from the biz is just what I need right now.'

She dried her hands, studying my face for the slightest trace of irony.

'And once you do your number on that little house –'

'You realise how much work it's going to take to just make it livable,' she said.

'It'll be fun. You love a fixer-upper.'

'I must, I married you.'

'Hey, I wasn't that bad.'

'Oh, please. Those green corduroy pants. And those Back-to-School shirts?'

'So, you fine-tuned my look a little.'

'And those Hush Puppies.' She raised an eyebrow in mock horror. 'How did I ever go to bed with you?'

'Drugs.'

She laughed and the room filled with the warmth of burning logs.

I could always make her laugh. I even took a perverse pride in making her think that buried beneath my near-addictive need for glitz and glitter lay a caring, sensitive soul. Someone so in touch with his softer, feminine side that perhaps deep down, I was a lesbian. She slid into the oversized chair I was sitting on. Her hair had the teasing smell of crushed flowers and I could feel her warm breath on my neck.

'Know what would make you feel better?' she asked.

Yes, I did, and it was something that both a man and a lesbian could enjoy. I started to caress her.

'Italian lessons,' she said, reaching for the phrase book. 'When I first came here, I found it a lot easier to cope if I could complain to somebody. Not that it did any good.'

'Do we have to do this now?'

'When?'

'OK,' I said, taking my hand off her thigh. 'But instead of all those verb tenses that just give me a headache, how about some common, everyday phrases I could really use?'

'Well . . . we're going to be dealing with a lot of workmen, so here's some things they always say when you ask them a question.'

'A question?'

'Yeah, you know, like: "When will the work be done?" or even "Can it be done?"'

'OK.'

'Now, their first response will always be, 'No, impossibile,' which means . . .'

'Pretty much what it sounds like.'

'Right. Then the second thing they say is '*Speriamo bene*,' which means, 'I really hope so, but . . .' Like in, 'Please, Tiziano, winter's almost here; is there any way you can finish installing our boiler before we freeze to death?"

'*Speriamo bene*.'

'Bravo. Now, the last phrase is '*Magari*.' This is a bit more mystical and is usually said with an upward toss of the hand,' she said, illustrating the motion.

'And it means?'

'If only the heavens would allow it. Like when you say, "For God sakes, Claudio, our septic tank has backed up and it's flooding the house! Can you get over here right now?"'

'*Magari* . . .' I said with an upward toss of my hand.

'*Ti amo, tesoro*.'

'I hope you're not saying that to the workers.'

She kissed me. I kissed her back, and the phrase book dropped to the floor.

That afternoon Nancy went out to buy us a cellphone. While she was gone, I decided to dedicate myself to the serious pursuit of the Italian language. I opened the phrase book and began to study, vowing that this would be just like college. And just like college, within twenty seconds I started to doze off. Then I remembered that many immigrants to America learn their English by watching television, which certainly explains why so many people fresh to our shores can intelligently discuss 'yellow waxy buildup' and 'the heartbreak of psoriasis'.

I turned on the set and up came one of the staples of Italian

TV, the game show. These programmes, sporting titles like Sarabanda and Furore, are not game shows as we know them, but rather frantic, high-energy quizzes featuring a bevy of attractive young women in scanty outfits furiously shaking their *culos* every time a contestant does something noteworthy. After an hour of watching, however, I realised that I had become so distracted by all the furious culo-shaking, I had pretty much forgotten that I was supposed to be learning Italian.

I switched over to the news, where the anchorman was speaking with such velocity, I couldn't understand a word. I was able to pick up what he was reporting on from the graphics, but my attention was drawn to the movements of his hands. I watched in fascination as he punctuated each story with an appropriate gesture: raising a fist to the heavens while he chronicled the latest villainy of the Sicilian Mafia, tapping his heart in sadness as he described a train wreck outside Milan, and kissing his fingertips in appreciation of the pulchritude of the new Miss Palermo.

I then realised that in all my years of watching American TV, I had never once seen Tom Brokaw's hands.

5. ALL IN THE FAMIGLIA

We parked on a narrow street lined with elms and walked towards a house we knew to be Dino's from the incessant yapping of dogs. It was a large neo-Palladian structure with sturdy brick walls and narrow windows cross-hatched with an ominous grid of iron bars. A common feature in a country intensely paranoid about crime, these bars tended to make the houses of most well-to-do Italians look like a home for the criminally insane.

I rang the doorbell and 'Brindisi' from La Traviata chimed out over the barking of hounds. Dino opened the door, his face aglow with good cheer. I handed him the bottle of Chianti Riserva we had paid far too much for at our local *enoteca*. He examined the bottle and concluded that it was of sufficient vintage to merit an appreciative nod, although being store bought, it could never compete with the home-made Chianti he had just decanted for the occasion.

He welcomed us in and as he helped Nancy off with her coat, he asked her about her fungus. I thought this was a rather intimate line of questioning but I soon realised that he was referring to a disease that was attacking our olive trees up at the *piccolo rustico*.

We pretended that we knew about it and casually asked him what he would do. He told us that we should immediately hire his cousin Faustino, who was renowned throughout Tuscany as a mighty warrior against the *fungi*. We were in luck because cousin Faustino was coming for dinner and Dino would arrange for him to help us.

We thanked him for his kindness, and he looked at us in shock that it should be any other way. After all, we were *famiglia*. Dino expressed himself with such sincerity that we almost forgot he was constantly hustling us.

We followed Dino down a narrow stairway, unable to tell where the baying frenzy of the dogs ended and the overheated babble of human voices began. As we descended the stairs, the scent of fermenting grapes grew so intense, it smelled as if this part of the house had been marinating in red wine for centuries. We were entering the *cantina*, the heart and soul of every Tuscan home. And to dismiss this as an Italian version of the American den, the English drawing room, or the French parlour is to miss a vital facet of its character.

Every Tuscan home, no matter how humble, is guaranteed two things by law: a *forno* for baking bread and a *cantina* where the family can make wine. No one is guaranteed a bathroom, but every citizen must have their *pane e vino*. For that reason, it was usually the first room built, and many houses in this part of Tuscany were literally constructed around it.

As modern life encroached and winemaking evolved into more of a hobby, albeit a deadly serious one, the *cantina* was used less for its original purpose and more as a place for social gatherings. Because the *cantina* is subterranean, it's the coolest place in the house, so in addition to be being an all-purpose party room, it's also used for the storage of food. Along with racks of hundreds of dusty wine bottles, every shelf, tabletop, and nook in Dino's *cantina* was stocked with glass jars of red peppers, marble-white chunks of mozzarella, silvery anchovies, and olives in every shade between green and black, all preserved in olive oil as golden as Mediterranean sunshine. The net effect of all this stored food and wine was to give one the feeling of being at a party held inside a large pantry.

Dino's *cantina* was dominated by an aircraft-carrier-sized banquet table and an authentic *pietra serena* fireplace large enough to spit-roast a baby elephant. A dozen people lounging on rickety pine furniture were gathered around the *stufa*, a cast-iron potbellied stove. The guests were drinking wine and munching on bruschetta. Their shrill voices, as well as the scratchy accordion music playing on a phonograph, were harshly amplified by the low ceiling and the lack of either curtains or carpets for muffling.

'*Ascolta, tutti, ascolta, eccoli Americani*,' Dino said, announcing our entrance as if we had personally liberated their village from the Germans.

Everyone stopped talking and turned to us in a moment of rare silence for a roomful of Italians.

'*Benvenuti nella nostra casa.*' A stout woman in a batik muumuu greeted us with kisses that felt wet on our cheeks.

'This is my wife, Flavia,' Dino said.

Flavia was an energetic lady who, had circumstances been different, could have enjoyed a flourishing career in public relations, given her fondness for throwing in flattering soubriquets for each person she introduced us to. Thus, the dour, cantankerous old man muttering to himself in the corner became the 'irrepressible' Uncle Carmuzzi. The hulking, barrel-chested guy stuffing his face with crostini was the 'urbane' Cousin Aldo. The three black-shrouded old women huddled together like a scene out of Macbeth were the 'convivial' Nina, Nona and Nana. And finally, the pompous aesthete holding court on the sofa was introduced as the 'genial' Dottore Spotto, with his wife, the 'pious' Monica, and their 'mythically gifted' children Leonardo, Rafael, and *la bimba* Artemisia.

'*Piacere, piacere*,' Nancy and I said with each introduction, our heads bouncing like a couple of bobble-head dolls.

'Cousin Faustino will be here later,' Dino said, taking us aside. 'He's still in the olive groves, such a hard worker. And the best part is: he is my cousin, so if he screws up I can strangle him.'

'So he's bonded,' I said.

Dino beckoned over a small, chinless man who had been staring at us from under his continuous eyebrow. 'I want you should meet Cousin Spartaco.'

'*Ah, piacere*, Spartaco. *Apprezziamo molto la sua bellissima casa.*' Nancy shook his hand and told him how much we appreciated living in his beautiful house – the one whose walls, it must be remembered, had been covered with alternating images of Jesus Christ and naked women.

Nancy kept addressing him, but Spartaco seemed incapable of speech because his eyes were riveted on her chest.

'A-hem.' I cleared my throat.

Cousin Spartaco realised I was staring at him. He clutched at the crucifix hanging around his neck and slinked off, either to pray or masturbate.

Nancy joined the group of women oohing and ahhing over *la bimba* Artemisia as Dottore Spotto came over and poured me a glass of home-bottled Chianti. I took a sip and felt the fullness of the Sangiovese grapes permeate my palate like a long, slow seduction. I held the taste in my mouth as long as I could and then swallowed. I raised my glass in appreciation. *Il dottore* gave me a celestial smile and went off to dispense his ambrosia to the other guests.

No sooner had he left than Uncle Carmuzzi approached. Swooping his weathervane of a nose uncomfortably close to my glass, he made a face as if I had been drinking raw sewage. He then produced his own labelless bottle and poured me a glass of garnet-red *rosso*. I took a sip while he stared at me in anticipation. The wine was so lush, it was like holding the liquid essence of a Tuscan forest in my mouth. I twisted my index finger into my cheek where a dimple might have gone, using the Italian gesture to describe something too delicious for words.

Dottore Spotto strolled past and, seeing me delight in another man's wine, grabbed Uncle Carmuzzi's bottle and swirled it around, disturbing the sediment. This caused much agony for Uncle Carmuzzi, who had been handling his wine with the delicacy of one carrying a vial of anthrax. *Il dottore* peered at the billowing clouds of sediment and clucked as if he were examining a tumorous kidney. Incidentally, I have no idea what kind of *dottore* he was, the Italians being so lavish with that title, they often bestow it on anyone who's knuckled their way through four years at a university.

Sneering at the sediment as proof of the wine's inferiority, Dottore Spotto retrieved the wine I had started and refreshed it. Then, standing arms akimbo in a stance vaguely reminiscent of Mussolini, he stared at me until I began drinking. Uncle Carmuzzi glared angrily when I showed pleasure in the *dottore's* home brew, and the good *dottore's* lips twisted in rage when I gestured that I liked Uncle Carmuzzi's as well.

Both men stood facing me, vigorously extolling the qualities of their particular wine, two sets of hands emphatically flying in the air. Uncle Carmuzzi's hands occupied the horizontal plane, while Dottore Spotto's the vertical. And like airliners stacked up over a busy airport, there were many near misses, but miraculously, no collisions.

I could see no diplomatic way out of this, so I brought the wineglasses over to Nancy. She sampled each as the men stood in rapt anticipation like two Miss America finalists. Addressing them in Italian, she explained that both wines were equally excellent. And just as one couldn't determine the superiority of a sculpture by Donatello over one by Tullio Lombardo, one could not, in good conscience, rate one wine over the other. Both were masterpieces in their own right. This seemed to satisfy them.

Nancy later explained that their rivalry was not just based on wine, but upon the fact that Dottore Spotto was a Florentine, while Uncle Carmuzzi's family was originally from Ravenna. Her clever use of Donatello (who was from Florence) and Lombardo (who hailed from Ravenna) gave each a face-saving way of accepting the quality of each other's vino.

To understand why the citizens of these two cities despise each other, you have to go back to AD 1309, when Italy's most renowned poet, Dante Alighieri, was exiled from Florence for political reasons. For years he wandered Tuscany, venting his fury by writing the Inferno and peopling hell with all the Florentines who had done him wrong. He finally wound up in Ravenna, where he died and was buried. Centuries later, the Florentines realised their mistake and demanded the return of their favourite son's remains. The Ravennese refused, and to this day there is bad blood.

I have a lot of problems with Italy. It's chaotic, confusing, and oftentimes incomprehensible. But I must confess that I find unabashed delight living in a society where people still get *furioso* over the bones of a poet who's been dead for seven hundred years.

'Come here, I show you something.' Dino led me over to a wall hung with hunting rifles, antlers and the large, snarling head of a wild boar.

'I shot him last month.' He patted the pig on the snout. 'On your land.'

'Whoa, he's big.'

'And vicious. Gored two of my dogs. Had to shoot them too.'

I suddenly realised that a scorpion sleeping in my shoe might not be my most serious wildlife problem.

'Do you hunt?'

'Haven't for a while,' I said, thinking about the time eight years ago when I had killed a spider in the bathtub while Nancy screamed in the background.

'What do you do?'

'I'm a writer.'

'Really? What do you write?'

'I've worked on a lot of television shows back in America.'

'I can't believe it, you're a celebrity!'

'No, no, I'm just –'

'Mamma mia, how many movie stars do you know?'

It made me smile that Italians really say 'mamma mia'.

'Do you know Frank Sinatra?' Dino demanded.

'Isn't he dead?'

'Al Pacino?'

'No.'

'Robert De Niro? Sylvester Stallone?'

'Actually, him I've met.'

'*Attenti, attenti tutti!*' Dino hollered out. '*L'Americano conosce* Sylvester Stallone!'

I was instantly surrounded by everyone at the party eager to hear all the intimate details of Stallone's life, except for Cousin Spartaco, who urgently needed to know if Britney Spears had had breast implants. Despite Dino's best efforts to translate, it was impossible for me to share the highly nuanced concept that my position in Hollywood hardly afforded me access to the pantheon of movie stars and their sordid little secrets. I was just a behind-the-scenes guy who had worked on a lot of TV shows, some good, some bad, and some too embarrassing to mention.

But the first maxim of show business is to give your audience what it wants, so I just made things up. I told them that, contrary to his dynamic screen persona, Sylvester Stallone was a man of towering intellect and profound depth, prone to reading Kierkegaard in the original Danish and spending long hours in his candlelit study ruminating over the duality of human nature.

As for Cousin Spartaco's burning interest in the after-market enlargement of Britney Spears's chest, I told him I had no firsthand knowledge. I could only offer my own personal philosophy towards beautiful women, which is: 'Just fool me, I don't much care how you do it.'

'*Buon appetito, tutti, la cena è pronta*,' Flavia announced as she came down the stairs leading a parade of women bearing platters of steaming food.

'Can I help?' Nancy asked.

'No, no, you sit right here by me.' Dino herded us to a table that was now spread, from sea to shining sea, with mammoth mountains of *manicotti*, cavernous canyons of *cannelloni*, and roiling rivers of *rigatoni*.

'So, where's your son Rudolfo?' I asked as we sat down.

'He's coming. He called to say that he's going to be late because he got some important Buddhist thing to do.' A wave of misery washed over Dino's face.

I wanted to say something consoling, but I was distracted by Uncle Carmuzzi and Dottore Spotto insisting I take bread from the baskets each was holding. Of course, one basket was full of the *pane toscano* favoured by the Florentines and the other, an oregano loaf loved by the people of Ravenna.

I took a piece from each man and, forking a slice of prosciutto, made myself a sandwich. I took a lusty bite and smiled at both of them, indicating that I was enjoying the top slice every bit as much as the bottom.

'*Mangia, mangia*,' Flavia commanded, plopping a huge serving of what she described as a 'rhapsodic' *tagliatelle ai porcini* on Nancy's plate.

'*Per favore, signora*,' Nancy protested. '*Non posso mangiare così tanto.*'

Flavia reacted as if Nancy had just desecrated a church, launching into a lecture condemning her, and most American women, for being too skinny. And by denying her body the food it needed, Nancy was all but guaranteeing herself a series of crippling illnesses and most assuredly an early death. Faced with such dire predictions, we put our heads down and ate until our underwear felt tight and it was difficult to breathe.

Unlike the French, who tend to sink into reverential silence when the food arrives, the act of eating merely increases the Italian need for volume and drama. Somewhere between the *primi* and the *secondi* a row broke out between Cousin Aldo and Dino, which Nancy translated for me.

'*Porca miseria!*' Cousin Aldo slammed his cellphone down on the table hard enough to wake up *la bimba* Artemisia.

'Hey, we are eating,' Dino said with indignant rage. 'Stop acting like an animal!'

'Don't bother me, I'm under a lot of pressure,' Cousin Aldo roared. He was a big, thickset guy with the huge, triangular upper body of a cartoon bully.

'What's wrong?' Dino said.

'Leave me alone.'

Dino thrust out his chest. 'Tell me or I swear by the Virgin, I'll take you out back and beat some sense into you.'

'It's Mamma,' Cousin Aldo said. 'We had a fight. I keep calling to apologise but she won't pick up the phone!'

'You must do something.' Dino grabbed Aldo by his large sawhorse shoulders and shook him. 'This is your mamma!'

'I know!' A tear waddled down Cousin Aldo's cheek.

'My God, what if the old woman is lying dead by the phone, her head split open from the fall?' Dino's own tears started to well up. 'And she died before you had a chance to apologise!'

The two big men embraced in a cumbersome bear hug and sobbed, as Cousin Aldo cried out, 'Oh, Mamma!'

Oh, brother, I thought. If these two guys get up and start dancing, I am outta here.

Cousin Aldo bolted out of his chair to go home to Mamma. As we got up to bid him goodbye, the renowned *funghi* fighter Cousin Faustino arrived. He was a toothless, misshapen little man with three fingers missing from one hand and a thumb from the other. His left eyeball was strangely blackened, and his right eye seemed to meander off to the side, as if he were trying to see who was behind him. Moreover, he looked drunk.

Dino introduced us, and Nancy greeted him warmly. She told him that she had heard great things about him, and now that our olive trees were being threatened, we urgently needed his expertise.

'Would you be able to come up to our house tomorrow?' Nancy asked.

'*Magari* . . .' Cousin Faustino said with an upwards toss of his four-fingered hand.

6. IN BOCCA AL LUPO

It was one thirty in the morning and I was wide awake, or as the Italians say, *in bianco*, in white. I was staring at the ceiling waiting for the antacids I had taken to help digest Flavia's dinner . . . and wondering what I was going to do with the rest of my life. I began to sense that the source of my anxiety was how ill prepared I was to make any kind of change. During the times Nancy and I were apart, she had been addressing the issue and evolving. She had deliberately sought a life peaceful enough for her to hear that small voice within that unerringly tells us what we should be doing, while I was doing my best to ignore mine. I felt my competitive juices flow and found myself slightly angry with her. Hey, I could be just as centred and serene as she was, goddammit! I tasted blood in my mouth and I realised I had been chewing on the inside of my cheek.

I closed my eyes and tried to picture myself picking olives. I was wearing a straw hat and a red bandanna, and in the background somebody was playing 'O Sole Mio' on a wheezy concertina. My sister was in the kitchen stirring a huge vat of pasta, while Nancy had her skirt hiked up as she stomped grapes, throwing back her head and laughing lustfully like a young Anna Magnani.

Everything was a script to me. I was incapable of experiencing life without trying to rewrite it. But maybe that was a good thing. After all, writers from as far back as Goethe have been coming to Italy for inspiration – why not me? Maybe I should tackle something big, like a book or a play. Let's see, what did I used to be interested in before I started working twelve hours a day, six days a week?

Unable to come up with anything beyond a vague fascination with the History Channel, I began composing an e-mail in my head diplomatically asking my agent if he'd had a chance to read my script. All at once I became aware of a steady tapping noise. At first I thought it was Nancy's teeth chattering from the cold, but then I realised it was coming from downstairs. I climbed out of bed and bundled on my robe. Nancy stirred and, in a groggy voice, asked where I was going. I told her that somebody was here.

Flipping on lights as I went, I followed the tapping to our front door. Through the peephole I spied a young man hopping up and down to keep warm.

'*Buona notte, Scrittore*,' he called out, addressing me by my title, Writer. I realised that this was Dino's son, Rudolfo. I opened the door and he entered, apologising for the lateness of the hour. He explained, in almost accentless English, that he had just gotten home when his father insisted he come right over and turn on our heat.

He headed for the thermostat, and as he peeled off his jacket, I could see that he was sporting all the prerequisite totems of his generation: the small silver earring, the hieroglyphic tattoo, and the bizarrely cut facial hair.

Italy leads the world in young men with funny beards. Rudolfo's particular cultivation consisted of sideburns that tapered into a pencil-thin line running down both sides of his jawbone, then stopping just short of the chin, where they formed a set of apostrophes and then suddenly ascended into a narrow rattail of a Fu Manchu moustache.

I looked at his beard in wonder, knowing that, if I were to try to maintain such a creation, between the unsteadiness of my hand and my myopic eyesight I would wind up slicing off my nose one fine morning.

Nancy entered, her cheeks pink tipped from the cold. Rudolfo introduced himself and assured us that he would have our heater working in a minute ... *bocca di lupo*. I looked to Nancy, who informed me that the phrase meant 'mouth of the wolf', and the Tuscans used it to say 'good luck'.

'Let me see what you're doing,' I said as I watched him tinker with the control panel.

'This button here, marked *Gravenungafürlenspielen*, is the main on/off.'

'*Gravenunga* . . .' I squinted at the console, wishing I had put on my reading glasses.

'And this one marked *Kleisterwahlfunghausen*' – he pushed another button – 'is the –'

The house plunged into blackness.

'*Maledetto* Italian circuit breaker!' Rudolfo let fly a bilingual string of expletives as he dug a cigarette lighter out of his pocket and used the flame to see his way down into the cellar.

Nancy and I stood alone in the dark. From downstairs we heard Rudolfo knock over a bookcase and cry out in pain as his disposable lighter burned his hand. Over the howling of Italian curses Nancy commented that, for just having spent a week at a Buddhist retreat, young Rudolfo didn't seem very Zen.

Just then the lights came on, and as Rudolfo clomped up the stairs, we heard the pleasant whoomp of a burner igniting.

'Bravo, Rudolfo,' Nancy said, clapping her hands.

'Yeah, nice work, dude.'

'No problem,' Rudolfo said through the burned thumb he was sucking on.

Nancy took down a bottle of Vin Santo. 'Can I make you a sandwich?'

'Oh, no, thank you, signora. Mamma fed me when I got home.'

'We really appreciate you coming over,' I said.

'Well, I just wanted to meet the people who bought the Bunker and say *bocca di lupo*.'

'We're screwed, huh?' I said.

We sat and Rudolfo proceeded to give us a brief history of our house, starting with how the young men of the village had been using it for years as a place to take their girlfriends. He slyly intimated that he himself had been deflowered on the very floor of our *rustico*.

Turning to weightier matters, he told us that Mario Pingatore had been trying to unload the house for as long as he could remember. Offered it to everybody. Even his father, Dino, had held a *compromesso* on it for a while. He went on to explain that since the house needed a road to be of any value, Pingatore had to find a buyer who didn't understand how things were done around here. In other words, he needed *stranieri*.

This is a word Italians use a lot. It literally means 'strangers' or 'tourists', but more accurately it connotes 'outsiders'. And in Tuscany that can mean somebody from the next village over. For example, one of our neighbours is a 72-year-old man who came here from Milan when he was ten. He married a local girl, had five children and twelve grandchildren. But to this day they still refer to him as Il Milanese.

Nancy poured drinks, and we passed around a tin of biscotti while Rudolfo summed up our dilemma. Pingatore owned a house that was worthless because there was no road leading up to it. He sold it to a couple of 'outsiders' and a road mysteriously appeared. Then his sister, Vesuvia, filed a complaint. This stopped all construction, rendering the house uninhabitable, so we poor *stranieri* would probably have no recourse but to sell it back to Pingatore.

'At a bloody loss, of course.' Rudolfo dipped a biscotto into his amber dessert wine with a raised pinky in a send-up of Mario Pingatore's English airs.

'How can he get away with this?' I demanded.

Rudolfo shrugged. 'We're Italian. We live with a million laws and no rules.'

'We're so screwed.' I was starting to get overheated from our now throbbing radiators.

But Rudolfo suggested that being *stranieri* might actually have a benefit. It seemed that everybody in town knew we had been conned by Mario Pingatore, and since nobody liked him, they would enjoy seeing us prevail if we could just give them a good reason.

'I have a good reason,' Nancy said. 'And I've been trying to get in to see the mayor for days to tell him about it.'

'Oh, you've got to go much higher than that,' Rudolfo said. 'You got to get to the mayor's wife.'

The following day the cold snap broke. The sun came out and it turned hot enough to blister paint. Unfortunately, the German behemoth in our cellar continued to heat our radiators to a white-hot pitch despite my best efforts to push the *Kleisterwahlathingee* and fiddle with the *Gravenungamajig*. I called Rudolfo, only to learn that he had left for Corsica to go surfing and would not be back until the end of the week.

I was sitting in my underwear, dripping sweat on the laptop, when Nancy came downstairs. She was dressed in black, her wild mane of blond hair was tamed into a prim bun, and she was sporting a large crucifix.

'You're going to burn in hell for this,' I said.

'I'm just going to church.'

'You haven't gone to church in ten years.'

'Then I've got a shitload to confess.'

So for the next two weeks, she went to Mass every day in hopes of accidentally running into the mayor's wife. Nancy spotted her several times but was unable to approach because the mayor's wife was either with somebody (once it was Vesuvia Pingatore!) or so deep in prayer that disturbing her seemed sacrilegious.

Burning with the need to corner Cambione's first lady alone at the right moment, Nancy dragged me out of bed early one morning to drive her to the Chiesa de Santa Maria della Pieve.

I parked the car and sat under the faded green awning of a café across from the church. Swarms of Vespas sputtered past me as I sipped a *caffè macchiato* to the steady rhythm of an old woman sweeping the sidewalk with a twig broom. I watched a young couple drift by and stop at the condom vending machine under the very shadow of the church. After discussing the relative merits of each product, they pooled their coins and made a selection.

I was thinking about what a great example this was of how unfazed the Italians are about the basic incongruities in their lives. Then I realised that this would make a terrific hook for a travel article. I started fleshing out the piece with the idea that I might run it by a buddy of mine who worked at the *Los Angeles Times*.

I was just contemplating a quick trip down to Rome to see if there were any such machines on the walls outside the Vatican, when I spotted a squat tugboat of a woman steaming down the street. In spite of the heat, she was wearing a wool dress and a thick black shawl. Arriving at the church, she stopped at the doorway and crossed herself. Then she bowed her head and entered.

Later, Nancy described what happened when the mayor's wife stepped inside the near-empty chapel. How the heavyset woman marched to her usual spot at the side altar of Santa Dominica. Dropping to knees sheathed in brownish-orange support stockings, she lit a candle and began to say her rosary in the fat, waxy smoke. But she quickly became distracted by the muted sobbing of the woman next to her. She tried to keep praying, but the weeping grew louder. Nancy apologised for the disturbance, prompting the mayor's wife to ask what was the matter.

'*La mia mamma*,' Nancy sobbed. She didn't know how much time her mother had, and tragically, Nancy could not be at her bedside, because we were unable to leave town on account of a legal matter we were ensnarled in (sniff, sniff). And the whole thing only happened in the first place because Nancy wanted a little house here so her saintly mamma (sniff, sniff) could spend her last days in her ancestral homeland.

'*La sua mamma è italiana?*' The mayor's wife asked with sudden interest.

Eyes glistening with tears, Nancy described how she had grown up listening to Mamma's stories of La Bella Italia, and how Nancy had vowed to someday buy a little *rustico*, just like the one Mamma was born in, so Mamma could (sniff, blow) be buried here.

Nancy dropped her head and wept into her hands. The mayor's wife, walking on her knees, scooted closer. 'You're such a loving child, I wish my daughter felt that way about me!'

I was eating the most delicious frittata, made in the shape of a fish and colourfully embedded with green chives and chunks of sweet red peppers, when I spotted Nancy and the mayor's wife coming out of the church arm in arm. They spoke for quite a while, with many comforting nods and reassuring pats on the arm, all followed by their kissing each other on both cheeks about forty times. I could tell by the look on Nancy's face as she crossed the street just how successful this gambit had been.

'She's going to talk to her husband and he's going to review our case and if he finds out Pingatore pulled a fast one, he'll overturn the whole *denuncia!*' she said without taking a breath.

'Brava.'

'And once that's lifted we can begin construction.'

'Isn't there one small hitch in your master plan?' I asked as Nancy sat down and started eating my frittata. 'Eventually your mother's going to have to show up.'

'I have a mother.'

'Your mother is a little Irish lady from New Jersey whose idea of fine Italian dining is a jar of Dolmio.'

'But my aunt Rose is Italian, and ever since Uncle Kenny died, she and Mom have been travelling everywhere together. So who's to say which lady's my mom and which one's my aunt Rose?

'I don't know . . .' I said, shaking my head.

'Look, I feel bad about using Mom like this, but it's the only way.'

'You mean bribery no longer works around here?'

'Remember when I first started coming to Italy? I was staying in that little apartment the next town over?'

'Uh-huh.' I speared the last bite of *frittata* and popped it in my mouth.

'Mom wanted to visit me, but I didn't have a bed for her. You can't rent something like that here, so I ran all over town looking for a cheap one to buy. Well, you know how things are here . . . everything was closed, or everything was the wrong size, or too expensive, and it was just hopeless. Time was running out and I was getting frantic. Finally, the day before she arrived, I found one that was perfect. But when I told them I needed it that day, they told me that it was impossible to have it delivered until the end of the month. Well, I guess it was so hot and I was so aggravated, I started to cry. I was sobbing my head off and blubbering that it was for my mamma and if I didn't get it today, she'd have to sleep on the floor!'

'Wow, what'd they say?'

'Nothing. They threw it on the truck and delivered it that afternoon. And that's how things get done around here. They'll do anything for the mamma.'

We came home to find our heater still running full blast, causing every radiator in the house to glow like the fuel rods of a nuclear reactor. We promptly decided that we had accomplished enough for one day and that we richly deserved an afternoon in the pool.

Under the shade of the backyard awning we spread out a lunch of *insalata alla caprese*. Slices of plump, vine-ripened tomatoes alternated with wedges of creamy bufalo mozzarella cheese made from the milk of Asian water buffalo brought to Italy a century ago to graze in the marshy wetlands around Naples. The fiery red of the tomatoes and the porcelain white of the cheese were garnished with green sprigs of basil. We felt like we were eating the Italian flag.

Then we settled onto our Pokémon rafts with thick novels to float in sun-splashed serenity. The sun warmed my skin to the point of tingling. I put my book down, closed my eyes, and let my breathing fall into harmony with the sucking of the pool skimmer. I must have dozed off, because the next thing I knew our cellphone was ringing.

I called out to Nancy to pick it up, but she had gone inside. So I rolled off my raft, dunked my head in the water to wake up, and climbed out of the pool just as Nancy was coming out of the house. I picked up the ringing cellphone and flipped it open.

It was my agent calling from L.A. He was speaking so rapidly, I felt as though we were not only in different time zones, but in different dimensions. He told me that he had liked my script very much and that he'd sent it to some producers who wanted to buy it. His words shot through me like electricity.

Nancy stared at my head, which was bobbing in idiotic delight while my agent described how excited they were about my script and how they want to be in production by the end of the year. This meant I had to get back to Hollywood immediately for meetings and rewrites. I was practically stammering when I told him I'd be on the next plane.

'Congratulations.' That was all Nancy could say. And she said that very flatly.

'I've come back from the dead!' I squealed, taking her in my arms. 'Can you believe it?'

Her sad little smile said it all. She was happy for me because it was something I wanted so desperately, and, yes, we could use the money, but this was happening just when it looked like we were trying to live another way.

I swore to her that this time was going to be different. The last few years of struggling to find work had changed me. And being here in Italy, even for such a short time, had opened me up to new ways to live. Even though I was going back into the anus of the beast, I vowed to her that I would not let it consume me as it had before.

I was hoping that she believed me, but I'm sure she didn't because even as I said it, I was picturing the size of the office they'd give me and how I might wrangle an associate-producer credit, so I could be more involved in the production. Or, no . . . on the basis of this sale my agent should be able to get me other writing assignments. I was so electrified by the sudden wealth of possibilities, I barely noticed how Nancy's shoulders slumped as she trudged inside the house.

I'd try to smooth things over before I left, but first I had to book a flight. I quickly discovered that it wasn't going to be easy. Tourist season was in full swing, and every seat was sold, unless I wanted to go standby or spend a fortune flying first class.

After repeated calls to an assortment of airlines and travel agencies, I was able to cobble together a schedule that would put me on an express train to Milan, where I would catch a midnight flight to Frankfurt, then shuttle off to Amsterdam, where I would hop aboard a charter to Toronto, and, if everything took off and landed on time, I would finally arrive in L.A.

I dreaded the impending fifty hours I would spend in transit, and the hell of spending most of it in middle seat coach, but I was buoyed by the fact that after travelling through a hodgepodge of foreign countries, it would certainly be good to get back to Los Angeles, where everybody speaks the same language. Korean.

7. THE COMEBACK KID

For most of my series of flights I sat in muted anticipation of my newfound success. I read a book, four magazines, saw three movies, and was served breakfast eleven times. On the last leg of my journey, just hours out of LAX, I took out the script I had sold. It was called *Son on the Moon*, and it was a thinly veiled account of my life as a shy kid with an overheated imagination, coming of age in a small midwestern town during the pre-Beatles sixties.

I read it twice. First for pleasure and then in a defensive mode so I could fend off any arguments to change the parts I really liked. I did this with the full understanding that I was breaking a cardinal rule of show business. When I first came to Hollywood, an established writer gave me this advice:

'Don't ever fall in love with your own stuff, kid,' he said. 'They'll only break your heart.'

As soon as I stepped off the plane and into a terminal full of my countrymen, I began to notice seismic differences. Americans looked heavier, more serious, more racially mixed, and not nearly as happy as a random crowd of Italians. Little details began to accrue, like how in Europe those luggage trolleys are free, but here they charge you a dollar and half, like, yeah, I just got off the plane after a month in Borneo, so I certainly have a pocketful of quarters.

I caught the SuperShuttle, and the driver updated me on the weather and the Dodgers in an accent that was either Bangladeshi or Guatemalan. Sleep overcame me so suddenly, I wasn't aware of dozing off, but I awoke with a start to cheery ranchero music on the radio as we inched along a freeway clogged with soccer-mom minivans and SUVs the size of armoured personnel carriers. Through sleep-caked eyes I studied the layer of smog that constantly blankets the freeway like permafrost. It was orangish-*grey*, smelled of unburned motor oil, and was as unlike the *sfumato* as cabbages are from calla lilies.

The shuttle turned down the tree-lined street where Nancy and I had lived for the past ten years. It all looked strange and unfamiliar, as if the shadows were on the wrong side of the street and our house was now oddly inverted. I unlocked the door and disarmed the alarm. The house smelled stale and slightly metallic. I flicked on the air-conditioning and the TV, because silence gives me the creeps. I listened to our phone messages, as cool, moist air filled the house and Connie Chung interviewed a panel of women and their plastic surgeons about designer vaginas.

It was good to be home. Seven big rooms with TVs and phones and surround sound in every one of them. A garbage disposal. A dishwasher. And a California king-sized bed, even though I was going to be in it alone.

I picked up the phone and dialled.

'*Pronto*,' Nancy said.

'Did I wake you?'

'It's three in the afternoon.'

'Oh. I thought . . .' It was too complicated to explain what I thought.

'How was the trip?'

'Long, but uneventful.' My eyes felt sandy. I rotated my palm in one of my eye sockets until it made a squishy sound. 'How're you doing?'

'Well, the big news here is that Dino came over and managed to shut off the heater.'

'But now it's turned cold,' I said.

'It's still hot, but the only way he could do it was to switch off a circuit breaker, which means that the pool pump isn't running.'

'How green is thy algae?'

'Not as bad as our fungus,' Nancy said. 'Cousin Faustino finally took a look and said that half our trees are infected and their olives won't be any good.'

'Land o' Goshen, Maw, if we lose the harvest, the ranchers'll get our land!'

'I know you see this as one big joke.'

'Well, the funny thing is, you know how much I love America and everything American like Taco Bell and sushi, and I know I just got here, but I swear everything seems so loud and vulgar and in your face.'

'Then you'd rather be here?'

'I'd rather be with you.'

'I'm sorry I gave you such a hard time,' she said. 'That wasn't fair.'

'No, you're worried about me.'

'I just have to understand that as much as I want to drag you out of there by your hair, your heart's in Hollywood and mine's –'

'I'm sick of us living parallel lives,' I said. 'This is the time we should be together.'

'That's what I want.'

'Me too. We're just going to have to find a way to make it work.'

I had an uncharacteristically good night's sleep and awoke feeling fresh and not at all jet lagged. I ran out to the market and bought milk, juice and bagels. Yes, bagels, hot and delicious. I ate breakfast watching ESPN. Life was good.

I left early for my meeting to allow myself plenty of time so I wouldn't have to rush. I tend to drive very carefully in L.A., because I'm always afraid that if I'm in too big a hurry, the one car I cut off will be driven by a guy who's fresh from some impulse shopping at a gun show because those goddamn anger-management classes are just not working out.

On my way to the studio I concentrated on staying calm. By

relaxing my facial muscles and slowly breathing in and out, I was able to generate a certain level of serenity. But as I pulled under the Moorish archway that greets both the meek and the mighty to Paramount Studios, I felt the old anxieties creep into my chest. My innards started vibrating like a hornet's nest and my mouth went dry. While the guard looked for my name on the list of drive-ons, I told myself that this time it was going to be different. I wasn't coming here hat in hand. They were excited about my script and they wanted me.

I was directed to an opulent waiting room richly panelled in exotic wood from some endangered rain forest. After a wait long enough to infuse me with the proper degree of humility, I was escorted to an even more munificent office covered in even rarer environmentally threatened wood.

Two people rose to greet me. A tall young man with cornrows and the long, tapering fingers of either a concert pianist or a point guard entwined his hand in mine in a soul shake. His partner was an attractive if Rubenesque Jewish girl in her twenties with hennaed hair cut in a futuristic, triangular wedge.

After the introductions, the sitting down, and the offering of mineral water, we devoted a moment of foreplay to my house in Italy and its cornucopia of problems. I told them that whether you want it or not, Italy gives you a lesson in patience every day. After all, Rome wasn't built in a day and apparently neither was anything there. They laughed, but I could tell from their comments that, like most Americans, even the more sophisticated ones, their image of Italy was mostly macaroni and mandolins.

Pleasantries aside, we got down to business. It's important to understand that these script meetings tend to have a structure as tightly forged as a Kabuki theatrical. The performance invariably opens with a ritual praising of your writing. How much they were moved by your 'searing insight' and your 'compelling narrative'.

But just as day follows night, their faces darken and they reluctantly voice their concerns. My script was just too time bound in the late fifties/early sixties and relentlessly mired in a type of factory town that just didn't exist anymore. They feared that those two elements would make the film inaccessible to the all-important male teenage audience.

Then, acting like his idea was completely spontaneous, the cornrow guy suggested we update the story by placing it in the present day.

'OK . . .' I said, mourning all the wonderful stuff I'd have to lose.

'And instead of a small town, how about setting it in the inner city? Uh, like Harlem, for instance,' the girl with the triangular hair said.

I pursed my lips and nodded as if I were thinking about it. But I wished I were wearing a Kabuki mask to keep them from seeing my left eye starting to twitch.

They were congratulating each other over these improvements when I first heard the name Charlie. As in, how Charlie could play the living hell out of a present-day kid from the hood.

'Charlie?' I wondered.

Hope piled upon hype as they buzzed over the possibility of casting Charlie.

Apparently Charlie had read the script and expressed interest. But now with these changes . . .

Charlie Sheen? Charlie Chan? Charlie Manson? I had no idea who Charlie was, but rather than betray my woeful lack of hipness, I grinned back in mindless delight.

'The songs Charlie could do for the soundtrack!' the girl cooed.

'Totally,' her partner said, suggesting they go for a mix of Charlie's classic rap hits with some new stuff.

They slapped hands and she broke into an impromptu riff of

what appeared to be one of Charlie's songs. It was as familiar to me as the Bulgarian national anthem.

Of course with the casting of Charlie, I needed to rewrite most of my scenes to highlight the Charlie persona. For example, they singled out an easy change I could make. It was in the part where the kid went out to dinner with his parents every Sunday. The parents were morbidly obese, and their favourite restaurant was a place called Paul Bunyan's, an oversized, all-you-can-eat smorgasbord whose motto was 'Big Food on Big Plates'. One Sunday, as they pulled up, the owner spotted them, turned out all the lights, and pretended to be closed so they wouldn't eat him out of business.

They loved that scene but thought it needed to be edgier. So perhaps, outraged at Mom and Dad getting dissed, Charlie could kick open the door and spray the restaurant with an AK-47.

This is madness! I thought. But I said, 'Well, that's certainly interesting, but don't you think that such sweeping changes will destroy the essential spirit of the work?'

'Not at all,' the guy was quick to say. 'Charlie's acting will bring such poignancy, it can only make it better.'

'And with Charlie starring, we're talking about a whole new thing here,' the girl said in a scolding tone. 'Not just a TV movie. This could wind up being released as a feature!'

And so, like many Kabuki performances that stress the importance of one's duty over one's conscience, our play ended with the promise of untold riches and eternal happiness for all. As I started for the door, they suggested we meet the following week so I could pitch out the changes I'd made. I indicated I would look forward to that, but first I had to go home, cleanse my hands, and slit open my belly with a hari-kari knife.

I drove down Sunset Strip. My stomach was churning and my brain bubbled with rage. If I worked in this town a hundred years, I'd never understand why they buy a script they love and proceed to change it beyond all recognition. There are fifty thousand scripts floating around – why don't they just buy one that already has what they want? And if they can't find one, why don't they just grab one of the ten thousand writers hanging around Starbucks and tell him to write down what they're saying?

For God's sake, after twenty-five years of shovelling jokes in the sitcom boiler room, aren't I entitled to something real and heartfelt? How could they take this away from me?

I stopped pounding on the steering wheel long enough to realise that I was stuck in that knot of traffic that always jams up around Tower Records. I decided to put aside my self-pity and at least see who this Charlie was. The guy must have some talent or they wouldn't get so excited. Who knows, maybe he was the next Denzel Washington. Or, failing that, the next Ice T.

After much browsing through the Rap/Hip-Hop/Urban Top 40 Section, I couldn't find anyone named Charlie. But I did come across a whole rack devoted to Charylie. So Charlie was a chick! *Son on the Moon*? I couldn't even keep my own title!

I picked up a CD and studied the angry young lady glaring at me. She was wearing a doo-rag and camouflage overalls. Her hair bristled in every direction, as did her facial piercings. I flipped over the CD and saw that it featured such classics as: 'Yo' Mama Is a Hootchie Ho" and 'F.T.C.H.C.P. (Flush the Crack, Here Come the Pigs).'

I lay in bed surrounded by books on hip-hop culture. I was staring at the TV, where a movie I had rented was playing. It was a teenage slasher flick called Is the Noise in My Head Bothering You? Part II. One of its stars was Charylie, and the best thing I could say about her performance is that she screamed very effectively.

I had been working for days and everything I wrote was bad. The words I put in Charylie's mouth seemed leaden and contrived. I was supposed to meet with the producers in a couple of days, and I was starting to panic.

Had I lost my fastball? Was I so busy pouting over these changes that my heart wasn't in it? Throughout my career I had moved easily from show to show, writing for casts that were black, Hispanic or female. Each time I was able to submerge myself inside the characters. I would start talking like them and soon I could hear them chattering away inside my head, until all I had to do was jot down what they were saying.

But not this time. This time I was just a middle-class, middle-aged white guy trying to sound like an angry teenage girl from the projects.

Maybe they were right. Maybe I was too old.

I stopped the movie. The TV was set on the Discovery Channel, where a dry, PBS-type voice was narrating the cycle of life as played out by a herd of wildebeest on the Serengeti Plains. How they frantically fought off the fiercest adversary to protect their young, but callously left the old to fall behind and be eaten.

Just like when I was a young writer coming up, and my peers and I snickered at the old guys and their talk of Jack Benny and Fred Allen. How could these old farts understand our generation? How could they ever know how we thought and spoke and felt? If there was anything more ridiculous than how we dressed in the seventies, it was the sight of some old man in a bad toupee, his saggy butt squeezed into a pair of bell bottoms and his belly bulging under a psychedelic T-shirt. How we laughed at them in our eagerness to take over their jobs.

Now it was happening to me.

I needed to talk to somebody. I couldn't call any of my fellow writers, even to ask if they knew whether or not Britney Spears had had breast implants. They'd be so envious I had this deal, they'd think I was calling to rub it in. Which perhaps I was.

I started to call Nancy when I reminded myself that I couldn't tell her about the struggles I was having. She'd see it as my way of saying that I really didn't want to be here anymore.

And even if she were right, what did it matter? What choice did I have?

I dialled up my sister, Debbie, who still lived in the town we grew up in. Debbie and I talked for about an hour, chewing over all the latest comings and goings back there. Things like the old greasy spoon next to the high school suddenly becoming an upscale Thai restaurant, and how ancient Mrs McCauly up the block had finally passed away. Our conversation only underscored how lost I felt. I knew that small town and its people in ways I would never know Charylie. Sure, I could write her anger, but where was her humanity?

I decided to talk to my agent, but I had to handle this delicately. After two years of my bugging him, he had finally sold something, and now here I was bitching about it. Of course he would be sympathetic, but in Hollywood you never knew who was in bed with whom. He, or his agency, might represent the producers. Or Charylie.

I got an appointment to see him the next day. In the meantime I put in a call to the producers. About an hour later they called back. I started with the prerequisite pumping of sunshine about how well things were going. I tried to sound carefree and confident, but I could hear my own voice and it sounded full of wrong notes. They asked me if any parts were giving me problems, which opened the door for me to be honest. But I was so terrified that this gossamer thread my career was hanging by would dissolve with one wrong word, I just mumbled that everything was going great.

The following morning I drove to Beverly Hills and was valet-parked at my agent's office. It was hot and sticky, and I picked my shirt away from my skin as I walked across the vast marble plaza. I passed a towering fountain my years of work had helped pay for. The cooling mist of its spray glazed my face and I felt slightly reimbursed.

I took the elevator up to his floor and stepped out, to be

greeted by his assistant, Greta, a disturbingly pretty California girl. You just knew that there had to be tan lines under that Prada suit. She told me that he was on a conference call and would be with me shortly, but in the meantime would I like some mineral water or a cappuccino? I chose the latter, settling into one of those plush, oversized chairs they have to make you feel insignificant. I picked up Daily Variety and thumbed through it. As I glanced at the articles, I thought about getting a little ink for myself. A blurb about me selling my script, blah, blah, blah. But what if the whole thing blew up in my face? Better wait. Plenty of time for some big-time pub if and when.

Greta returned with my cappuccino and a smile. She told me how happy she was to finally meet me after we'd spoken on the phone so many times. She had always wanted to tell me how much she loved a certain show I had once worked on. I thanked her, privately grateful she hadn't mentioned that she was in junior high at the time.

She went on to say how much she loved the writing, and how she believed it had actually sparked her ambition to try and break into the business. I knew it was all boilerplate bullshit. Knew she probably said that to everybody who sat in this oversized chair. I knew all that, but it still felt good.

Greta trotted off to check on his conference call, and I took a sip of my cappuccino. It looked beautiful but tasted like coffee-flavoured dishwater. I desperately yearned for a caffè macchiato from that little place with the green awning across from the . . . I suddenly wondered what the hell I was doing. When I was in Italy I kept thinking about L.A., and now that I was in L.A., I was yearning for Italy. What was up with that? I forced myself back to the trades, flipping past all the articles about those younger and more successful than me.

But when I got to the obituaries, something caught my eye.

Remember the guy who told me never to fall in love with my own stuff? There he was, dead at sixty-three. The obit listed the shows he had written, which were impressive, and the awards he had won, which were numerous. I drifted back in time. About ten years after he had given me that advice, I was producing my first network show. I had heard that he was out of work and I wanted to repay his kindness, so I called him. I explained that the star of our show had packed the writing staff with his relatives and his running buddies, so I didn't have the title or the money to give him what he deserved. But I'd love to have him involved, perhaps as a consultant who came in once or twice a week.

The offer was demeaning for a guy of his stature, and the show was, quite frankly, one of those idiotic eight o'clock family comedies that I'd built a career out of writing. He thanked me for thinking of him and a few days later showed up at one of our run-throughs. Out of the corner of my eye I watched him grimace at the over-the-top acting and the sophomoric writing. He left as soon as it was over, muttering something about being too old and too rich for this.

I saw him again three years later. I walked into a restaurant and spotted him at the bar. I sat down and tried to make conversation, but all I got was a drunken rant against every prick who'd ever screwed him. Here was a guy who had made a lot of money, won a shelf full of awards, and had achieved about as much acclaim as any TV writer can ever hope to get.

I still remember how he looked at me with unfocused eyes and said, 'In the end, kid, no matter how big you are, this town won't leave you with one shred of dignity on your bones.'

His death made me realise how lucky I was. I had my health, I had about as much sanity as I'd had when I first got here, and most importantly, I had somebody who loved me so much, she wanted to drag me out of L.A. by my hair. Maybe she was right. Maybe I needed to get out now before I became that bitter, drunken bastard on the barstool.

Wait a minute . . . was I actually thinking of walking out on all this? Me, who never quit a job in his life? Me, whose working philosophy can best be described as just leave the money on the dresser and if you had a good time, tell your friends?

Then, for no reason whatsoever, Charylie popped into my mind. It was just a fragmentary image. The way she cocked her head or curled a lip. But it was so dead on, the tumblers clicked and her entire life opened up to me. I saw her as a baby, a child and a woman in one vast, continuous panorama. I had to stop myself from shrieking with excitement.

I scrambled for a pen. My hand was a blur moving across the paper as I tried to follow her rap about society. It was something about how we're all suffering from 'strangulation by communication' because we'd been 'massmedia-ised like some fries that have been supersized.' Then I stopped writing, because I realised she was talking to me.

'Yo, man,' Charylie said, plopping her purple Doc Martens down on the coffee table. 'What you be comin' up in here all whinin' and cryin' like some little punk bitch?'

'I'm not whin –'

'Look at you, sucka. You be all wah-wah-wah, oh, please, Mr Agent-man, don't let 'em change my script. I loves my script.' She was laughing at me.

I looked over at Greta. She was on the phone and hadn't noticed that I was having a conversation with a person who wasn't there.

'What you even doin' comin' up here at all?' Charylie's eyes were on me like an arraignment.

'Trying to make a living.'

'You done made a living. Ain't you got money?'

'Yeah. Some.'

'Ain't you seen your name on TV enough?'

'Yeah.'

'Then move your sorry ass over, nigga, and make room for somebody else. You been feedin' at this trough long enough.'

She was right. It wasn't the money or even the ego strokes anymore. I was mindlessly chasing stardust, because without show business, I had nothing else in my life. No hobbies. No interests. No real friends outside of the people I worked with. I was condemned to spend the rest of my days trying to fill a hole that was essentially bottomless.

Charylie was now on my lap. She wrapped her arms around my neck and whispered, 'Listen, boy, you ain't so old, you just got to be a little more bold.'

Yeah, maybe I could change. Maybe I could build my life around something else. Nancy was offering me a chance to reinvent myself, if only I had the –

'He's ready to see you now,' Greta announced.

How could I see him now? I was right in the middle of figuring out what I wanted. Why I was here. Not here in my agent's office, but here on earth. Oh, God, I'm no good at these vast, imponderable questions. I'm good at writing jokes and ordering Chinese food, but when it comes to everything else, I'm pretty clueless.

'He's ready,' Greta repeated, as if I had a hearing problem.

I stood up and looked at the door to my agent's office, and then at the elevator.

'Sir?. . . Sir?'

8. GIORNALISTA

I was standing in front of our bedroom mirror, my face turning a fire-engine red as I struggled to fit into my loosest pair of pants. After taking a breath, I groaned, sucked in my gut, and made one last attempt. I had just about gotten my zipper closed when I saw Nancy standing in the doorway.

'Are you OK,' she said, 'or are we going to have to use the jaws of life to cut you out of those?'

'I know ... I'm getting a little heavy,' I said, rummaging through the armoire for something with an elastic waist. 'And do you know why?'

She pursed her lips in mock concentration. 'Could it have anything to do with you eating like a cow?'

'Because in this wonderfully modern country of Italy, there's no such thing as a garbage disposal, that's why.'

'Oh, this should be good.'

'OK, I'm having pasta or risotto or whatever you've made, which, incidentally, is delicious, but I'm getting full. I still have stuff on my plate, but there's really not enough to stick in the fridge, which is so tiny, there's never any room anyway.'

'So it's the refrigerator's fault.'

'So ... I start thinking about having to scrape off my plate, first with a fork and then with my fingers because a fork just can't get up all those stubborn little scraps, and then shovel the whole gooey mess into that leaky paper bag we're using for garbage, which is going to get all slimy and smelly, which'll attract ants, not to mention spiders, which you'll insist I kill, and then I'll claim that as a devout vegan I'm against the killing of any living thing, and you'll say since when am I a devout vegan since I just inhaled enough meat to gag a timber wolf. It'll turn ugly, we'll get into a big fight, and so to avoid all that, I just eat everything on my plate, and, OK, maybe I am getting a little lunchy, but as you can see, I'm only doing it for you.'

'Why, thank you, Tubby, that's so considerate.' She giggled as she took me in her arms and hugged me in a way that said she was glad I was back from L.A.

And I hugged her back because I was just as glad.

'You must stay up nights thinking these things up,' she said.

She was right. I was staying up nights, but it was mostly to try and figure out what to do with my life now that I had decided not to sell my script to those producers. Remarkably, my agent had been very supportive over my sudden display of integrity, and if I hadn't known any better, I could have sworn he was treating me with a modicum of respect. He told me to go back to Italy, start writing something new, and not to worry about my script. He'd sold it once and he could sell it again.

That was three and a half weeks ago and I hadn't heard from him since.

After Nancy left to go to the market, I made myself a little lunch, and, yes, I ate everything on the plate, because I happened to be a little depressed, you know? What was disheartening was this new script I was working on. When I was in Hollywood I had seen how hungry they were for big-budget action-adventure films. Lots of exploding tanker trucks and Uzi blowback, and every time the hero immolated a neo-Nazi skinhead, an anthrax-wielding Chechnyan, or a Colombian drug lord, he uttered some macho catchphrase, like 'Hasta la vista, baby,' or 'Feel lucky today, punk?'

So after lunch I sat with a yellow legal pad on my lap, trying to find that one catchphrase so testosterone fired it would rip through the Ritalin haze of a generation of teenage boys and entice them to plunk their Slurpies into the cup holders of every multiplex in North America.

I wanted to write something I didn't have any emotional

connection to, so when the inevitable changes and rewrites came, I would feel no pain. But apparently this was not sitting well with me, because when I looked down at the catchphrases I was working on, I saw that I had written:

I AM A WHORE

I felt alone and adrift. I needed to write something to keep my brain from devouring itself, but what? I thought about turning on the TV for inspiration, but the idea of surfing through all those Italian-language channels flayed me. I think at that point I would have sat through a documentary on the Phillips screwdriver if it were in English.

I was mindlessly staring into space when I became aware of the absolute silence. I looked around and realised that the kitchen tap had stopped dripping. This was odd, because that constant plunk, plunk of the Italian Water Torture was something we'd come to count on, like the neighbourhood rooster who suffered from some form of cock-a-doodle-do dyslexia, causing him to start crowing when the sun went down, continue through the night, and be left in poor voice for the sunrise.

I went to the sink and turned the handle, and, sure enough, it was dry. I went into the bathroom and tried that tap with the same result. We'd had water before lunch. Had we forgotten to pay our bill? Was there a broken pipe? I picked up the cellphone and dialled Dino. A recorded voice from TIM (Telecom Italia Mobile) came on, urgently telling me something I couldn't understand. I was musing over the possibilities of living in a world where we had no water and the phones were down, when I remembered having seen a flier or something from the Agenzia dell'acqua. I seemed to recall throwing it out, so I proceeded to dig through the bag of stinky garbage.

I felt a soggy piece of paper, but when I pulled it out, it was yesterday's list of macho catchphrases covered in coffee grounds and pesto sauce. I went to rinse off my hand, only to remember we had no water.

'Goddammit!' I screamed to the mute faces of the Jesus Christs and the naked ladies staring down at me from the wall. 'Why is everything here so difficult? Why is even the simplest thing such a struggle?'

Then I remembered the article I was thinking about pitching to that buddy of mine at the *L.A. Times*. I bet it would really make him laugh to receive an e-mail titled: 'Ten Things I Hate about Tuscany'.

At that moment Nancy entered, heaved a sigh, and let the bag of groceries she was carrying drop to her feet.

'I can't do this anymore. . . .'

'What happened?' I said, trying not to show my delight that she might have an item to add to my list.

'I swung by the church, hoping to catch the mayor's wife,' Nancy said, as she took off her rosary. 'Of course, she wasn't there, but I had to sit through the entire Mass anyway, because the priest was staring at me and I couldn't leave.'

'The sacrifices we make.'

'I'm so sick of these games, I decided to grab the bullshit by the horns and go see the mayor himself.'

'You went to his office?'

'He was right there! I could see him through a crack in the door, doing a jigsaw puzzle, for God sakes, while his assistant's telling me I can't see him because he's in a meeting.'

'How about I get us a meeting?' I said.

'You're going to get us a meeting?'

'Well, you dressing up like Jennifer Jones in *The Song of Bernadette* and running to church six times a day isn't getting us anywhere.'

After apprising her of our water situation, I had her phone the mayor's office and translate exactly what I said. As I dictated, Nancy explained to the mayor's assistant that she was calling for her husband, a *giornalista* on assignment for the *Los Angeles Times*. Nancy went on to explain that I was doing a story about the town, and because I was on a deadline, I needed to interview the mayor as soon as possible.

Without a moment's hesitation the mayor's assistant gave us an appointment for the following day. Nancy hung up and wrapped her arms around me. For this brief moment I was her overfed knight in shining armour.

And I was right about my friend at the *Los Angeles Times*. I e-mailed him that evening, and the following morning I received an enthusiastic fax from his editor authorising me to go ahead with the story.

9. IL SINDACO

The next morning we arrived at the Comune di Cambione in Collina. It was a blocky three-storey building of medieval origin, rebuilt after every war until its last reincarnation in the 1950s left it looking like the unholy marriage of a high Renaissance palazzo and a Texaco service station. At the top of the building fluttered an Italian flag so sun bleached, its red and green bars had faded into the pastels of orange and lime sherbet.

We walked through the lobby, past the feudal banners and the heraldic crests of the local noble families. But just as those icons symbolised the historic grandeur of the town, there were also images of her more tragic recent past. A row of photos chronicled the carnage wrought during the war. Between the retreating Germans and the advancing Allies, the city was heavily damaged. In ghostly black and white these pictures captured the haunted, shell-shocked faces of refugees wandering through the bombed-out rubble searching for food. These were the parents and the grandparents of almost everyone we were dealing with, and their faces were testament to the events that have shaped the lives of three generations of Cambionese.

As we headed down the hall towards the Ufficio del Sindaco (Office of the Mayor), I began hearing something I hadn't heard in twenty years – the staccato clacking of an electric typewriter. We entered the waiting room and the mayor's assistant, a cheerful woman bedecked in African jewellery, stopping pecking on her Olivetti and welcomed us. After making sure we were comfortably ensconced on the sofa, she scurried off to make us cappuccino.

I had just begun leafing through a brochure entitled 'Cambione in Collina – City of Yesterday, Today, and Tomorrow', when a door opened and *il sindaco* himself appeared. He was a thick, broad-shouldered man with an aerodynamically shaped head as bald as a light bulb. *Pelato*, the Italians call such a skull. Peeled. I wondered . . . does every language have to take a shot at those with hair problems?

He greeted us with a politician's handshake that featured the clasping of your hand with both of his for an added touch of sincerity. He escorted us into his office, which, in addition to the usual self-congratulatory plaques and framed documents, was oddly hung with completed jigsaw puzzles that were lacquered and framed, while a half-finished one sat on his desk.

'So how may I be of service?' he asked, as Nancy translated.

'As my wife explained to your assistant,' I said through her, 'the *Los Angeles Times* travel section wants me to do a story about Cambione.'

'Such a big, important newspaper for our humble little town,' he said.

'Well, that's all part of its charm,' I said, as I handed him the fax I had received that morning. 'This is from my editor authorising me to write the article and kindly requesting your cooperation.'

'Of course, anything we can do.' He scanned the paper as if he could read it.

'What really intrigued him was a story about this village by someone who actually lives here,' I had Nancy tell him.

'You live here?' the mayor said, his eyes brimming with innocence.

'We bought the old *rustico* up on the hill,' Nancy said. 'The one people call "the Bunker".'

'Oh, I know it well. As I child I often played there,' he said, gazing nostalgically at a framed puzzle of a lacquered Tahitian sunset.

'Then you know how much work it needs,' Nancy said, '. . . and some of the problems we've encountered.'

'Well, I really don't know all the details.' Nancy didn't have to translate how evasive he was becoming.

'The point is, sir,' I said, boring in, 'I can't write an article as someone who lives here, because due to this *denuncia* business, we don't. And my paper's kind of a stickler about things like that.'

'I see.' He tilted back in his chair but kept level eye contact.

'Of course, the sooner this little problem is solved . . . the sooner I can begin.'

'From what little I understand, your *denuncia* is a rather complicated situation. With many different facets to consider.' He carefully pushed his jigsaw puzzle aside to make a little room on his desk for his elbow.

'And you haven't even heard our side of the story,' Nancy added.

'Indeed,' he said, staring down at the unfinished board. 'And that only makes it . . . uh, more of a puzzlement.'

Nancy tried not to smile when she translated.

'Some pieces fit and some don't,' he said.

'Well, sir, just because some of the pieces may be missing,' I said, 'doesn't mean there isn't a big picture here.'

'True.' He held up a small piece shaped like Florida. 'But even when you have that missing piece in your hand, do you always know where it goes?'

Nancy and I craned our necks to study the board and see where Florida went.

'We feel that you're very skilled at solving puzzlements,' I said, handing him a piece shaped like a bird wing and pointing to where I thought it might fit. 'So we were hoping you'd get involved.'

'I'd be happy to look into it for you, *signore e signora*, but really there's not much I can do until it's been processed by the proper committee.'

'I'm glad you brought that up' – I took out my notepad – 'because I think our one point seven million readers would be very interested in how that process works. And especially how long it's going to take.'

'That's hard to predict,' he said. 'But I can assure you that the Comune di Cambione is known far and wide as one of the most modern and efficient in Tuscany.'

'With all due respect, sir, I saw your office equipment and it made me nostalgic.'

'Oh, this mania for computers is so wrong,' he said, interrupted by the jangling of African jewellery on his assistant, who had entered with our cappuccinos.

'Really?' I clicked my pen and poised to write. 'Why's that?'

'We Italians tend to make a lot of mistakes.' He winked at his assistant, who backed him up with a smile. 'With a computer, once you make a mistake, poof, it's gone! But a typewriter is slow. You make a mistake and there's time to catch it before it goes out in the world for everyone to see.'

'That's terrific,' I said, writing furiously. 'You know, sir, it'd be a damn shame if I couldn't do this article and the world missed out on reading about such a quotable civic leader as you.'

'Sì, *che peccato*,' he said. Yes, what a shame.

'And what's an article without pictures?' I said, taking out my camera.

The mayor sat up and adjusted his tie. 'Could I be doing my puzzle?'

'I don't see why not,' I said, as I composed the shot.

The following day we got a call from the mayor's assistant, and over the jangling of African jewellery, she informed us that the *denuncia* against us had been overturned.

10. TRAPASSATO PROSSIMO

Buoyed by our success at the mayor's office and the prospect of actually living a life here, I vowed to achieve some level of competence in the Italian language. I was no longer content to let Nancy do all the talking while I remained a grey eminence on the periphery of the conversation, like some immigrant grandfather in a 1940s movie, grinning idiotically while his smooth-talking grandchildren helped him file his citizenship papers.

I was eager to strike out on my own and make friends, develop relationships, and by God, reach out and touch somebody. To that end I enrolled at the Giosuè Carducci Language Academy, where my classmates and I were tutored by a young lady with the intoxicating name of Ms Margarita Martini. Three times a week we were drilled on verb conjugations in the *trapassato prossimo* tense and encouraged to memorise the inane conversations of Paulo and Maria, until there began to grow in me a sapling of confidence that would someday be a sturdy enough oak to allow me to have a conversation in a language I did not grow up speaking.

I studied diligently and began to see results. Within a month I was able to carve out a crude version of Survivor's Italian, assuring me that if anything ever happened to Nancy, I could at least get myself fed in a restaurant and then ask directions to whatever hospital or morgue they had taken her.

Of course, I still got a lot of things wrong. Once Nancy and I were at the post office to take care of some bills, a place most Italians go to directly pay a clerk, saving them the anguish that, thanks to Posta Italia, their payment will never get delivered. Nancy presented our water bill and our electricity statement, along with the correct amounts of cash, to the man behind the counter. As he was processing our payments, I heard him use the word *gamba*, which I had just learned was the word for 'leg'. OK, she was wearing shorts, but what was he doing talking about her legs? When I asked her about it, she laughed. What he had said was that she was *in gamba*, a phrase used to compliment someone on their efficiency . . . the Italian equivalent of 'on their toes'.

Mistakes aside, my confidence kept growing until I decided to attempt a conversation with a woman I saw every day, our neighbour Signora Cipollini. A short, stocky old woman who was invariably dressed in a faded brown housecoat and apron, babushka, and huge rubber galoshes, she looked if she'd just stepped out of a Khrushchev-era documentary entitled Heroic Farm Workers of the Ukraine Celebrate the Glorious Five-Year Plan.

I admired how the signora had taken what was essentially a small scrap of land and converted it into a life-sustaining source of food, as self-contained as a terrarium. Her land teemed with rigid rows of carrots, butter lettuce and beets. There was a microgrove of apple and pomegranate trees, flanked by tomato vines and rows of *rapa rosa*, a fat, bloodred turnip the Tuscans eat in the winter. Every square millimetre was under cultivation, in such an efficient manner that those plants not bearing fruit provided shade for those that did, like the line of tall cypress trees that blocked the *tramonto*, a feverish wind that comes howling out the Alps and was thought to cause headaches and homicides.

In addition to her cash crops Signora Cipollini kept a flock of chickens. Eight plump white hens, with an ever-changing number of chicks in tow, all overseen by a speckled rooster who strutted among them like the cock of the walk he was. What was interesting about her approach to livestock was her frugality in feeding them. Instead of squandering money on feed, she would simply take her flock out so they could graze on whatever garbage her neighbours had dumped that day.

It was on one of those walks that I struck up a conversation. I had just done a load of wash and I was in the process of hanging it on the line when Signora Cipollini and her poultry came clucking past our house.

'*Buona sera*, Signora Cipollini,' I said with all the confidence of one quoting the first page of a phrase book.

'*Sera*,' she muttered, eyeing me warily.

'*Molto bello oggi*.' I pointed up to the sky so she would know I was talking about the weather.

'*Troppo caldo*,' she said, indicating her displeasure with the heat.

'*Sì*,' I said agreeably while I composed my next thought. '*Allora, come sta, signora?*'

'*In somma*.'

I didn't know what that meant, so I just plunged on. '*Prendere mangiamo . . . uh, uh, suoi polli?*'

She flashed me a look of horrified indignation, quickly huddled her brood together, and ushered them away with such alacrity, I knew I had said something wrong. As they receded in a flurry of swirling pinfeathers, I leafed though my phrase book and discovered that instead of asking if she were taking her chickens out to eat, I had asked if I could eat her chickens.

And we wonder why nations have such a hard time hammering out peace treaties.

I had gone back to hanging out the laundry when Dino's truck pulled up. He hopped out, casting a baleful eye at a man too busy washing his wife's undies to go out with the boys and gun down a wild pig.

'*Ciao*, Dino,' I said, nonchalantly turning the lacy front of Nancy's pink panties away from him.

'Is your wife sick?' he said, sliding open the hatch and letting his pack of hounds bound free.

'No.' Then I realised that had to be the only explanation for what I was doing. 'Yeah, a little touch of the flu.'

'Oh, too bad,' he said, 'but, listen, I need to talk to you about something.'

'Our water?'

'Your water's OK, huh?' he said pulling a chewed-up clothes peg out of Luna's mouth before she could choke on it.

'Sort of. Ever since they turned it back on, there's been no hot water in the shower.'

'Just in the shower?'

'That's the strange part. Like maybe there's an obstruction, or a broken –'

'I take care of it.'

'How soon?'

'Today, tomorrow.'

'Today would be better.'

'Today is impossible.'

'Tomorrow?'

'Tomorrow I will call my cousin Turrido, one of the finest plumbers Italy has ever produced, and if he can do it, he will do it, and that's a promise.'

'Thanks.'

'But you must help me with my son.'

'What's the matter?' I put on the properly serious expression, which was difficult because of the sudden raspy wetness of Ninja's tongue on my bare foot.

'I am a worried sick. Rudolfo don't want to marry Pia.'

'*Pia?*'

'*Pia Tughi*. They be together since they was kids. Our families are very close. We all expect them to marry, but now he refuses.'

'Well, I'm sure he's got his –'

'No, he don't! You got to talk to him.'

I winced.

'He likes you. He thinks you're *moderno*.'

'Look, Dino, I don't think you can talk anybody into getting married.'

'You and Nancy have no kids, no?'

'No.'

'Then how do you know what you can't talk anybody into? Especially a son who is killing his mother to death because she don't have no grandchildren.'

'Rudolfo is thirty-four years old,' I said, cupping my privates as Cosimo came sniffing up to me. 'He's old enough to know what he wants.'

He looked at me with pity. '*Ai*, you *Americani*. You know how to get to the moon but you don't know how to get to anybody's heart.'

I was truly at a loss to respond to such an observation, but mercifully, we were interrupted by Signora Cipollini coming around the corner. Her unexpected presence sparked an instant, violent confrontation between Dino's pack of dogs and her flock of chickens. Amid a swirling dust storm of clucking and barking came the piercing shrieks of Signora Cipollini and the angry bellowing of Dino trying to separate bird from beast.

Signora Cipollini was screaming that her chickens were being murdered when, in reality, the fighting fowl were inflicting heavy damage on the dogs. The rooster had jumped up on top of Ninja, dug his claws into the dog's fur, and was pecking him on the head. One of her pluckier pullets clamped a beak around Scheherazade's tail and would not let go. The rest of the emboldened hens attacked in an echelon of clawing and scratching until the poor dogs were reduced to a disoriented pack of howling mutts. Dino finally grabbed a broom out of his truck and managed to separate the combatants.

'Promise me you talk to Rudolfo!' he hollered over the barking and clucking, as he herded his mutts towards his truck.

'*Vai! Cretino con sue bestie!*' Signora Cipollini screeched, huddling her hens under the hem of her mud-stained apron.

'What about our shower?' I yelled.

'I speak to Cousin Turrido,' Dino cried as he pushed the last of his dogs inside his truck and slammed the hatch. 'He come over soon as he can.'

'What do we do in the meantime?' I asked as Dino jumped into the cab.

'You come over to our house anytime you want,' Dino called out as he sped off. 'And while Nancy's taking a shower, you can talk to Rudolfo!'

'Now, there's a fine plan,' I said to the rooster, who had no comment as he pecked at the gravel around my feet.

11. IL DIPARTIMENTO D'AUTORIZZAZIONE DELLA LICENZA EDILIZIA

There's no such thing as junk mail in Italy, at least not yet, and since our friends and family wrote to us by e-mail, the arrival of an actual letter, especially an official-looking one, was such an occasion that the postman hand-carried it to our door. Nancy invited him in for coffee, and as he sipped, he watched us read the document overturning our *denuncia*. He congratulated us, then he did what most Italians do. Looking up to the heavens as he tapped on his heart with his fist, he shared his tale of woe dealing with the Comune, specifically how he'd been waiting six years for them to approve the rebuilding of a *ruvinato*, a ruined house, so he, his wife, and their three kids could move out of his mamma's place.

Judging by his and many other stories we'd heard, we were lucky. For two *stranieri* to get this far this fast was remarkable. But we needed to begin rebuilding quickly, because things could turn against us in a heartbeat. So while I loaded up the postman with cookies for his kids, Nancy dialled Umberto. She told him that we had just received the official notification that we could proceed with our renovation, and we'd like him to start immediately. Then Nancy's eyebrows furled over something he was telling her. She tried to get in a word but he kept insisting that we meet in person at a café in the main piazza.

As we got ready to go, Nancy fretted about losing him. Long before I got to Tuscany, she had spent weeks driving around looking at other *rustici* that had been restored. Time and time again the best work had been done by Umberto and his crew.

She contacted him, and when they sat down to talk, she realised how deeply he loved these old stone houses and how well he understood what she wanted to do.

I, meanwhile, was ruminating over how much the Italians hate the telephone. During the course of rebuilding our house, we got calls from our *ingegnere*, the *geometra*, the carpenter, and so on asking us to come to their office or workshop. Invariably, we'd discover that whatever they wanted to discuss could have been dealt with over the phone. But that's not the Italian way. They need to see your face, look in your eyes and use their vast array of hand gestures. So dependent are they on hand gestures that an Italian with a missing finger is thought to have a speech impediment.

So it came as no surprise that as we sat down, Umberto greeted us by placing his palms together, fingers extended towards us, and rocking them up and down as if he were praying. This was the Tuscan way of saying, 'I'm begging you to understand my situation.'

None of the workers we hired ever apologised for not showing up, being late or installing something wrong. When confronted ever so gently, they immediately went on the offensive, getting angry with us for not appreciating how difficult their lives were. In Umberto's case, his face reddened with indignation as he enumerated his woes, which began with his truck breaking down right after he had spent three hundred euros having it serviced! Then, kissing his wedding ring, he told us how his dear wife had fallen out of a tree picking peaches and broken her foot. Without a truck, his work was hampered. And with a plaster cast on her foot his wife could no longer do her duties, forcing him to hire a woman to cook, clean and take care of the kids. So even though we had told him the *denuncia* was going to be lifted, he had taken another job because he wasn't sure ours was ever going to happen.

But even as Italians are disappointing you, they hope to

make the situation acceptable. So Umberto insisted he could do both jobs at once by splitting up his crew and working them overtime.

'It's not right to make your guys work like that in the summer,' Nancy said with a scowl.

'*Loro sono bestie*,' he proudly replied. They're beasts, they like the heat.

'Besides, how can you supervise two jobs at once?'

'I do it all the time,' Umberto said.

Nancy placed the thumb edge of her palm against her forehead and waggled her fingers at him in a gesture reminiscent of the Three Stooges, which meant, appropriately enough, 'You're crazy.'

'*Quanto tempo ci vuole finire nostra casa?*' I haltingly said, asking how long he thought our house would take using a smaller work force.

'Don't worry, *signore*,' Umberto replied in Italian. 'My guys are trained to work quickly, efficiently and, in spite of anything man and nature throws against them, do the most magnificent work in all of Tuscany.'

The words shot out of Umberto's mouth with the velocity of a bullet train, which made it hard for me to follow. At this point I was able to understand about half of what people were saying if they didn't talk too fast or stare down at their shoes when they were speaking.

'Besides, my other job's right next to yours,' Umberto said, turning to Nancy, 'so I can be at two places at once.'

'You're working at Vesuvia Pingatore's?'

Umberto looked up to the heavens, made a fist and pounded it on his chest. 'After I finished work on her brother Mario's villa, she made me promise to do hers next.'

Nancy grimaced.

'Come on, it's no big deal. I'm just doing her outside wall.'

'She already has an outside wall,' Nancy said.

'She wants it higher.'

'So she doesn't have to look at us?' Nancy said.

'I swear to you that no matter what it takes, or how much rain we get, you'll be able to move into your house by the end of summer. OK?'

'Soon as you're done with hers, do you promise you'll put your full crew on ours every day?' Nancy said.

'You have my word,' Umberto replied.

Nancy and I looked at each other and considered the alternatives, which were few. Then she turned to him, put the tip of her index finger on the tip of her thumb, and made a downward movement as if pulling a lamp cord. She was using the Italian gesture that says, a posto . . . 'OK, all set.'

Before we went to the Comune to pick up the building permits, we had some banking to do. One of the conditions of lifting the *denuncia* was agreeing to keep the amount of money needed to cover the cost of the construction in an account at our local bank. Anytime our balance fell below that sum, the bank was obligated to inform them. This was their way of making sure we weren't going to cut and run. We had wired the funds over and now we needed the bank to give us the documentation that the required amount was in place.

The bronze plaque that displayed the name of our bank also announced that this particular institution had been founded twenty years before Columbus sailed for the New World, and every time I walked in, I felt like there were still customers from the fifteenth century waiting for a teller. The bank had computers, but they seemed to be mostly used for sending e-mails and playing video games, often during business hours. Instead, bank workers could be seen using the traditional scissors-and-glue-pot approach to commerce.

As usual, the bank was crowded. There were about a dozen people in a line that was moving at a glacial speed. Italian lines, by the way, are not straight, but round. They tend to coalesce into a loose mob, where everyone seems to be able to follow the threads of many simultaneous conversations at once while never losing track of who goes next.

The wait was endless, but Italians can endure anything as long as they can talk. And their preferred way is everybody at the same time and at a volume we usually reserve for telling somebody the building's on fire. It got so deafening in there that the tellers had trouble understanding their clients. The bank manager started hollering, '*Silenzio!*' but it was so noisy, nobody heard him.

We finally got to a teller. We explained our need and handed him our chequebook. He then disappeared for the exact amount of time it takes to have a cappuccino and a cigarette at the café next door. He reappeared with a document verifying that we had the proper amount on deposit and handed us back our chequebook.

A word about Italian chequebooks and that word is drab. Unlike America, where you can order your cheques in lots of twenty thousand and get them printed with everything from Sunset Over the Mojave to a field of Happy Faces, Italian cheques come in only one colour: a faded, plain institutional brown. When you open an account, they hand you a slim packet of fifteen cheques, stapled together, without even one of those cheesy plastic covers. After you've used up your allotted amount, you return to the bank with your chequebook. They tear it in half, giving you back the part where you recorded the information on the cheques you wrote, and then give you a fresh pack of fifteen.

In a country recognised for style and design, the very birthplace of the Renaissance, this is an appalling lack of *sprezzatura*, or what the Italians themselves call 'the art of living'. Perhaps they are content with having their cheques in sober, solid hues and leaving images of Michelangelo's David and

Raphael's angels to adorn the Jockey shorts and potholders that are bought by the tourists.

On our way to the Comune, we spotted a homeless man headed in the same direction. I fumbled for some change, but as he came closer, I realised it was Mario Pingatore! His face was covered in day-old stubble and he was wearing a frayed shirt, paint-splattered overalls, and a battered little sailor's hat that looked as if it belonged to a child. His only concession to fashion was a threadbare mackintosh he wore over his shoulders, Vittorio De Sica style.

Instead of regaling us with his pip, pip, cheerio British, he spoke little and what he did say was in Italian. He was angry for two reasons. First, he was miffed that we were actually going to fix up the *rustico*, which he had had every opportunity to do. In fact, before putting it on the market, he had done his own remodel. But instead of turning it over to professional workers with power tools, he did it on the cheap, hiring four Albanians with putty knives to mortar up some cracks and install glass in the windows.

His second source of irritation was that he had to come to the Comune to receive his tax assessment. Hence, the wardrobe of a Dumpster diver over his usual natty English tweeds.

As Mario trudged off to the tax collector, we climbed two flights of marble stairs and headed for the Dipartimento d'Autorizzazione della Licenza Edilizia. When we entered the office, I thought it was interesting that the department charged with the supervision of all construction and remodelling in the city was, in fact, under construction. Bare wires hung from the ceiling and large sections of the walls had been opened up. As we stepped around ladders, idle power tools, and buckets of plaster, Nancy told me that this was exactly the way it had been when she was here two years ago.

A common feature of every government office in Italy is a

constantly ringing phone that nobody ever bothers to answer. This office, being bigger, had two phones ringing maddeningly out of sync. On top of that the FM radio piped in to soothe us had drifted off its station and was now broadcasting pure static.

'*Buona sera*,' Nancy and I said in unison when we finally reached the man behind the counter. He was movie-star handsome, with chiselled features and a magnificent Roman nose. His face made me grateful I hadn't been born here, because with so many good-looking men around, I would never have found a woman. But he was rather short, and he immediately put on his hat so he'd be Nancy's height.

We handed over our documents, and he glared at our papers like a man reading that his bank had just gone under. Then he took off his hat and disappeared. We waited patiently, but when his absence stretched way past the time it took to have a cappuccino and a cigarette at the café next door, we knew there was trouble.

'We cannot issue you your permits,' he said in Italian as he snapped his hat back on and stood up on his toes.

Nancy's face whitened with shock. 'What?'

'What'd he say?' I asked.

'Did we fill out something wrong?' she asked in his language.

'The house has no address,' he imperially replied.

'What's he saying?' I implored.

'He can't give us the permits because we have no address,' she said in my direction.

'Tell him that's why we're here,' I urged.

'That's why we're here,' she said sweetly in Italian. 'To get an address.'

'Yes, but we can't give you one, because we can't find any proof your house exists.'

'What's going on?' I asked.

'Please ...' Nancy muttered between clenched teeth. Then,

turning to him with a smile, she said, 'I'm sorry, *signore*, but we don't understand what the problem is.'

'I'm trying to tell you that we've searched everywhere and there's no indication that your house was ever registered.'

'What? What?' I demanded.

'He's saying that there's absolutely no proof our house ever existed.'

'Huh?' I turned and glared down at him. 'What are you talking about? People have been living there for hundreds of years.'

'He can't understand you,' Nancy said.

'I think he can and I think he's speaking Italian just to piss me off.'

Nancy closed her eyes and bobbed her head back and forth, as if she were smashing her forehead into a brick wall.

'Just tell him what I said,' I hissed.

Nancy flicked her smile back on and spoke to him in Italian, until I stopped her.

'Wait a minute, you just used the words *mio marito*. What are you saying about "your husband"?'

'That you don't mean to be an asshole, but you missed lunch.'

'OK, go ahead.'

She went on to ask how people could have been living in the *rustico* for hundreds of years if it didn't exist.

'Back then it was common to build a structure and not register it,' he explained in Italian, 'and over the years no one's ever bothered. So according to law, if it's never been registered it doesn't exist.'

'Why hasn't this come up before?' Nancy asked.

'No one's ever tried to remodel it,' he replied.

'Come on, man, how can it not exist?' I said, elbowing Nancy out of the way. 'Everybody in town knows it's there!'

He said something to me in Italian that was so indignant, he jerked his head and his hat went askew.

I dug a paper out of our folder and handed it to her. 'Show him the title. Doesn't that prove something?'

He didn't even look at it, replying to Nancy, who turned to me and said, 'Their position is: a title signed over to us is only a bill of sale. Nothing more.'

'Well, if it doesn't exist,' I said to Nancy, 'ask him what difference does it make what we do to it?'

Nancy asked and was answered. Holding her throbbing temples, she told me that the law says it's illegal to alter or change an unregistered property.

'Well, it's immoral to approve the sale of something when you know damn well you're not going to allow any improvements,' I said.

'Honey . . .' Nancy said, tugging on my arm.

'We're only trying to make something nice out of a place no one can live in!' I cried. 'Improve the neighbourhood, build up the tax base and – and . . . wait till the *Los Angeles Times* hears about this!'

Nancy dragged me away before I could finish my indictment of how they ran things in this Tuscan Hooterville.

'You can't get anywhere arguing with them,' she said as we stepped over a trough of wet plaster.

'The hell you can't! Goethe lived here, you know. In Italy for three years. And he once said, "Be bold and great forces will come to your aid."'

'Listen, honey, they've been here two thousand years and they never invited you, me, or Goethe. So forget bold, that doesn't work. Let's just relax and try to figure out how to do things their way, OK?'

12. L'AVVOCATO

I have no trouble lying to the Italians, because they're a highly imaginative people who have an ethereal relationship with the truth. They are a nation of natural-born storytellers who love to wrap you up in their yarns. Interestingly, they tend to label such a narrative as *una storia*, which implies that what they are telling you can be true, made up or a combination of the two. Often these anecdotes are long and quite intricate, carefully crafted to elicit your sympathies, or, failing that, exhaust you so you'll go away.

For instance, we have an English friend in Italy who once called a repairman because he wasn't getting any heat in his house. After examining the furnace the repairman blithely told him it was working perfectly. Trouble was the outside air was too cold.

We had a similar experience after we moved into the *rustico* and had a satellite dish installed by Telepiù Italia so we could watch CNN and the BBC World Service (which, incidentally, aired a documentary on the Phillips screwdriver that was quite fascinating). A few days later, however, something malfunctioned and we couldn't get any reception at all.

After many phone calls, with me screaming in Nancy's ear, a cable guy finally showed up. He looked at our equipment, jiggled a few wires, and concluded that everything was working fine. But, as I pointed out, we still had no picture or sound, strongly suggesting that he climb up on the roof and try repositioning our dish.

Since he didn't want to do that, he told us that the problem was with the transmission of our signal. Being in the communication business myself, I pressed him for specifics. He was vague and evasive enough to make me think he was vamping, so I kept grilling him because I didn't want to go another day without TV.

Finally, he leaned in close and in a confidential tone told us that the company didn't want their customers to know this, but they were having trouble with their satellite. I asked him what they were doing about it, and as he packed up his tools, he told me to just be patient. The satellite would soon be functioning again because Telepiù Italia had the best technicians in the world.

I immediately pictured Telepiù Italia's secret launching pad high in the Alps. A rocket blasts off with two pastanauts and they dock with the satellite. The hatch pops open and Luigi says to Giovanni, 'OK, pass me the wrench.'

Giovanni says, 'Hey, I thought you brought the wrench.'

'Doh!'

We didn't want Umberto to know the real reason that our building permits were delayed, so in the grand tradition of *una storia*, we informed him that there'd be a slight holdup because the paperwork had to be routed to the city of Lucca for somebody's signature. It was a lie, of course, but it was a good explanation because this kind of a delay could take anywhere from two weeks to two years to resolve.

Truth was, we had made repeated appeals to the Comune to issue us an address, but we had been flatly turned down each time. We realised that we needed help, so we sought out a lawyer. After sifting through a number of recommendations, we settled on one who had the exact qualifications I always seek in an attorney: He was cheap and he spoke English. But despite his reasonable rates, when we drove up to the office of Avvocato Bonetti, I found myself agitated about paying good money to somebody whose title sounded like the key ingredient in guacamole.

The office itself was on a run-down commercial street sandwiched between a shoe repair shop and a store selling clocks. The walls were thin, so as you sat in his office, you had to conduct your business with the steady tapping of the shoemaker's hammer in one ear and the constant barrage of bells, gongs and cuckoos in the other. If this weren't enough, Avvocato Bonetti had three cellphones on his desk, one of which was always ringing. The constant barrage of phone calls was all from members of his family. His wife called (twice), followed by his daughter, his brother-in-law and, of course, his mamma.

'You think you have problems?' he said, picking up one of his cellphones. 'It's nothing compared to what I have with my family. Excuse me.'

'Of course,' I said, as a clock next door bonged eleven times, even though it was only twenty after two.

Each time he spoke to someone, I noticed that l'avvocato propped his cellphone under his chin, freeing up both hands so he could make hand gestures that the other party would never see. And he had good reason to gesture emphatically, for, as we were to learn in the course of that hour, he was struggling to find a job for a brother-in-law who hadn't worked in two years, cart around a teenage daughter who had to be driven to a clinic in Siena three times a week for an eating disorder, and console an elderly mother who kept waking him in the middle of the night to find a Siamese cat that had been dead for twenty years.

'You seem awful busy,' I said, getting up and gesturing for Nancy to follow. 'Maybe we should come back some –'

'No, no, no,' he assured me, opening a desk drawer and sweeping all of his cellphones into it. 'You have my complete and undivided attention.'

Nancy tugged on my shirtsleeve until I sat back down, and we proceeded to lay out our story. Avvocato Bonetti listened intently, never once distracted by the muffled rings of the various cellphones from inside his desk drawer. Then he leaned back in his chair, rubbed his chin, and told us that the problem we were facing could take months to resolve. Maybe years. But not to worry, over the course of three centuries our house must have been identified in some surveyor's report or perhaps a geological survey. There had to be a record of it. And once we had that, we'd have enough evidence to file an appeal, which we could win!

By now I had the makings of a fine headache brewing behind my eyes, and with the few brain cells I had left, I was ready to summon my arm to throw in the towel. But Nancy was smiling, her eyes glinting like a bird of prey's at the prospect of proving that, at least in this part of Tuscany, you can fight City Hall.

Avvocato Bonetti buzzed his intercom, and a moment later a young lady entered. This was his sister, Avvocatessa Bonetti, apparently the only person in his family he wasn't at odds with. She would help us search the old city records to find any trace of such a transaction. Meanwhile, Avvocato Bonetti told us that he would speak to the head of urban planning for the entire Frazione di Lucca. Perhaps he could be persuaded to look the other way.

We were perplexed. Was he suggesting a bribe? And if so, did they take American Express? He was vague, even though influence peddling is not illegal in Italy. The only crime associated with such an action is if you take money on the promise you can fix something and you fail to do so.

We arranged to meet Avvocatessa Bonetti at the Comune archives, thanked them both, and said our goodbyes.

My head was ringing louder than Big Ben at high noon, but as we headed for the car I was determined to tell Nancy how ready I was to dump the house. I decided to soften her up by first telling her about my headache, but before I could get to the part where it was most likely an inoperable brain tumour, she suddenly wrapped her arms around me.

'Do you know how great it is that you're here with me?' she said.

'Me? What do I do?'

'A lot, and even if you did nothing, just you being with me makes me feel like I'm not fighting everybody all by myself. I know this is hard on you, but I just want you to know how much I really appreciate you being on my side.'

'Hey, that's what being a couple's all about,' I said.

She smiled and my brain tumour was miraculously healed.

13. UN GIRO

My behaviour at the Dipartimento della Licenza and the lawyer's office made Nancy feel that I was becoming as stressed-out here as I had been in Hollywood, and she worried that I was in danger of missing all the joys of living in Italy. A change of scenery might help, so when I managed to scorch the Teflon off our favourite frying pan, it gave us the perfect excuse. We decided to splurge and buy a new one in *rame*, copper. And when you buy copper, everybody knows that you must take a giro (a trip) to Montepulciano and buy from Signor Mazzetti.

The drive to Montepulciano took us through some of the most serenely beautiful wine country in all of Chianti. Soft, rolling hills, as sublimely curved as a Stradivarius violin, spread out before us as the land pulsed with the greening of early summer growth. Rigid rows of grapevines ran like spokes to the horizon. Tall, spindly cypress trees swayed in the wind, and from everywhere at once came the smell of sun-warmed earth and budding Sangiovese grapes.

I was trying to let the palpable sensations of the land wash through me and sweep away my cares, but the very vehicle we were sitting in reminded me of our problems. Without an address to register it, we couldn't buy a car. So for the past two months we had been renting a Fiat Punto at twenty-four euros a day. Do the maths and you'll quickly discover why Avis owns a sixty-seven-storey high-rise in Manhattan and you don't.

A more imminent threat, however, was not money but death. Italians drive with a ferocity usually connected to a blood sport – horns blasting, brakes screeching, gears grinding – and that's just getting out of the driveway. Two thousand years ago these maniacs would have been racing chariots around the Circus Maximus, but today all their horses are under their hoods, as they roar past each other in pursuit of a laurel wreath from some long-forgotten past.

I was grateful that Nancy was behind the wheel and not me. Being far more familiar with both the terrain and the temperament, she did the driving and navigating, while I was charged with the all-important tasks of selecting the appropriate CD and turning off the air conditioner when she went to pass somebody on a hill.

The problem with driving in Italy is basically this: Cars and Vespas come at you so suddenly and from such unexpected angles that a driver all by himself is easily overwhelmed. My theory is, to drive safely in this country requires at least two other people in the car, a tail gunner and a wingman. Even then, it's precarious because 85 per cent of the drivers in Italy drive much too fast, while 15 per cent drive much too slow. Of course, the too-fast drivers are obsessed with passing the too-slow drivers on roads that are ancient, narrow and winding. This would be dangerous enough, but throw in the inordinately large number of huge trucks and those odd little three-wheeled putt-putts, comically overloaded with bales of hay and various farm implements, and you begin to get a sense of the peril.

We were stuck behind such a putt-putt, chugging along at eleven kilometres an hour, as we followed the road up to Montepulciano, the biggest and highest of all the hill towns in southern Tuscany. The town sits atop a narrow ridge of volcanic rock and as you approach, the ancient fortifications seem to lean down on you in their full medieval menace. We entered the city through the Porta al Prato, driving past the three hanging balls that signify that these gates, and much of this city, were once the property of the Medicis.

We then began the search for a parking space. Whenever you plan a trip in Italy you must double the time you've allotted, because it takes the same amount of time to find a parking space as it does to travel to your destination. The problem is so acute that as soon as an Italian spots a parking space he grabs it, then leaves his car there, preferring to get around by bus and taxi for the rest of his life. On the off chance that a parking space actually does open up, chaos ensues. The situation is best illustrated by one of those flat puzzles we all played with as kids, the one where you moved the tiles around because one space was free. Whenever anyone leaves a parking space, every car in Italy moves to adjust, because, like nature, Italian drivers abhor a vacuum.

We finally found a space so ambiguously marked, we had an equal chance to get or not get a parking ticket. We walked down the Via di Gracciano as it looped through the monumental area of the old town, changing names four times. We strolled past churches and palazzi built of warm, salmon-coloured stone and supported by graceful curvilinear pediments.

The street, now calling itself Via di Voltaia, widened as it gently ascended upwards. It was a stunning walk, because as you strolled in shade past the upmarket boutiques and gourmet wine shops, you'd come to a break between the buildings and you'd be suddenly dazzled by a slice of golden-green countryside.

Finally, we came to the establishment known as Signor Mazzetti's Rinomata Rameria (Copper Store of Renown). It was a small, densely cluttered shop where every square inch was occupied by something made of, or covered with, copper. Pots, pans, kettles, clocks, jelly moulds, colanders, wine stoppers, mailboxes, doorstops, hat racks, weather vanes and irons, back-scratchers and letter openers, all in copper. The only things not covered in copper were the elderly Signor Mazzetti and his cat, Beppe.

He spoke passionately about *rame*, his white mane of hair bristling with excitement at the idea of copper-coating an object he had not yet thought of. Did I mention he sold a copper-coated fly swatter?

We told him we were in the market for a cooking pan, and

sensing we were new to his world, he took delight in explaining the three different grades we could buy. He showed us his best, a heavy-duty, restaurant-grade pan three millimetres thick with an inside coating of quicksilver-coloured tin. I grasped the long bronze handle and imagined that when full of pasta it would be the equivalent of bench-pressing one of those three-wheeled putt-putts.

He showed us the medium grade, which was two and half millimetres thick and was intended for large families. Again, it would take a large family to lift it off the stove and haul it to the table. We finally settled on the most popular one, measuring two millimetres thick. It had the graceful classic shape of an Etruscan bowl, and with its bulged-out bottom and hammer-pounded surface, Nancy liked the way it would look hanging on the kitchen wall. Signor Mazzetti was pleased with our choice, commenting that whichever one we selected, we would be getting an authentic piece of copper work that was *fatto a mano*, made by hand.

As he wrapped our pan and prepared the bill, we browsed his store for any of our other copper needs, coming frighteningly close to buying a copper-handled toilet plunger.

The copper bell above the door rang and Signora Mazzetti entered with their four-year-old grandson, Lorenzo. While Lorenzo chased Beppe around the store, she reminded Signor Mazzetti that he had promised to take his grandson for a haircut. He told her that he first wanted to show us his workshop. We suggested that if he wanted to take Lorenzo to the barbershop now, we'd go have lunch and come back afterwards to see his workshop when we picked up our pan.

He asked us where we were going to eat. When we told him we had no idea, he insisted we go to a little *osteria* around the corner, because they were making one of their specialties today, *pici all'aglione*, thick spaghetti in a garlicky tomato sauce.

Allow me a moment to explain the various designations of

eating establishments in Italy, and what the differences are between a *ristorante*, a *trattoria*, and an *osteria*. Although the lines have tended to blur over the last few years, any place called a *ristorante* is bound to be fancy, with white tablecloths, heavy silver, and a menu that usually takes classic Italian dishes and tortures them with a fusion of sauces until they are beyond recognition. Although they often serve excellent food (one has to be profoundly unlucky to get a bad meal in Tuscany), many think it's unnecessary to pay those prices, because great Italian cooking is simple, especially in Tuscany, where the cuisine is essentially peasant food, honest and delicious. For that reason, you may be better served by eating at either a *trattoria* or an osteria.

A *trattoria* is a family-style restaurant. It has chequered tablecloths, and Chianti bottles hang from the ceiling. It's the original of what the rest of the world thinks of as Italian dining. Meals are served *a la famiglia* on large platters, and not surprisingly, the ambience is noisy, smoky and brimming with life.

An *osteria*, which actually means 'tavern', is the least expensive of the three and is primarily a place where workingmen take their meals, with long wooden tables covered with butcher paper, benches without backs, and food far greater in quality and quantity than you'd ever expect to find in such humble surroundings. There is a rough conviviality that welcomes you, but as many old-timers are sad to report, white-collar workers, ladies in hats, and even yuppie scum have recently discovered the delights of *osteria* dining and bestowed upon it the highest compliment an Italian can give an eatery, '*Si mangia bene, si spenda poco.*' Here, one eats well and pays little.

We didn't have dessert at the *osteria* since Signor Mazzetti advised us to go to a certain wine shop down the street, and enjoy their famous baked ricotta cheese smothered in local honey. This proved to be one of those remarkable instances of just when you thought something couldn't get any better, it did. The *pici all'aglione* we had for lunch was hearty and superb, the sweetness of the garlic elegantly melding with the natural tartness of the tomatoes. Just like the syrupy smoothness of the honey found its perfect complement in the warm brick of baked ricotta cheese it was poured over at the wine shop he had recommended.

Like many of the *enoteche* (wine shops) in town, this one invited you to go down into their wine cellar and see the Etruscan tombs. This part of the old city had been built over a honeycombed maze of basements and underground tunnels that once connected all the palaces and cathedrals. So with the ambrosial taste of ricotta and honey still in our mouths, we descended the mouldy staircase that led down to the wine cellar, examining a collection of medieval torture devices, household utensils, and chastity belts bolted to the wall. We walked down long, darkened corridors, passing rows of fat oaken vats lying on their sides, as big as four-door sedans and filled with wine aging in the cool silence. The scent of wine was so pervasive, it seemed mixed in with the very moisture sweating through the ancient brick walls.

We finally came to an expansive chapel-shaped area. It was a barren space, but when we looked closely we could make out indentations on the floor that might have been the outline of an altar. To this day no one can figure out how old this room is or what it was used for, but it's located directly under the altar of the Chiesa di Gésu above, leading to speculation that it was once an Etruscan place of worship.

We returned to Signor Mazzetti's shop to find our pan wrapped and Lorenzo sporting a new haircut. After paying and saying goodbye to Signora Mazzetti and Beppe the cat, we followed Signor Mazzetti and Lorenzo out the back door and down a flight of broken concrete stairs. We navigated the narrow medieval alleyways as Signor Mazzetti, holding Lorenzo by the hand, told us how his father had come to Montepulciano from a small village north of Perugia to set up the store in 1910.

Signor Mazzetti and his wife took over the shop after the Second World War. It prospered and they raised a fine, healthy family. But now that they were ready to retire, they didn't have anyone to leave it to. He lamented that we were living in an age when young people weren't interested in the old crafts anymore. His sons and sons-in-law had no desire to work the copper, but he was praying that he might plant a seed in Lorenzo.

Crossing one of the perpetually gridlocked streets that led out of the city, we approached a padlocked garage. He opened it, and we entered a cramped, dark workshop smelling of sulphur. He turned on the bare hanging bulb to illuminate a world of drill presses, workbenches, kilns, stacks of copper ingots, and boxes of every imaginable size of fitting, hinge, and rivet. But the star of this constellation was the anvil. Dark, silver-grey, and battle scarred in its invincibility, it sat on a concrete pedestal and even though it was only about the size of a sewing machine, it occupied the centre of Signor Mazzetti's workshop with the permanence of a mountain range.

He sat Lorenzo at a workbench with a battered piece of copper and smiled as the child gleefully pounded on it with a small hammer. Then Signor Mazzetti selected a flat copper disk about the size of a DVD and took it to his anvil. He began using various taps and dies to engrave the copper as he asked us about ourselves. We told him how we had come to Tuscany to try to make a new life together and about the problems we had run into along the way. As we told our story, people started wandering in.

First it was Francesco, who owned the glass-blowing workshop next door. The two men, obviously old friends, commiserated over how the rising price of natural gas for their furnaces was bound to drive them both out of business. Then two Senegalese men popped in, wondering if we wanted to buy any colourful woven baskets.

Next to arrive was Lancellotto, Signor Mazzetti's best friend. A bottle of ruby-red Vino Nobile di Montepulciano appeared, and it all turned convivial. As Lorenzo hammered on his little piece of copper and Nancy bargained with the Senegalese, Lancellotto performed the story of how his father had helped Signor Mazzetti's father bring this very anvil across Lake Trasimeno in a small rowboat. A storm came up, and the men had had to struggle mightily to keep the anvil from winding up at the bottom of the lake with them under it.

A busload of Chinese tourists appeared and, thinking they had stumbled onto to some kind of crafts fair, began taking pictures. They handed Nancy and me their cameras and posed by the anvil with Signor Mazzetti.

Finally, we told everyone that it was getting late and we had a long drive back to Cambione. But before we left, we watched Signore Mazzetti use a metal cutter to trim the copper disc into the shape of a heart. After cutting it in half and polishing the rough edges, he handed Nancy and me the two pieces. When we held the two halves together, we could see that our two names were linked together by a chain of engraved hearts. We thanked him profusely, and after a round of handshakes and hugs, we left with our new pan, two woven baskets, and a copper heart.

Things happen in Italy that happen no where else on earth. A magical friendliness is spread all over the place like pixie dust. Sure, the salesman in America who greets you when you walk into Circuit City is as affable as a sheepdog, but isn't that well-practised camaraderie all part of their corporate policy? In Italy, especially in the small family-run shops, they don't just go for friendly, they actually seek to engage you as a person.

And this can take so many forms, like the local shoemaker who examines your heels and tells you that you don't need new ones yet. Just walk around on your old ones for *quaranta giorni* (forty days), and then come back. Or your favourite *fruttivendolo* who stops you from selecting the shiny red apples and steers you to the ugly brown pugs that wind up tasting more delicious than any apple you've ever eaten. When you tell him that you want four, he puts five in your bag because four is an unlucky number in Italy, while thirteen is not.

Delighted that our windshield wasn't plastered with parking tickets, we drove back to Cambione with the setting sun splashing riotous shades of reds and golds in our eyes. I looked at my half of the copper heart and realised that, when I wasn't having an 'I Hate Italy Day', this place had actually started to tug on my heartstrings.

Nancy downshifted to pass a three-wheeled putt-putt and I slid in a CD of Italian love songs.

14. L'ESTATE

Summer was here. Streams and creeks roared with snowmelt from the Alps rushing down to the Mediterranean. Every night there were *sagras* and *festas*; concerts in churches and castles. Every day l'estate got a little hotter. In a month the winds would go into a kick-stall, causing the trees and the cornstalks to stand as motionless as if they were in a vacuum.

We were also in a vacuum. Every morning, we met Avvocatessa Bonetti at the Comune archives to continue clawing our way through a dingy basement full of file cabinets and cardboard boxes. Some of the documents were ancient, written in a form of Italian that's no longer spoken, and forcing us to enlist the services of a professor of linguistics at the university in Pisa to translate them into the modern vernacular.

During the course of our investigation we discovered why the Tughi and the Tartughi families hated each other, why the former capo of the local *carabinieri* went to jail, and that when Rudolfo was born, Dino and Flavia had only been married for two months.

But there was not a single word about *il piccolo rustico*.

I was squatting over a box of dusty documents, using my pocket dictionary to try and figure out whether they were geological surveys or death certificates, when I heard someone addressing me.

'I say, old sport, frightfully dank down here, eh, what?'

I looked up to see Mario Pingatore standing over me in a crisp white linen suit and a creamy Borsalino hat.

'Worse are the spiders,' he said for Nancy's benefit. 'Mind the little grey buggers. One bite and you're dead as mutton.'

'Thanks for the warning, Mario,' Nancy said, 'but if you'll excuse us, we've got work to do.'

'Sorry. Didn't mean to disturb. Just here to pay my taxes,' he said with a sly little grin. 'Must have taken a wrong turn looking for the bloody loo.'

Mario had reason to smile. His hobo costume had somehow convinced the Comune to reduce his assessment. He had money to play with and he was in no hurry to leave.

'Find anything?' he said, looking over Avvocatessa Bonetti's shoulder.

'*Nulla*,' she said. Nothing.

'Call me an old softie,' he said, turning to me, 'but I feel bad for you and Nancy, stuck down here when you two should be out larking in the sunshine.'

'The California sunshine?' I suggested.

'And paying a solicitor by the hour, on the odd chance you'll –'

'If you're thinking about us giving up,' Nancy said, 'forget about it.'

'Oh, come on, you Yanks put up a good fight as you always do, but you've surely come a cropper here. Now, I'm willing to make you a very decent offer. Pay you full whack.'

Hmm, I wondered: How much is full whack?

'Not for me, mind you, but Vesuvia's keen to keep the old place in the family name. Sentimental rubbish and all that.'

'We're not selling,' Nancy said with utter finality.

'Very well.' He shrugged. 'Good hunting. Hope you find something.'

'Maybe we'll find something on you,' Nancy said provocatively.

'Trust me, dear girl, I have nothing to hide.'

We worked in silence for the rest of the morning, interrupted only by Nancy calling me over several times to kill little grey spiders. The Comune closed at one, and after swinging home to eat lunch and change, we headed up to the *rustico*. We couldn't do anything about the structure right now, but Nancy and I agreed that we'd at least clear away all the stones and weeds, so that when we finally did get the paperwork straightened out, Umberto and his guys would have a clear area in which to work.

Nancy was on weed patrol and I had challenged myself to see how many stones I could lift before I got a hernia. At first I thought heaving stones would be fun in a mindless way, and a good workout to boot, but I quickly discovered how gruelling this was. Filling and hauling wheelbarrows full of stones, day after day under the blazing sun, was hell, and I vowed never to squawk about a bill from Umberto, because whatever we were going to pay these guys, it wouldn't be enough.

At the end of our labours Nancy and I sat in the shade with our backs propped up against a stone wall, too exhausted to speak. We passed a bottle of *acqua naturale* back and forth, taking long swigs, holding the bottle gingerly with hands raw from hard labour. From across the way we could see Umberto and his crew leaving Vesuvia Pingatore's house. They saw us and waved. We feebly waved back. From behind a window we saw a shadow, and we could just imagine the severity of the *malocchio* (evil eye) she was casting in our direction.

While Nancy muttered some unflattering comments about the Pingatores, Super Mario's offer kept eating through my brain like battery acid. How tempting to get out now while I was feeling so bruised and achy, physically beaten, and stymied at every turn. I knew Nancy was in for the long haul, but was I?

We drove back to the rented house and took showers ... short ones timed to end before we ran out of hot water. After picking at some cold cuts we were both too exhausted to eat, we dragged ourselves to bed. Nancy fell asleep immediately, but I lay there trying to sort out my feelings. They all seemed to be bound up around the observation that life in Italy was hard, but it was easy; while life in L.A. was easy, but it was hard. I felt confused and conflicted. I wanted clarity and a pure vision of my future, but my brain felt numb and burned out by all the exasperations and exhilarations of living here.

I was listening to the soft purr of Nancy's breathing when I drifted into a hypnagogic state, and somewhere between staying awake and falling asleep, my screenplay started to write itself.

INT. WAREHOUSE – NIGHT

Dark, spooky, water dripping.

CRACK DEALER pops out of the shadows and fires a LARGE assault rifle at ROCK.

ROCK whips out a LARGER rocket launcher and fires back at the CRACK DEALER.

There's a shattering EXPLOSION.

Smoke clears, revealing a stain on the wall that was once the CRACK DEALER.

ROCK

The dog with the biggest bone always wins.

My eyes popped open and I accidentally knocked over a water glass fumbling for my notepad.

'Shit.' I tried to mop up the spill with the edge of the blanket.

'Hunh?' Nancy mumbled, waking up. 'What're you doing?'

'Sorry, I had this idea. Go back to sleep,' I said, drying the pen off on my T-shirt.

'Idea for what?' She rolled over to face me.

'You know, that action-adventure thing.'

'You still doing that?'

'Sort of,' I said, scribbling in the darkness.

'What happened to "I'm a whore"?'

'I think at these prices we're technically referred to as call girls.'

'Did you ever finish that article for the *Times*?'

'Still working on it.'

'I'd rather see you spend your time on that,' she said, sitting up. 'And why is the blanket wet?'

'Problem with the article,' I said, 'the reader's got to be thinking if I have so many complaints about Tuscany, what am I doing living here?'

'Well,' she said through a yawn, 'maybe you need to explain

that you're just cranky because we're living this weird gypsy existence, and that you'll be a lot happier when we move into the new house.'

I thought for a moment about the wisdom of pursuing this. 'I'm not trying to rain on your piazza, but has it occurred to you that we may never live in that house?'

'Go to sleep.' She rolled over and pulled the covers up to her shoulders.

'We're working like galley slaves, haemorrhaging money, in search of some scrap of evidence that probably doesn't even exist. I mean, at some point we might have to admit that we've come a cropper here, whatever the hell that means.'

She rolled over, propped herself up on her elbow and stared at me.

'What?' I innocently asked.

'I can't believe that Mario Pingatore . . .'

'It has nothing to do with him!'

'He wants it back,' Nancy said. 'Doesn't that mean something to you?'

'Yeah, he's a bigger schmuck than we are.'

'How about he knows there's a way to get an address?'

'Then why didn't he do it?'

'Because he needed us to buy it first so we'd put in the road. Then he buys it back, gets the address, and enlarges it. Any idea what that could be worth?'

'At this point I don't care anymore.'

'Really?' Even in the dim light I could see her eyes go icy and hard.

'Really.'

'OK, fine. Let's sell it.'

'I mean, we've given it a good try here, you know.'

I was expecting an argument, but she got real quiet.

'And it doesn't mean we're giving up on Italy,' I said, trying not to sound like I was pleading.

'I'll call Mario tomorrow.'

'Look, I don't want you to think that I'm just some spoiled yuppie who's whining because I have to stick my hand in garbage and I can't watch *Friends*, because –'

'It doesn't matter what I think.'

'– because I know the house means a lot to you but, Jesus, honey, for the money we're spending, we could rent a villa and live like –'

'The house means nothing to me. Nothing! What means something is that you and me were finally doing something together. Standing for something, committed to something!'

'Come on . . .'

'For twenty years we lived parallel lives, which was fine. But I really thought this was our last chance to do something like this.'

'Oh, stop being so dramatic.'

'How many more years do you think we've got where we're strong enough and healthy enough to haul rocks and take on the powers that be?'

'A lot.'

'Don't kid yourself. In ten years we'll be sitting in wheelchairs, wondering what room we left our teeth in. That's why we've got to do this now!'

'I don't know. . .'

'Unless this is just too much reality for you.'

Her words stung me like a slap across the face with a riding crop. Righteous anger started to rise, but it had nowhere to go, because I knew she was right. All my writing, the scripts, the articles, were just my way of retreating into the playground of my mind. I've lived my whole life in fantasy land, and only pure dumb luck and/or divine providence enabled me to make a living out of it. Nancy knew I was no good at reality, because, just like Peter Pan, if I had bad thoughts I would no longer be able to fly. Once again, I was guilty of what she had always charged me with . . . being absent from my own life.

15. LA PROVA

Despite my misgivings I was earnestly trying to improve my language skills, fit into small-town life and wean myself away from living inside my own skull to the exclusion of everywhere else. I discovered that a daily walk through Cambione was a good way to address all of those needs. Without Nancy, I had to rely on my own abilities to do my shopping and converse with the people I saw every day.

One ritual I grew to cherish was breakfast, Italian style. There were more cafés in Cambione than churches, and there were a lot of churches, indicating a preference for the worship of strong coffee and a flaky cornetto over the usual path to salvation. I had no favourite, gravitating to the café that had the liveliest crowd dishing the freshest gossip. People came to know me as I tried my best to join in. Gratefully, Italians are very forgiving about the mangling of their mother tongue. If I got anywhere close, they helped fill in the blanks. Much of their banter, however, was lost on me because they'd often lapse into a local dialect, full of 'shushes', for their s's and chopping the ends of their verbs . . . something Ms Margarita Martini failed to cover at the Giosué Carducci Language Academy.

If the café wasn't crowded enough to support conversation, I borrowed an Italian newspaper and tried to understand why the sports reporter wrote that the local soccer team had been playing like a pack of *mutilati* (handicapped people).

After breakfast I took a leisurely stroll down the walking street on stones smoothed soft as mascarpone cheese by a thousand years of foot traffic. The main walking street, officially known as Via Vittorio Emanuele, is about twenty feet wide and six blocks long. It is slightly humped to help the rain runoff. Its ancient paving stones, arranged in a herringbone pattern, are terrazzoed with the remnants of innumerable cigarette butts and the million amoeba-shaped ghosts of wads of hardened chewing gum.

I'd marvel at the houses painted in the lunatic colours of apricot, parchment yellow and a highly saturated dark red they call *sangue di bue*, oxblood. I studied these colours, trying to understand why they worked here, but if any suburban house in America were painted those shades, the neighbours would throw rocks at it.

I continued past the *panificio* with its warm, yeasty fragrance of baking bread drifting unacknowledged past the lowered heads of the off-duty ambulance drivers playing dominoes next door. The next heady aroma I encountered came from the Gelateria di Pinocchi. It was too early for them to be serving their home-made ice cream, but when I passed the life-sized statue of the eternal wooden boy sitting in the shop window, I went weak at the smell of the wafer cones they were making, one at a time, on a tiny, ancient waffle iron.

I turned left at an icon on an ancient wall that featured a muscular Jesus carved in concrete that looked like a certain governor of California with long hair and a beard. I strolled past the Confused Store, to gaze once more in the window in hopes of trying to figure out what led them to sell only items made of wicker and boxes of chocolates. If I had to stop for something at the hardware store, I hoped that Mina (whom Nancy and I called Mean Girl) wasn't on duty, but that her brother Nicola (Nice Guy) was.

I entered the Piazza Maggiore and hailed the clump of old men hanging around the fountain, arguing about politics and football just as they had done every day since they were ten. At the news kiosk, I ritually gave the signora a two-euro coin. She handed me the *Herald Tribune*, and glancing at a headline she couldn't read, she would cluck, '*Che casino!*' (What a madhouse!)

There were times, however, when I needed to downplay my

burgeoning language skills. Like if I happened to bump into the mayor's assistant and she tried to pin me down as to when the *Los Angeles Times* was going to publish that article I was writing. In those instances I simply did what had been done to me hundreds of times. I just pretended that I didn't understand what she was talking about. No matter what she said or how clearly she said it, I merely shrugged, smiled and said, '*Non capisco.*' She would then walk away muttering under her breath what an idiot I was, but at least I didn't have to tell her that I hadn't even started it yet.

If it were a hot day in the height of summer, I would pass the local swimming pool and gaze at it wistfully. This clean, modern facility was the jewel in the crown of Cambione's municipal works. When I arrived in the spring and Nancy brought me for the first time, I was delighted to have such an opulent place to cool off and exercise. We quickly fell into a pattern of using it two or three times a week, but one day I noticed a sign somebody had just put up. My Italian wasn't very good in those days, but I did recognise the word *chiuso*, closed. Soon as Nancy came out of the ladies' dressing room I pointed it out and she told me that it was there to inform the patrons that the pool would be closed for the months of July and August.

I was confounded. They were closing the swimming pool during the two hottest months of the summer? Nancy was disappointed but willing to let it go. I, however, wasn't, and I insisted she act as interpreter as I grilled the *bagnino* (pool boy) about their policy.

He patiently explained that they had to close the pool then because that was the time the employees took their vacations. Here's a radical thought, I posed: Why don't half of you take your vacations in July and the other half in August? That wouldn't work, he explained, because July and August are the months when everybody who belongs to the pool prefers to go to the beach.

I'm condensing this conversation, of course, but it was from episodes like this that I slowly came to accept a way of thinking that at first was totally incomprehensible. The best I could do was learn to live with it by putting it in the category of things I'd never understand, like why some people enjoy bagpipe music.

As I came to the end of the piazza, I had to slip past the small market that the townspeople referred to as *Alimentari Brutti* (the Shop of Ugly Groceries). This place presented a rather ticklish problem for us, because Nancy had become chatty with the daughter of the elderly lady who owned it. Mother and daughter had pretty much given up on getting any of the locals to patronise them, but they were always urging us to shop there. Nancy tried to wriggle out of it by explaining that, as Americans, we were more used to big supermarkets, which is why we drove to Lucca once a week to shop at the *supermercato*.

Truth was, their store displayed a foul-looking assortment of produce that looked to have been fished out of a compost heap, and the canned goods were dented in a way to make you think about botulism. But the old lady and her daughter were such nice people, and besieged us so earnestly, that we tried to shop there when we needed items that wouldn't poison us, like wax paper or clothes pegs.

Another constant feature of my daily walk was the small, brown, excitable mutt that Nancy and I had dubbed Horn Dog for his penchant for humping anything that moved across his field of vision. Dog, cat, goat, squirrel, mailman, it mattered little to him. If it could fog up a mirror, Horn Dog would try to screw it. When he saw that I was not interested in his advances he would chase after me, yapping at my heels in a frenzy of sexual tension. I would have gotten angry at him, but he so reminded me of myself when I was fifteen.

There are things I'll always miss about the States, but I can say with reasonable certainty that when I return to L.A. after a long absence, and walk into Sav-On Drugs, the employees will not drop everything and rush over to me with hugs and double-cheeked kisses. Yet, this was precisely what happened when I returned from Hollywood and walked into Gilberto's Farmacia. And I had only been gone three weeks.

There is a fabric of life here, a texture that enfolds you in a way that as a young man I might have found smothering. I grew up in a small town and I couldn't wait to get out. But the years of faceless anonymity in Chicago, Los Angeles and London must have chilled me in a way that made me receptive to the warmth of Tuscan cheer. Maybe I'm mellowing as I get older, but I find myself no longer judging a place by its theatres and its clubs – or its lack of them. It is no longer vitally important to me to be able to buy an onion bagel at three in the morning, and for someone who has lived his life by staying out of the impact zone of human emotions, I have come to find life here oddly nurturing.

One Friday, after my daily walk, I joined Nancy and Avvocatessa Bonetti at the comune archives. I had picked up some Perugia chocolates at the confused store and placed the opened box on the table where they were working. The avvocatessa thanked me and took one, but Nancy kept right on working without so much as a glance at the sweets. She was still upset with me for wanting to give up, and this was her way of letting my know that it would take more than a box of cream caramels to persuade her to forgive me.

I plopped down on a stool and hauled a thick, mildewed ledger onto my lap. Numbers swam in front of my eyes as I tried to focus on the 2.930,00 lira that had been paid in property taxes by Lot 7BY-2 on 08/06/66. That was the lot right next to ours, and like all the land around us, it was owned by the Pingatores. What stuck out was that this amount was higher than that paid on the surrounding plots, which were purely agricultural, perhaps indicating that a structure existed there. Was that a mistake? Could that structure be on our lot, and in fact, could it be our house? It was a slim chance this would come to anything, but we were desperate and we had to go down every avenue.

Just then Nancy screamed. I whipped around to see her jump out of her chair and hysterically flick a spider off her arm. The little grey spider landed on Avvocatessa Bonetti, who also started to scream. I rushed over to make sure nobody had been bitten. They were unpunctured, but in shaky voices they urged me to hurry up and kill it. I told them I didn't know where it went. They pointed in the direction of a stack of cardboard boxes piled up in a corner.

They were far too upset for me to invoke my vegan creed, so I picked up the heavy ledger and advanced. I started moving away boxes amid Nancy's cautions to be careful because there were probably thousands of spiders under there. In fact, two did scurry away, but unable to identify either one as the perp, I held my fire. I was pushing aside a half-buried box with my foot when I noticed that stencilled on the side were the words U.S. Army Air Force.

I dropped the ledger and pulled the box free. Brushing away the spiders, I ripped it open. As Nancy and Avvocatessa Bonetti timidly approached, I discovered it was full of large black-and-white photos. I took out several and realised what I had found. They were aerial reconnaissance photos from World War II. All thoughts of spiders forgotten, we tore through them until we found one that showed some familiar landmarks, and there, right in the middle of the photo, was our house! Of course the air force had photographed the Bunker. The Germans were using it as a gun emplacement!

At last, we held *la prova* in our hands . . . the proof that our house existed. We were shouting with glee and pumping our fists in victory when I glanced at the clock and realised that the Dipartimento d'Autorizzazione della Licenza Edilizia would close in about fifteen minutes. And this being Friday, it would-n't reopen until Monday afternoon, maybe. We bade a hasty goodbye to the avvocatessa, grabbed the photo, a handful of chocolates and raced for the car.

Thanks to the unusually light traffic, we made good progress until we were flagged over by two *carabinieri* standing on the side of the road, machine guns hanging from their shoulders. Despite the show of ordinance, this is a common occurrence in Italy, where motorists are routinely stopped to have their papers checked. So while Nancy showed them her passport and a smile, I anxiously stared at my wristwatch and groused about this lack of 'probable cause' and their violation of 'due process'.

One *carabiniere*, who was thick and muscular with the neck of a weightlifter, examined the car's rental agreement, while the other, tall, skinny with a big Adam's apple, looked in our trunk. The weightlifter seemed pleased that we were Americans and informed us that he had relatives in Philadelphia. When the tall, skinny one heard that we were from southern California, he dropped whatever he was doing in our trunk, and came over to our window to rhapsodise about surfing and California girls, repeatedly using the one word of English he knew, Baywatch.

I think they would have stood there all day chatting with us, but Nancy told them that we were running late for a very important appointment. They handed us back our papers and we left amid smiles and friendly waves.

I checked my watch and realised that the office would be closing in less than five minutes. Nothing else runs on time in Italy, but the door locks of every store and office in this country are obviously connected to a chronometer at the Specola Astronomica at the Vatican, so everything can close up tighter than a fist at the exact stroke of one.

We raced through town, squealing tyres through the roundabouts just like real Italians. Double-parking in front of the office, we jumped out just in time to see a police car bearing down on us. We froze at the thought of how many traffic laws we had broken. Nancy was preparing her excuses, when we recognised the tall, skinny *carabiniere* getting out of the police car. He approached our car and sheepishly asked us to open our trunk. Then he reached in and retrieved his machine gun. He apologised for having left a deadly firearm in our vehicle, but the thought of all those surfer girls in bikinis had made him a little absentminded. We told him there was no problem, if he'd just watch our illegally parked car for a few minutes while we dashed inside.

We chugged up the stairs and managed to slip in the door just as the handsome guy behind the counter was putting on his hat to go to lunch. Nancy blocked his way, and I held the photo in front of him. He vigorously protested that office hours were over for the day. Nancy argued back that a government office must deal with everyone who is waiting before they can officially close. The argument escalated, until the good-looking guy's boss, who was also trying to get out the door, saw that we had no intention of moving. Finally, they stopped quarrelling with us long enough to actually look at the picture. Then they looked at each other in disbelief.

After briefly conferring, the boss left for lunch, turning us over to the good-looking guy. Muttering something about *stranieri* lacking any respect for a worker's hours, he went back to the counter and handed us the forms to fill out so we could petition for an address.

This called for a celebration, so we left the Comune and went to an obscenely expensive *ristorante* for lunch. I ordered a bottle of Sassicaia, and as we lifted our glasses, I made a toast to that little grey spider, hoping that in its honour, Nancy would never make me kill one again.

16. IL SENTIERO

Having proved that our house existed, we were not out of the woods yet. In fact, the woods were causing our latest problem. This dilemma reared its ugly head when we first met with our *geometra*, Gigi. Despite the image the name conjures up, Gigi was not an adorable little French girl like the type Maurice Chevalier would have sung to. Gigi, the common nickname for Luigi, was our land surveyor – a burly Goliath of a man with a forehead wide enough to show home movies on and thick locks of long hair that curled around the sides of his face, giving him the appearance of a rather alert-looking musk ox.

Gigi had hauled his surveying equipment up to our land so that he could take the necessary measurements and file the proper documents with the Comune. When all that was approved by everybody who had to approve it, we could get down to the hard business of turning this pile of . . . well, crap . . . into a house. Nancy had driven some stakes into the ground to mark off how we wanted to expand the structure to include such things as a closet and a bathroom. But no sooner had Gigi squinted into his surveying level than he started shaking his woolly head and telling us that what we had planned could not be done.

Gigi unrolled an ancient, yellowing map that looked like something Vasco da Gama might have used and pointed out a small grove of olive trees sitting at the top of our hill. The map clearly showed that the only way to get to that piece of land was to come through our property. By law the owner of those trees had the right of access, which in this instance meant a footpath (*un sentiero*) that happened to run right though the area where we wanted to expand. We followed Gigi's thick finger as he traced the course of this path, pointing out how it had been worn down by centuries of use, and that its ancient heritage made it all but untouchable.

All of the obvious questions ensued, followed by all the obvious answers. No, the path cannot be obstructed in any way. No, the only way to change the course of the path was to petition the Comune and get permission from the owner of the trees. And, yes, the owner was none other than our neighbour, Vesuvia Pingatore.

Nancy fumed and stomped all over the disputed strip of land, trying to figure out how she could enlarge our house while still allowing Vesuvia to get up to her land. As she did this, I studied the ancient map, looking for a loophole. Unable to make any sense out of the renderings of property lines so arcane, I half expected to see illustrations of dragons in the corners to show what would happen when you fell off the edge of the earth.

I walked over to where Nancy was talking to Gigi about how we might reconfigure our design in light of this new development. Not that I could be of any help, but the sun was really starting to beat down, and I wanted to stand in some of the shade Gigi was casting. I watched them carry on for a while, then Gigi walked away – either because the conversation was over, or because he was feeling uncomfortable that I was standing so close.

'What does he think?' I asked.

'Well, as it stands now, Vesuvia's footpath will run right through our new shower stall.'

'That'll be cosy,' I said, studying the terrain around as if I actually knew what I was looking at. 'I don't suppose we could open up the area behind the house.'

'Solid bedrock. It would cost a fortune. The only way we could grow the house is in this direction, and now we can't even do that.'

I looked over at Vesuvia's house, and unless the sunlight was playing tricks on my eyes, I thought I saw a figure moving behind one of the shaded windows. She was watching us and probably enjoying the heck out of our latest problem.

I nudged Nancy and directed her attention to Vesuvia's window. 'What if we offered to buy it from her?'

'She's not going to sell to us,' Nancy said.

'It's worth a shot.' I looked uphill at the clump of trees in question. 'It's a such a small plot, she probably doesn't even use it anymore.'

'All our money's tied up, remember?' she said.

'Maybe we can put it on a credit card,' I said.

'Look, don't worry about it.' Nancy started pulling up a wooden stake and repositioning it. 'Maybe there's a way to alter the design so we –'

'No, why should you?' I said. 'You spent time working this out, let's see if we can't get it the way you want.'

'How? Just call her up and ask her how much she wants?'

'I was thinking more of a peace offering. Suppose we give her a gift. Something nice. And in the note we say that since we're going to be neighbours, would she consider selling us that piece of land?'

Nancy thought for a moment, chewing on her lower lip in concentration. Then she looked over at Vesuvia's window, where our neighbour was now in full view. 'Think you could get me a photo?'

This took a little figuring out, but I was finally able to give Nancy what she wanted by using my camcorder. I set it up on a tripod behind some foliage so it was surreptitiously aimed at Vesuvia's house. I zoomed in tight on her side porch and locked it down. Then, using the remote, I started taping whenever she appeared there to shoot another *malocchio* in our direction. It took a few days, and there were times I felt as if I were filming a nature special for the Discovery Channel, but at least I wasn't standing hip-deep in a piranha-infested river waiting for two tsetse flies to start mating.

What Nancy wanted was a nice clean profile, almost a silhouette, which I was able to get. I then used the software on my computer to clean up the edges, sharpen the image, and enlarge it. I printed it out for her, and Nancy took it to her marble studio. She selected a small, flat piece of moon-white alabaster, and working freehand with an air hammer, she carved out a bas-relief showing Vesuvia's face in profile.

The carving was a remarkable likeness, even though Nancy took pains to turn Vesuvia's flyaway hair into smooth, flowing locks and make her hawkish nose look aquiline and aristocratic.

When it was complete, we carefully composed a note saying how much we were looking forward to being her neighbour, and how, in the spirit of friendship, we'd like to give her this gift. We ended the note with the humble suggestion that perhaps she would consider selling us the small plot of land at the top of our hill. We arranged to have the package dropped off at Vesuvia's door, and then waited for her response.

It would prove to be a long wait.

17. TITO TUGHI'S AUTO MUNDO

Working at a speed that undoubtedly made them dizzy, the Comune approved our petition for an address, and within a week *il piccolo rustico* was forever to be known as 42 Via Serena. I liked the number because it was easy to remember, but Mario Pingatore was particularly delighted, for as we learned from Umberto, who heard it from Vesuvia, forty-two was the year he was born, and he wasted no time spreading the word that this was an omen the house would soon be his. And this portent apparently had enough street mojo to prompt several customers of Lucca's Barbershop to set up a pool establishing Mario as the eight-to-five favourite.

The force of superstition in Italian life can never be minimised. It seems to exist with equal potency up and down the boot as well as the socioeconomic ladder. Some of these superstitions exist without any trace of explanation, like the one decreeing that the head of your bed must never touch a wall that faces out to the street, or you'll die of brain fever. Some have a twisted connection to science, like the adamant Italian belief that no water, not even the amount involved to wash your face, can touch you after you eat, or you will die. This is probably related to the avoidance of swimming after eating, which can cause cramps. And some superstitions, as crazy as they sound, may actually have a basis in logic, like the phobia about eating freshly baked bread. This came from the hard years after the war when Italian mothers, wanting the loaf they had just baked to last a few days, told their kids that eating bread while it was still warm could cause, you guessed it, brain fever.

With the exception of rubbing the head of an occasional dwarf, I have little regard for superstition, having lost any respect for the occult when as a teenager I was unable to reconcile, from an astrological standpoint, how Soupy Sales, Cardinal Richelieu and my girlfriend Marsha could all share the same birthday.

Perhaps my scepticism has softened, for I was grateful to whatever mysterious powers now favoured us because, thanks to our having an address, we were able to turn in our rental and buy ourselves a car.

True to the idea that a rising tide lifts all boats, Dino was quick to insist that we could get preferential treatment and the best deal only by shopping at his future in-law's establishment, Tito Tughi's Auto Mundo. In addition to keeping the money in the family, Dino saw this as an opportunity for me to spend some quality time with Rudolfo and convince him to marry Pia Tughi, guaranteeing that there would be a family to keep the money in. I wanted no part of this, preferring to stay focused on our goal of not winding up with a vehicle that didn't need a horn because you could hear it two blocks away. But in Italy, where nothing is business but everything is personal, my objections were in vain and we soon found ourselves in the backseat of a van, our faces being licked by dogs, while Dino drove us to Signor Tughi's car lot.

To Americans the words car lot conjure up a very specific image. A crisp, asphalt-paved expanse of real estate, festooned with flapping flags and neon signs fluttering and flashing over rows of gleaming cars, while a fast-talking guy in a loud sport coat earnestly tells us that he's not authorised to go that low, but he'll go talk to his manager. That was exactly what Tito Tughi and his Auto Mondo were not.

The lot itself was a meandering patch of land partially concealed by an outcropping of bramble bushes. Not only was it unpaved, but it dipped and dived into flat-bottomed gullies and shallow ravines, so that all vehicles on display sat at various heights and angles, as if they were bobbing on the surface of a rather choppy body of water. Additionally, the phrase hail fellow well met never has been, nor ever will be, used to describe Signor Tito Tughi. A dour man with tired, droopy eyes and a toothbrush moustache, he dressed in black and walked around with his hands clasped behind him in a manner more befitting a gravedigger than a used-car salesman.

There wasn't a vast assortment of cars to choose from, but after navigating up and down the terrain and kicking the tyres of various Fiats, Lancias, and Opels, we gravitated towards a red sedan that was parked at such a steep angle, we could see without a doubt that no fluids were seeping out. When we asked Signor Tughi the price, his hangdog expression became positively funereal.

'Do you have any young children?' he asked.

Nancy told him we didn't and proceeded to translate.

'Then this would be a good car for you. For when you have that unfortunate traffic accident' – Signor Tughi held up a closed fist with his pinkie and thumb sticking out in the shape of horns – 'you won't have to worry about them being killed.'

His use of the hand gesture the Italians call *le corna* to ward off bad luck did little to soften the fact that he was speaking of a car accident as if it were as much a part of driving in Italy as an oil change.

'Much safer to be inside this,' he said, patting the fender of a VW Polo with one hand as he made *le corna* with the other. 'If and when . . .'

Signor Tughi went into great detail extolling the solidity of the frame and the dependability of the airbags, with the tacit implication that any *macchina* built by the Germans had to be superior to anything manufactured in Milan, Turino, Detroit or Yokohama. A begrudging respect for their engineering skills is about the only good thing the Italians can find to say about their Teutonic neighbours. That's because the atrocities committed by the Germans during the war seem as fresh in people's minds as if they happened last Tuesday, and even a carefree stroll around the piazza takes you past a plaque marking the spot where the Nazis lined up eight partisans and shot them. Resentments run deep, for as our neighbour Annamaria so succinctly put it, 'How can a nation that belches understand a nation that sings?'

After the Germans failed to occupy Italy by force, they turned around and conquered it with Deutsche marks, and now euros. This fact also riles the Italians to the point where if a German and a French customer are in a store, the Italian clerk will often choose to wait on the French one, only because they hate them slightly less than they hate the Germans.

Over and above the car's excellent bloodlines, Signor Tughi presented us with the most compelling reason to buy it. The original owner was Father Fabrizio of the Chiesa della Madonna dell'Acqua, so not only had this car been actively engaged in the charitable acts of visiting the sick and the needy, it was also featured in the annual parade honouring Our Lady of the Autostrada. Clearly, here was a car whose history of pious service would long protect its occupants. I, for one, didn't feel worthy to own such a hallowed vehicle, but events were pushing us along and we found ourselves following Signor Tughi through the bramble bushes back towards his office.

When Nancy asked him the price, he led us over to the garage to talk to his sales manager, who turned out to be his daughter, Pia, a lively blonde in a short skirt that seemed better suited for a disco than a service bay. She signalled that she'd be right with us, but she was busy dressing down her two brothers for botching up the repair on an exhaust manifold. Signor Tughi looked away, and the boys all but hung their heads, as Pia showed them the proper way to remove the housing assembly without tearing apart the gasket.

Wiping her hands on an oil rag, she approached us. Dino made a great display of welcoming his daughter-in-law-to-be and introduced her to us. She shook our hands and told us how much Rudolfo liked us. We in turn told her how fond we were of Rudolfo, with Nancy commenting on what an adorable couple they made. Pia blushed and I was hard pressed to understand his reluctance to settle down with a girl who not only looked good in a miniskirt, but also knew how to rebuild a transmission.

The question of the price came up and Pia was almost apologetic, hoping we'd understand that, all religious implications aside, Father Fabrizio had taken very good care of the car, rarely driven it, and had had it serviced regularly. I figured this was the Italian way of letting us know it had once been owned by the Little Old Lady from Pasadena, so after a nod of agreement from Nancy, I was prepared to make a counteroffer.

Pia brought the offer over to her father. He took out his pocket calculator and she whipped out hers, and they stood, not ten feet from us, arguing as they plinked on their keys as if they were playing a duet. After a great deal of bickering Pia threw up her hands in resignation and returned to us with a new figure that was only a few euros less than their original.

We seesawed back and forth, but we were clearly at an impasse. Nancy finally took Signor Tughi aside and told him that as much as we liked the safety features of the Volkswagen, it was too expensive. We would have to settle for a cheaper car and pray that, when my sister visited with her grandchildren, any accident we had would not be fatal. As she said this, I stood behind her making the sign of *le corna* and looking to the heavens for divine protection. This moved Signor Tughi to relent. Not wanting the blood of innocent children on any car that came from his lot, he agreed to come down from his price and we split the difference.

Just then the roar of a motorcycle heralded the arrival of Rudolfo. Taking a bounce off of a ravine, he popped a wheelie and executed a flashy state-police stop right at our feet. He dismounted, and disregarding Dino scolding him for being late and needing a haircut, he shook everybody's hand and planted a polite peck on Pia's cheek.

By the time we had finished haggling over the price, filling out the paperwork, receiving the temporary registration and arranging for the insurance, it was dark. It had been a long day, but at last we felt that our lives were moving.

'He doesn't love her,' Nancy said as she downshifted the Popemobile and we whipped around a curve.

'You think?'

'I didn't feel any heat.'

'Well, they've known each other since they were kids,' I said.

'Hey, unless you're jumping out of your skin every time you see somebody, you shouldn't marry 'em.'

'You mean, like us?'

She smiled.

I was struck by how beautiful she looked, illuminated by the dashboard lights. 'You know, after all these years I'm still jumping out of my skin.'

'Yeah?'

I moved closer.

'Hey, stop that, I'm driving,'

'Pull over,' I whispered, indicating the wooded area ahead.

'No!'

'Come on, let's do something really sacrilegious in the back seat.'

'Leave me alone, you perve,' she giggled as she flicked on the turn signal.

18. ARCHEOLOGIA

The actual construction on our house began in a most inauspicious way. One morning we were walking up the hill to our *rustico* in the cool hours before the sun burned off the pink baby blanket of fog that lay across the town. As we approached, we began to hear a steady tapping noise that, if we hadn't known better, sounded like a woodpecker that preferred rocks over trees. We spotted the squatting figure of Carlo, one of Umberto's workers, chipping away at a softball-sized stone with a ball-peen hammer. With the dexterity of a Neolithic hunter fashioning a spear point, he was chiselling the stone until it was the perfect shape to fit into one of the many holes in the ancient stone wall that surrounded our property.

We called out to him and he waved. Carlo was a fleshy, wide-bodied guy with warm eyes and a shy grin. He told us that Ivano was also here working, and that after lunch Umberto himself would show up with Silvio, the other member of the crew.

We were elated. True to his word, Umberto was managing to be at two places at once, and how he was able to sneak his guys out from under Vesuvia Pingatore's nose, we had no idea. But work had started and we hoped the house would be finished before we got too old to climb up the hill to get to it.

Over the course of the time it took to restore the house, Umberto and his guys, Carlo, Ivano and Silvio, became a steady part of our existence. We ate lunch together under the shade of a gnarled old olive tree, met their parents, wives and children, and attended family weddings, confirmations and funerals. From the beginning we established a cordial relationship when Nancy asked if we could address one another as *tu*, because, as in many Romance languages, you must be granted permission before you can refer to an Italian in the informal manner. Unlike Americans, who are world famous for our informality, the Italians are very rigid about this, using the more formal *le* to address anyone older, more educated or in a socially superior position, unless he is the prime minister of their country – and then they speak to him as if he were the Antichrist.

We also gave each other nicknames. I became Fellini because of my penchant for videotaping the progress on the *rustico*. Nancy was *la donna della casa* (the lady of the house), but her confrontational style with the Comune and anyone else who stood in our way quickly earned her the nickname Rompicoglione. The verb *rompere* means 'to break' and *coglione* is slang for testicles. The expression these two words form, however, is somewhat less confrontational in Italian than it is in English. Over here, this appellation is most commonly bestowed on those with the ability to make themselves into a real pain in the butt. Either way you translate it, Nancy was so proud of her sobriquet, she often introduced herself by that title.

Of course we also gave as good as we got. We quickly noticed that Carlo and Ivano had decidedly predictable responses to anything that we asked. To the biggest and most complex problem Carlo would nod and say, '*Va bene*' – 'OK' – and to the smallest and most piddling request Ivano would gravely shake his head and reply, '*C'è un problema*' – 'There's a problem.' So they became respectively Va Bene and Problema.

Silvio, the third worker, came with his own nickname. Because he was a nice-looking guy in his late twenties with shaggy hair and Don Johnson stubble, who was mildly indifferent to his job and preferred to conserve his energies for club hopping and hustling women, the town had dubbed him Il Vagabondo.

Despite his penchant for coming to work from a different direction every day and nursing a chronic hangover until noon, I enjoyed his insouciant, lounge-lizard attitude and I was delighted when he told me that he wanted to learn English. We came up with a plan where I spoke to him in Italian, he spoke to me in English, and we both learned from each other.

I was impressed with his ambition, thinking that perhaps he wanted to get into computers or do carpentry work for some of the many Brits who had settled around Lucca. But his real need was far more pragmatic. Vagabondo's objective was to meet a rich American woman and become her gigolo. In time she would fall madly in love with him, take him back to the States, and they would live together in a mansion just like the one on the TV show Dallas. As a result of his dream my job was to teach him how to tell a woman that she was beautiful, they were meant for each other, and he had a *cazzo* the size of a baby's arm.

nostro amico   ...

There was never any discernible pattern to the work. Some days nobody showed up. Then suddenly the whole crew would be there with more heavy equipment than Hitler had when he invaded Poland. Mostly, though, when we took the ten-minute walk from the house we were renting from Dino to the *rustico*, we'd discover that Vagabondo was there by himself chucking broken terra-cotta tiles off the roof, or that Problema was using a hand axe to split apart a rotting beam, although he was quick to tell us that he was only doing this because Umberto had told him to, and that our house would probably fall down.

Coincidentally, the issue of our house falling down became a constant topic of conversation with Umberto. He minced no words in suggesting that the *rustico*'s collapsing was a distinct possibility. Once he tried to intimate that this could actually be a good thing, since building a new house from scratch would actually be easier, faster and cheaper. But Nancy shot him one of her *rompicoglione* looks, and the subject was never broached again.

To better understand the construction problem we were facing, try to imagine a two-storey structure made of thousands of stones held together by whatever form of mud, sand and ash they were mixing three hundred years ago. Over the years as the hill above the house eroded, vast amounts of earth slid down and piled up behind and on the sides of the house. So much dirt, in fact, that one could literally jump out the second-storey window and only fall six feet. Over the years this earth became hardened and impacted so it, more than anything else, was holding the house together.

You're probably way ahead of me in realising that in order to restore the house, the tons of earth holding it up would, of course, have to be removed. We began cautiously, with shovels and wheelbarrows, but it soon became apparent that doing the job that way would put us on a time frame comparable to the construction of the Great Pyramid of Cheops. So on a fine Sunday morning Umberto drove up in a flatbed truck that was hauling an enormous steam shovel. He somehow got the entire rig up our narrow little road. Climbing into the cab, he fired up the earthmover, drove it off the flatbed, and proceeded to carefully excavate the mound. Nancy and I did our best to haul away wheelbarrow-fulls of earth but the frenetic Umberto picked up his pace and started clearing dirt like he was on a mission from God.

Over the roar of the diesel and the whirring of the power arm came the ominous sound of stones being wrenched apart. Nancy and I gasped as a jagged crack suddenly appeared on our back wall, and for a moment the house quivered as if it were about to collapse into a pile of rocks and rotting beams.

Nancy accused Umberto of doing this on purpose, and he argued that he was just trying to get the job done quickly because they were charging us for the machinery by the hour. All of this was being hollered back and forth as Umberto turned the earthmover around until for a moment it was coming straight at us. We scurried out of the way just as he pivoted the arm so that the flat edge of the bucket rested flush against the sidewall of the house, literally holding the entire structure together.

After a moment to catch our breath in the haze of swirling dust and diesel fumes, the three of us cautiously entered the house. The crack had come completely through a wall that was over twenty inches thick. It ran like a hideous scar from about the middle of the kitchen wall all the way up to the roof. At its narrowest it was pencil thin, but it spread as it climbed until it was wide enough to stick your fist through without scraping your knuckles.

We stood there gazing at it as if we were seeing some vertical Grand Canyon for the first time. Then Umberto, who had been studying the crack up close, beckoned us over. He pointed to a clump of what looked like matted weeds imbedded in caked mud.

His eyes widened in reverence as he explained that we were looking at a mixture of straw and clay that made up a wall inside our stone wall. This was how we learned that our house had been built over the shell of a far more ancient structure, a primitive house with daub walls and a thatched roof where serfs had cowered in the darkness from capricious feudal lords and the Black Plague.

According to its cornerstone the oldest church in town was built in AD 1250, about a hundred years after Cambione was founded. People were obviously living here even before then, so we had accidentally discovered that our little *rustico* could be over a thousand years old!

Clearly this house had gone through many adaptations over the years, a fact made evident, for instance, by the faint outline of a wide opening that had once existed where one of the kitchen walls now stood. This opening was called the cattle door, and in cold weather the livestock was herded inside through it, so that they would not only be protected from the cold night air, but their bodies could also warm the house for the people sleeping on the floor above them. And all of this was done, mind you, hundreds of years before the invention of the room air freshener.

Another clear indication of its longevity was the four distinct patterns of stonework, one on top of the other, on the walls of the bedroom on the second floor. Each change marked a point where the roof had been raised because people kept getting taller. These renovations seemed to end somewhere around the time Lord Byron came drinking and debauching his way through these parts about two hundred years ago. There is no record, of course, that Lord Byron was ever in our house, since anyone he could have drunk or debauched with was too illiterate to write it down, and the goats weren't talking.

We were staring at the crack in our wall when we heard Umberto dialling his cellphone.

'Who are you calling?' Nancy asked in Italian.

'Well, my father, for one. He would be very interested.'

My Italian was good enough to understand that the way Umberto loved to gossip, the revised age of our house would be all over town before the church bells rang for noon Mass.

'We can't tell anybody about this,' Nancy said, as I nodded in agreement behind her.

'But this is important,' he said, as he reluctantly hung up. 'Big news for the town.'

We hadn't shared with Umberto any of our difficulties with the Comune for fear he wouldn't want any part of our troubles, but we had to let him know that this would only make things worse. If the Comune found out the true age of this place, they'd shut us down immediately and turn the whole site over to the Dipartimento di Archeologia.

'You know, Umberto,' Nancy said, 'I'll bet even the Pingatores don't know how old this is.'

'That's possible,' he mused.

'Which makes me think that if they did, Vesuvia would get even madder that her brother sold it. She'd yell at him, and who knows what she'd do to you for sneaking over here to work with us.' Nancy made a *malocchio* at him.

'So you don't want me to say anything?'

'Please,' she pleaded. 'At least until the work's done.'

Umberto darted his eyes around the room like a man who had just taken a picture of a flying saucer only to discover there was no film in his camera. 'What about the guys?'

'Well, if you patch the crack up right now, nobody will be able to see what's inside.' Nancy handed him a bucket and he stood there staring at her. 'I mean, Vesuvia could come up that footpath on her way to her trees at any time, and if she even suspects –'

'OK,' he said. 'If that's what you want.'

'In the meantime, how do we keep the house from falling down?' I asked in my broken Italian.

'It's complicated,' Umberto said, tearing open a sack of plaster. 'First we have to prop up the wall with wood beams, then we need to girdle the outside of the structure with pipes and –'

'Can you start tomorrow?' Nancy asked.

'I can't do anything for a week.'

'A week?' I moaned.

'What can I do? Vesuvia told me I got to finish her wall or else! Why do you think I'm here on a Sunday?'

'What's going to keep the house from falling over with the next stiff wind?' Nancy asked.

'I think the shovel will hold it up.'

'But we're paying for that by the hour,' Nancy said, throwing in an assortment of Italian swear words.

Umberto shrugged and went outside to get water to make plaster. Nancy followed to plead with him, leaving me alone with my crack. As I stared at it, I thought of the fifty generations of people who had lived here in the thousand years this dwelling had been standing in place. A faceless army of peasant farmers and milkmaids, doing the best they could, every day, to survive and raise a family, hardly noticing that the Crusades, the Dark

Ages, the Renaissance, the Reformation and the Industrial Revolution were happening all around them.

Did they recognise Michelangelo when he wandered through these hills looking for fresh veins of white marble? Did they even look up from their tilling when Napoleon's army marched right past here chasing the Austrians out of northern Italy? Did they wonder about the small group of English poets and writers on their way to pay their last respects to Percy Shelley, whose body washed up on Focetta Beach not ten miles from here?

The house creaked, and a thin finger of dust drizzled out of the crack. It resembled ashes, and I thought about the funeral pyre they had made on the beach for the drowned poet. Percy Shelley once wrote that Italy was 'the paradise of exiles', and that made me think about his widow, Mary Shelley, another expat writer trying to make a life in this alien culture. When I thought about the book that made her famous, I felt a strange kinship with her.

She had her Frankenstein and I had mine.

19. OMERTÀ

Having spent most of my adult life in an air-conditioned office, I was ill prepared for Nancy's insistence that we have an *orto*, a vegetable garden. Even though we were not living in the house, she felt that there was no reason we couldn't enjoy the benefits of fresh vegetables all summer long. I went along because I had no idea how much work it would take.

Apparently there's this whole procedure where you have to turn over the soil, dig up all the weeds, and spread (organic, of course) fertiliser, snail killer, plant food and mulch . . . whatever the heck that is. I did all of these chores, muttering under my breath every time I passed the steam shovel that was still holding up our house. After two weeks there had been no trace of Umberto or his guys to shore up the *rustico*, and any attempt to call him went unanswered.

We would see him every day, of course, working on Vesuvia Pingatore's walls. We'd wave, he'd wave back, but when we beckoned him over, he'd point to his watch and give us a sheepish little shrug. We knew he was sulking about having to keep quiet about the age of our house, but we had no choice, we had to carefully guard our secret against all intruders. And that included Cousin Faustino, who was locked in mortal combat with *fumagini*, a sticky black fungus that was ravaging our olive trees.

Cousin Faustino kept arguing that he needed to dig up a diseased tree that was close to the house so he could treat it with nitrogen. But we feared that in unearthing the root, he would see a section of the exposed wall and discover what we were trying to hide. So we distracted him. Nancy engaged him in taking us around the land and telling us about the various plants we had growing there, like *niebitella*, a feral mint that the Italians cook with porcini mushrooms to cut the oily taste, or *finocchio selvatico*, a form of wild fennel that Cousin Faustino broke off and ate raw. When we cooked up a batch, it gave us stomachaches and double vision.

I did my part in distracting Cousin Faustino, especially when Nancy wasn't around, by getting him to do my work for me. My soft, pencil-pusher hands were cracking and blistering from working the hoe, so I'd call him over, ostensibly to ask him about what we should plant when. He'd rattle off a list of things I couldn't understand, and when I pleaded ignorance he'd take the hoe and show me how to properly prepare the seedbed. Feeling a little like Tom Sawyer after he got his friends to paint the fence, I'd go in the house to fetch us soft drinks, while Cousin Faustino worked.

It was three-thirty in the morning. A lone Vespa whined through the narrow streets, provoking the village dogs into fits of barking. I flipped over my pillow, laid my face on the cool side, and tried to fall asleep, but the Vespa buzzed in my ears like a gnat that keeps flying around your head despite your best efforts to shoo it away.

I dragged myself out of bed and headed for the kitchen to see what there was to graze on. When I passed the laptop I remembered that I hadn't checked my e-mail today, so I switched it on. I was scanning over the spam when my eyes widened. There was an e-mail from my agent!

For weeks now I had been careful not to badger him about my script. In some weird way I felt that by my not contacting him, some good karma might accrue and I'd soon be surprised by another phone call. My heart was in my mouth when I opened it, only to learn that he and his wife were thinking of coming to Italy and could we recommend a good itinerary?

I ground my teeth in anger as I saw that there was not one single mention of my script. But I realised I needed to be cool, so I wrote him back. My reply started out as a dry, businesslike missive with a selection of picturesque villages and recommended hotels and restaurants, but somehow in the middle of it, my feelings about this place started to seep through, including the 'Ten (Now Seventeen) Things I Hate about Tuscany'. I ended with an invitation for him and Mrs Agent to come visit us in Cambione. They could stay with us if they chose, and there, in the soft azure sunlight of another perfect day, I could ask him face to face how come he hadn't sold my damn script?!

The village dogs had now settled down and the heavy night air seemed to heave, as if it were sighing right along with me. Why was I still obsessing over that script? Had I learned nothing from my last go-around? Did I really want to be thrust back into that world of oversized egos, vainglorious self-promotion, and monumental insincerity?

I knew I'd never get to sleep now and I didn't know what to do with myself. I was too agitated to read and I had lost my appetite. I thought about going back to bed, snuggling up to Nancy, and seeing if she wanted to fool around (but then I'd have to talk to her, because she'd want to know what was bothering me, and then she'd get upset because I wasn't letting go of things the way she wanted me to . . .), or I could just do what I normally do at four o'clock in the morning: stand in front of the refigerator with an eating utensil and sample things – an activity I like to refer to as 'sport forking'.

Not finding anything all that amusing in the fridge, I went into the living room and flicked on the TV in the hopes that some confluence of solar flares and atmospheric disturbances would conspire to send me a programme I'd actually like to watch. I sat through about four minutes of a hopelessly retro variety show that featured a baggy-pants comic cracking jokes with canned laughter on every punchline.

I was flicking through the channels when I suddenly

recognised Tony Soprano. 'Yo, Tone, what are you doing here?' I found myself saying aloud to the TV.

He was speaking in badly dubbed Italian, but I understood enough from the voice-over announcer to learn that *The Sopranos* would start airing here in the fall. I thought about all the episodes we had missed and I was delighted. Finally, I had a good reason to improve my Italian. Now, if they'd only start showing the Dodger games, I'd be in hog heaven.

When you come to Florence and you're in search of a magnificent view of the city, as well as a brutal cardiovascular workout, you must go to the Cathedral Santa Maria del Fiore and climb the 468 steps up to the top of the dome. The view is heart stopping, if the 468 steps alone don't do the job. Looking down through a labyrinth of ochre tile roofs you can see a dense warren of narrow streets richly clotted with life. Beyond that, to the north, lies the panorama of the hills of Fiesole, and to the east your eyes can follow the Arno River as it turns into a muddy trickle in its meanderings toward Pisa.

The church, commonly referred to as Il Duomo, has one of the largest and highest domes ever built. It is taller and wider than the Pantheon in Rome, which it's modelled after, and more than one-third larger than the Capitol Dome in Washington, D.C.

As you make your way up the endless, narrow stairway, you'll pass a level where the wall has been exposed so you can see how this marvel was actually constructed, since the architect, Filippo Brunelleschi, vowed never to use any scaffolding. The Romans had originally mastered this technique, but that knowledge was lost during the Dark Ages when the Church declared everything Roman to be pagan.

Brunelleschi went to Rome and, digging through the forbidden archives, unearthed the designs for the Pantheon dome. He learned that the Romans had conquered the effects of hoop stress on unsupported walls by surrounding a structure they wished to enclose with stout chains and heavy lead piping. This would enable them to reinforce the walls with concrete (which they invented, by the way) until the structure was sturdy enough to stand alone. So when Umberto and his crew showed up with lengths of pipes and chains, I was to learn that they would be using this two-thousand-year-old technique to hold together our one-thousand-year-old house.

The enveloping of our house in this girdle was done quickly but carefully. Scaffolding was put up around the *rustico* (with apologies to Filippo Brunelleschi, who built the Duomo without using any!). Vagabondo handed up lengths of pipe and Va Bene and Problema chained them together at the corners of the second storey, until the house looked as if it were wearing a headband. As they worked, Umberto used a plumb level to gauge how straight the corners were, and since one end was sagging because of the crack, he got into the earthmover and gently nudged the wall until it was straight enough for the guys to shore it up.

A cement mixer roared to life. Va Bene and Vagabondo dug away at the mound of earth behind the house, as Problema and Umberto slathered layers of concrete on the newly exposed foundation. To his credit Umberto was quick to cover up the foundation with concrete before his guys could take a closer look and discover that we had a wall within a wall.

Unfortunately, all this work was being done on one of the hottest days of the summer. We kept a steady stream of bottled water coming and insisted the guys take breaks in the shade. The only good part was that because it was so hot and dry the concrete set very quickly, and by the end of the day Umberto felt it was hard enough to take away the earthmover.

So as we gathered around, Umberto climbed in and gunned the engine. I readied my camcorder and we all looked at each other in anticipation.

Va Bene said, 'Don't worry, Signor Fellini, it's going to be fine,' while Problema predicted disaster, and Vagabondo gave me a wink and a thumbs-up as he continued chatting on his cellphone with a girl he had met at the beach.

We held our breath as the earthmover moved and the house didn't. A cheer went up and I produced a bottle of spumante I had picked up at the Alimentari Brutti, figuring that as long as something had a cork in it, we probably wouldn't get salmonella. As I poured us a round of drinks, I realised that I was becoming so Italian, I looked to celebrate at the slightest provocation.

With the structure stabilised work kicked into high gear, and within a week all the earth behind the house had been dug up and carted off. Additionally, they had patched up and reinforced the stone walls that buttressed the terraced land on our hill. Things were going so well, we were actually in a good mood when Umberto presented us with his bill.

It was enormous. At least twenty-five per cent higher than we had anticipated, and that didn't even include the rental on all the heavy machinery. There were so many zeros, at first Nancy thought he had given us the price in lira. If he continued to charge us at this rate, we would run out of funds long before the house was finished.

We had to do something, but we knew we had to proceed carefully. Italians are very touchy when it comes to money. Ironically, they consider it crass to even bring up the subject even when they are gouging you down to the marrow of your bones. They just don't like to talk about money, and you can see their reticence on the subject manifested in a thousand different ways. At a street *mercato*, for instance, when you ask a vendor about the price of something, he will go on at great lengths describing the quality of the item, until you have to say, '*Più parole, più costosa.*' The more you talk, the more expensive it sounds.

You also have to ask a waiter for your bill at least three times, until you're finally forced to get up, take out your credit card, and walk to the cash register. Italian restaurateurs consider it rude even to hint that you should leave, unlike some establishments in New York and Los Angeles, where they take away your silverware and the tablecloth while you're still sipping on your coffee.

We agonised over this problem for days before we finally spoke to him about it. And even though we did it in the most nonconfrontational manner, Umberto was an unsettling combination of vague and defensive when we tried to get him to explain why his bill was so much higher than his original estimate. Then it occurred to us. We were paying for his silence. The discomfort we had caused him by asking him to keep our secret was going to have to be compensated.

OK, if this is how he wanted to play it, fine. In the immortal words of Joan Crawford when the board of directors at Pepsi tried to get rid of her, 'Don't screw with me, boys, I've been to Hollywood.'

I went online and downloaded a picture of Tony Soprano and his crew. I printed it on photo paper and bought a frame. We found a prominent spot on the wall of Dino's living room, and after taking down a pinup of a topless blonde and a rendering of Christ healing a leper, we hung the framed photo of the Soprano gang.

We invited Umberto over for coffee and when he arrived we seated him so that Tony and his goombahs were staring down at him. When Umberto asked about the photo, Nancy explained that they were her uncle Tony from New Jersey and a few of his business associates. In fact, Nancy added, she was so confused by Umberto's bill she had faxed it to Uncle Tony, who was in the construction business, among other things. Nancy emphasised the 'among other things' part by putting her finger on her nose and bending it to the side.

Umberto smiled uncomfortably as Nancy went on to tell him that Uncle Tony had faxed her back, saying that he thought she was being overcharged and that somebody needed to talk to this Umberto. Umberto started visibly perspiring.

We were preying upon their common conception that all Americans, especially those of Italian descent, are gangsters. This stereotype is clearly fed both by the popularity of our movies and TV shows around the world, and by the images of cigar-chomping, Hummer-driving military personnel around the world. This gunslinger image the Italians have of us was brought home to me when I innocently visited a hardware store soon after I arrived in Cambione. As soon as the owner realised that I was American, he brought me over to the rack of guns he was selling, thinking that I would want to buy several.

Umberto fumbled with his bill and suddenly remembered that perhaps he had failed to tell us that this was the amount if we paid him by cheque, because then he'd have to report it. But since we were dealing in cash, it would be less. A lot less.

Some months later, on a Sunday night in the fall after the house was finished, Nancy and I were preparing our snacks for the premier episode of *The Sopranos*. The series had been heavily promoted. Tony, Carmela and the gang could be seen scowling from bus benches and billboards all over the country, so we had little doubt that by now, Umberto knew we had bamboozled him. You can well imagine our dread when, right before the show was to start, we heard the unmistakable sound of his truck chugging up our driveway. Was this just a strange coincidence? Or had he come here with a sawn-off shotgun to extract some measure of revenge?

Nancy turned off the TV. As I opened the door my trepidation increased when I saw how upset he looked. And he was holding a sledgehammer. Nancy and I looked at each other apprehensively, but after he asked us for '*permesso*' to enter, we had no choice but to let him in.

Once inside, his demeanour changed into profound sadness as he poured out the story of his missing wedding ring. This ring, the sacred symbol of his twenty-two-year marriage, had gotten lost some time ago, causing him and his wife no end of agony. After months of racking his brain he finally realised that he had last seen it when he was working on our house. Specifically, on the wall near the crack. It seems that he had taken it off and placed it on a crevice in the wall, and in the rush to patch it up, the ring must have gotten sealed up inside the crack. So he had come to ask if he could hammer open our wall and try to find it.

As Nancy and I exchanged amazed looks, he assured us he would try to be careful not to hit a water pipe that might result in somebody from the Comune having to come over and then, by seeing the inside of the wall, discover how old our house was.

'How much do you think the ring was worth?' I asked in Italian, which by now had gotten pretty good.

Umberto's face grew long and grave. 'Oh, one can never put a price tag on such an object.'

'Two hundred euros?' Nancy suggested.

'It means so much to me,' he said looking sorrowfully at his empty ring finger. 'It would be more like a thousand. . . .'

Nancy and I stepped aside and indicated for him to begin hammering apart our wall.

'But it was an old ring,' he said. 'Maybe not worth more than five hundred.'

I went to get my chequebook with the realisation that even though Nancy and I had still come out ahead financially, Umberto had left knowing that when it came to outsmarting each other, we were dead even.

20. ZUM ZUG

I like ice. I really like ice. One of my favourite things to do when I'm in the States is to go into a 7-Eleven, get a Super Quencher-sized cup, and fill it up with ice, which I suck on and chew all day long. My dentist also loves ice, since he was able to buy himself a new Volvo (which is also good on ice) for all the fillings I have cracked.

The last time I was in the States I was thrilled to discover that my favourite convenience store was now dispensing two kinds of ice, either minicubes or crunched. Or, I could have a combination of the two.

Is America a great country or what?

Italy is also a great country, but they have no ice. Well, they have it and it's called *ghiaccio* (gee-ACH-ee-o), but when you ask for some in your drink on the hottest day of the year, they'll plop in one dinky cube that melts down to the size of a baby aspirin by the time it gets to you.

Making ice at home is no easy matter either. If you want a built-in ice maker, you have to finagle your way into a kitchen at one of the military bases and buy a huge double-door frigo Americano that'll take up so much room in a typical Italian kitchen, there won't be any room for your sink. The only option left is to fill an ice tray like some pre-Betty Furness housewife and slide it onto a narrow shelf in the tiny freezer without dribbling half of it on the floor. My best efforts to make home-made ice cubes resulted in slopping so much water on that shelf that the entire freezer locked up in a sheet of ice and the fridge started making a noise that I think was originally developed by the North Koreans to torture downed American pilots.

Much has been written about the legendary heat of the Italian summer, and the Italians really do love to complain about it, but any attempts to cool themselves off are greeted with outright suspicion. They'll go the beach but avoid the water. They despise air conditioning and have no qualms about sipping a steaming cappuccino on a day hot enough to boil you inside your own natural juices.

But their worst fear is about moving air. You can be on a crowded train where the inside temperature could fuse glass, but if you dare crack open a window, someone will invariably say, 'Scusi, signore, mal aria, mal aria.'

It means 'bad air' and it's the origin of our word malaria. Their request for you to shut the window is usually accompanied by pointing to their throats, their sinuses, their kidneys, or any other vital organ threatened by the insidious movement of air. So intense is their fear of it that their houses, cars and offices are all but hermetically sealed. It may be a fiery cauldron of a summer day, but the most an Italian driver will do is roll down his side window just wide enough for him to dangle his hand out, so that to the uninitiated, it looks as if the country is full of people driving around drying their nails.

It was on such a hot day that Nancy and I went to the bank to withdraw the money to pay Umberto. The bank was crowded and stifling, full of heavyset, perspiring women and their crying children. There was a floor-standing fan off in the corner, but it was not turned on out of fear that it would stir up the air and disperse the cigarette smoke that was so thick, I could barely make out the No Smoking signs on every wall.

We finally reached a teller, and you could imagine our delight when she told us we couldn't have our money, because the Comune had frozen our account. I heard the word *ghiacciato* (to have frozen) and I got excited. I thought she was telling us that we had won a free ice maker and I couldn't understand why Nancy was getting so upset. But as the conversation between them grew more heated, they kept saying '*bloccato*', which I recognised as the word the Italians use to describe the stoppage of anything from bowel movements to bank accounts.

I then got the picture and joined Nancy in pressing our teller for the reasons. She claimed to have no further information. For that we needed to speak to the bank's vice president, Marco Mucchi.

This being the middle of the business day, Signor Mucchi was not in his office and the teller didn't know where he was. But we did. We promptly marched out of the bank and went across the street to the café, where we found the vice president sipping on a steaming cappuccino on a day so hot, you could fry a frittata on the pavement.

Marco Mucchi was of slightly less than normal height, but he was thick and wide, with a big man's head sitting close to his shoulders. His finely groomed black hair, slicked down and combed straight back, combined with a pair of no-nonsense wire-rimmed glasses to give him an air of gravitas far beyond his years.

'*Buon giorno*, Signor Mucchi,' Nancy said, apologising for our interruption as we approached his table.

Signor Mucchi half rose out of his chair and invited us to sit, never once taking his eyes off the clingy tank top Nancy was wearing. I'm not the jealous type, but I never cease to marvel at how Italian men will ogle a woman with a blatancy that would get you hauled into court on sexual harassment charges in America.

'*Caffè per te*?' he asked, beckoning a waiter. He had shifted into the informal tense, letting us know that whatever business we were here to discuss could be done on a friendly basis.

'*Troppo caldo*.' Nancy explained that it was too hot for coffee, then turning to the waiter, she told him that she'd love some bottled water.

'*Per me, una Coca-Cola con ghiaccio, per favore*.' I cupped my hands in abundance to show him I wanted lots of ice. '*Molto ghiaccio*.'

Without even the prerequisite chitchat required by Italian law, which dictates you must ask about the health and happiness of every member of a person's family, we launched into the inquiry about why our funds had been blocked by the Comune. Signor Mucchi responded with a well-practised vagueness, intimating that the Comune felt we had not honoured the spirit of our agreement. We prodded him for details, but he sidestepped our every inquiry.

I was running out of ways to ask the same question when I realised that Nancy had not been saying anything for a while. I looked over and saw that her face was contorted in agony like a Greek mask of tragedy. Her lips were quivering and she began sobbing as huge tears flowed down her cheeks.

'Honey?' I said, concerned.

'I don't know what to do,' she blubbered in Italian. 'My mamma's coming to spend her last days here and I have no place for her! Is that what the Comune wants? For me to put my poor, sick mamma in a hotel?'

Signor Mucchi was distraught. He handed her his handkerchief, patted her on the arm, and signalled for the waiter to hurry up with our drinks.

'We've followed their instructions to the letter.' Nancy sobbed. 'No matter what it cost us, no matter how difficult it was.'

The waiter arrived with our drinks. My Coke had one little piece of ice floating on the surface about the size of a ladybug.

'What do they want from us?' Nancy wept, her bare shoulders heaving. 'We're at the end of our rope!'

'Let me see what I can do,' Marco Mucchi said, rising. He stood over Nancy, telling her that he was going to call a friend of his at the Comune as he lingered for a moment to stare down her cleavage.

'*Grazie, signore,*' Nancy said in a trembling voice as she looked up at him with tear-sodden eyes.

He went off to use the phone, and I turned to her, frantic to know what had upset her enough to make her cry.

'Oh, relax,' she said, all dry eyed and chipper. 'I'm fine.'

I stared at her in disbelief.

'Italian men really relate to tears.' She craned her neck to make sure he was talking on the pay phone inside the bar. 'And if a mamma's involved . . .'

'I can't believe you were faking that.'

She gave me a cryptic smile, and for the first time in our relationship, I found myself wondering about orgasms.

Signor Mucchi returned a few moments later. He apologised for having taken so long, but he had been finally able to find out what the problem was, although he warned us that what he was about to say was off the record. We drew near in anticipation, and he revealed that the Comune had blocked our funds because they had heard that we were putting up a three-storey aluminum-and-glass California beach house.

That's preposterous, we sputtered. Except for making it slightly larger, we were spending a fortune trying to preserve the traditional stonework of the *rustico*. All they had to do was look at all the schematics and blueprints we filed with them, which their own architects had approved!

'What you file and what you build may be two different things,' Marco Mucchi said, giving Nancy a look that was both admiring and a little flirty. 'Everybody knows how clever you Americans are.'

'We're not that clever,' Nancy said indignantly. 'I mean, we love that old house and we want to honour it.'

'It's a rumour,' I added, happy to finally be able to use the word *chiacchiera*, even though I probably mispronounced it.

'Well, there's a little more to it than that,' he said, nodding gravely.

'Such as?'

He unhooked the wire-rimmed glasses from around his ears,

and as he wiped off the sweat with a paper napkin, he looked around to make sure no one was listening. 'Well, for one, why does Umberto get so mysteriously quiet when anybody asks him what's going on up at your house?'

Nancy and I looked at each helplessly. We had gotten trapped in the irony of trying to cover up one thing, only to have it come back at us in another form.

'I think he's just tired,' Nancy said. 'You know the heat's been so –'

'On any other topic you can't shut him up.' Marco Mucchi held his ears to indicate being barraged by a torrent of Umberto's words. 'But when it comes to your house . . .' He zipped his lips shut.

'*Chi sa?*' I said, showing off my fluency. Who knows?

'And what about Vesuvia Pingatore?' Marco Mucchi asked. 'Why does she suddenly decide, after all these years, to make her stone walls so much higher?'

'She hates us and she doesn't want to look at us,' Nancy countered.

'Or . . . maybe she doesn't want to look out her window every day and have to stare at a three-storey aluminum-and-glass California beach house,' he said.

'Look, signore,' Nancy said, reverting to the formal tense to let him know that this was all about business. 'We have been nothing but nice to that woman. And you cannot believe how rude she's been!'

Marco Mucchi shifted uncomfortably in his chair.

'Weeks ago we offered to buy that small olive grove at the top of our hill,' she told him as he nodded. 'And she never even had the decency to respond to our offer!'

'Actually, she called and asked if I would tell you that she respectfully declines your offer. She wants to keep that land in her family.'

'And what about the bas relief Nancy made for her?' I asked

indignantly. 'Did she also want to keep that in her family?'

Marco Mucchi shrugged. '*Boh.*'

'Signor Mucchi,' Nancy said, fighting back the tears like Meryl Streep in every movie she'd ever been in, 'if we wanted a three-storey aluminum-and-glass California beach house, we would have stayed in California. We love it here and we love our *piccolo rustico*. And we would never do anything to violate the tradition of that house. How can we prove that to you?'

Unfortunately, we couldn't. The only way we could prove we were honouring the house was to finish it and the only way we could finish it was for the Comune to unblock our funds, which they refused to do. The term zum zug came to mind. It's a German expression that's used in chess, and it means every way you move, you lose.

21. ZIZZANIA

'Ooooooooooooooommmmmmmmmmmmnnnnnnnnnnnnnn.'

I was meditating. Yeah, really. Sitting cross-legged on the floor with my eyes closed, I was concentrating on closing off my mind to everything but the flow of my own breathing. And according to this book I had ordered through Amazon UK, *Meditation for Morons*, I was well on my way to aligning my chakras, resonating my prana, and wandering serenely through the landscape of my own consciousness. Except the left side of my butt had gone numb, and there was a bird in the backyard making a constant, and I mean constant, Hoo-hoo-hoo-hoo-hoo-hoo sound.

I'll admit I don't know much about wildlife, but from watching things like Animal Planet I've learned that ninety-nine per cent of everything that animals (and presumably humans) do is to either catch food or procreate. In my wildest imagination I couldn't imagine anything that would allow this damn bird to get close enough to eat it or screw it when he kept going Hoo-hoo-hoo-hoo-hoo-hoo 24/7/365.

Did I mention that I wasn't supposed to be thinking about anything?

'Oooooooooooooooooooooooommmmmmmmmmmmmmmnnnnnn nnnnnnnnnnnnn.'

Hoo-hoo-hoo-hoo-hoo-hoo-hoo-hoo-hoo.

Aw, the hell with it. This was hopeless, I realised as I unknotted my legs and got up. Look, it's not as if I wasn't trying. I had gotten into this meditation thing when I started going to a yoga class taught by a Swiss lady. Her class was quite popular with Cambione's yuppies (or, as they pronounce it: YOU-pees), and on any given night you might find as many as twenty-five people there. But much to the dismay of our Swiss *professoressa*, the Italians approached this discipline with a rather cavalier attitude. While I was sweating and grunting in a comic attempt to twist my creaking body into shapes that would only be desirable if you wanted to have sex with yourself, the Italians were acting much as if they were in a café, laughing and chatting throughout the entire session. I half expected them to light up cigarettes and start sipping cappuccino.

My best efforts to view life through the tranquillity of my third eye had been singularly unsuccessful, and I found myself increasingly stressed out over our situation. As if that weren't bad enough, I was also feeling guilty for not being as happy as a loon because I was living in a place that most people can only dream about. Even in the best of times I'm about one broken shoelace away from a nervous breakdown anyway, so this was really taking a toll on me.

You see, the issue of money was ever on our minds, creating a state of *zizzania* (discord) between Nancy and me. With the Comune blocking the funds we had earmarked for remodelling, we had no other resources to draw from. We did our best to shield Umberto from our situation, so he and his guys would keep working as Nancy and I scrambled to turn up some cash.

I barraged my agent with e-mails and kept dreaming up more and more macho catchphrases. He wrote me back with the usual platitudes about being out there every day trying to sell my script, but how tough the market was these days.

The only encouraging thing he ever said was how much he enjoyed that e-mail I had written to him about Tuscany. In spite of the fact that I had chronicled all the charming ways things don't work around here, it made him and his wife even more eager to come. Unfortunately, he was so busy at the office (presumably with the clients he could find work for), they probably wouldn't be able to get here until late in the year. And by the way, did I know a cosy little B and B in Siena where he and his wife could enjoy a romantic Christmas?

These e-mails made me feel more like a travel agent than a writer, but at least they had opened a new avenue of communication between us. So I sent him back the names of a few B and Bs, as well as more impressions of Italy, like how every time I came back here from America it took me weeks to reset all my default commands. Expectations had to be lowered and appreciation widened so that I expected to do less in a day, but appreciated each thing more.

Meanwhile, Nancy rented a space at a local marble studio and began carving a statue she thought she might have a buyer for. The marble studio she worked in was a large open space the size of a warehouse. Yet it felt claustrophobic, due to the towering blocks of raw stone and the half-sculpted human figures that were scattered throughout the area like huge oak trees in a forest. There were life-sized angels and nightmarishly proportioned gargoyles. Fluted columns of creamy alabaster and ceiling-high pillars made from a Russian onyx as black as sable.

As many as a dozen sculptors and *artigiani* worked there at one time, and the din of air compressors and hammers striking chisels was thunderous. In the midst of all this glorious confusion and serious concentration, people laughed and shouted over the jet-engine howling of the machines and the unsynchronised clanging of hammers playing a version of the 'Anvil Chorus' at warp speed.

One wall of the studio was hung with a collection of body parts . . . arms, legs, torsos, hands and feet that would have been macabre if they weren't so beautiful. They were plaster models, some dating back to the fifteenth century, and the sculptors, using calipers to scale up or down to whatever size they wanted, used them for reference points when they couldn't get a live model.

I entered and ratcheted down my senses to adjust to the dim light, the mind-throttling noise and the burning smell of stone being ground into powder. Stepping around a coarse wooden trestle that was cluttered with chisels, mallets, drill bits and air hammers, I spotted Nancy. I tried to call out, but my throat was already hoarse from the marble dust that hung in the air like a cloud and was rendered in shades of ivory by the sunlight that streamed in through fly-specked skylights that were never opened.

'Hey,' I croaked as I approached.

Nancy smiled as she looked up from the torso she was smoothing with a rasp. I smiled back because she was so covered in marble dust she looked like she had been rolled in powdered sugar.

'You did a lot today,' I said, walking around the statue.

'It's getting there.' She took off her goggles to reveal the face of an albino raccoon.

I put my arm around her, and we walked over to the opened, garage-sized doors where it was a lot quieter.

'So?' she said, unzipping her jumpsuit and letting the top fall down around her waist.

'I've been crunching numbers.'

'And we're broke.'

'We will be if we keep going on like this.'

'So you're saying it's time to sell?'

I nodded and turned away to get a drink out of the water fountain, because I didn't want to see the look she was giving me. I swallowed, and with my head still down, I said, 'I know it'll mean taking a loss, but in the long run –'

'A loss? That house should be worth a lot.'

I straightened up and faced her with narrowed eyes. 'What house are you talking about?'

'Brentwood.'

'You don't want to sell the one here?'

'No! I thought you were talking about –'

'I don't want to sell the one in Brentwood!'

'It's the only thing we got that's worth anything,' she said.

I should have known it would come to this. For the past few weeks she had been talking about refinancing that house and pulling some money out. But I was nervous about taking on large monthly payments when neither of us had a salary coming in. She argued that it would be a short-term loan that we'd pay off when the Comune unblocked our funds . . . but what if that, like everything else in Italy, took years?

Then we started talking about renting it out, long term. That would certainly help with our cash flow, but do little to give us the amount we needed to finish the *rustico*.

'I'm not ready to sell that house,' I said emphatically. If I had been holding one of those sculptor's hammers, I think I would have banged on something.

'I knew it was too good to be true,' she said. 'You're still dreaming about Hollywood.'

'That's not it,' I snapped, even though it probably was.

'All right, honey,' she said soothingly. 'Let's not get all worked up over it.'

I took a deep prana breath like, yeah, that was going to help.

'I don't know, would it hurt just to find out what that house is worth these days?' she said. 'Couldn't we at least look into it?'

'I can't stop you, it's half yours.'

'Aren't you just a little curious about what the housing market's like back there?'

I knew what she was doing. When a frontal assault doesn't work, pull back, and come at it from the flanks. Introduce the idea and get the other person used to it little by little, like boiling them alive by turning up the temperature of the water very slowly. Oh, yeah, I knew what she was doing, because it was something I did all the time.

It was so beastly hot that only mad dogs, Englishmen and fools who owned broken-down houses in Italy were out in the noonday sun. Nancy was inside helping Umberto and the guys tear up the old flooring so we could put in terra-cotta bricks, while I was hauling debris down to where we were dumping it at the bottom of the hill.

I was mopping my brow in between gulps of water, as Vagabondo filled my wheelbarrow with shovelfuls of dirt and broken concrete. We were talking about women, and he was telling me about a girl he had met at the disco. Even though he liked her and they had really hit it off, he suspected that from the wild way she danced she was a *bicicletta*. That's a term the local boys use to describe a woman who's so easy, it doesn't take a car to get her into bed, she'd go off with a guy who only owns a bicycle.

Nancy, Umberto, Va Bene and Problema drifted outside. They were breaking for lunch, and as they sat down in the shade and unwrapped their sandwiches, Nancy motioned for me to sit beside her. I told her I was just going to take this last load to the bottom of the hill, because I was afraid once I sat down, I'd never get up again.

I turned the wheelbarrow around and pointed it downhill. I had to dig in my heels to keep it from dragging me headlong as sweat, mixed with sunblock, ran into my eyes and stung them. My sunglasses slid down my nose, and I had to squint because the day was as blindingly bright as an overexposed photograph.

I was feeling as oppressed by my worries as I was by the fierce Tuscan sun. I hated the idea of struggling this hard at my age. I felt that after a lifetime of work, things should have been easier. But here I was, bedeviled by financial worries due to the fact that we hadn't saved enough because I thought I would keep working forever. I knew that once I got to a certain age and my pension kicked in, we'd be OK, but the trick now was to live long enough to collect that pension before this house killed me.

I hit a bump in the heavily rutted road and the wheelbarrow swerved to the left. I tried to jerk it back on course, but my hands were so raw, I lost grip of the handles. The whole thing pitched over and started to fall. I lunged after it, but I couldn't hold on. I fell to my knees and could only watch helplessly as the wheelbarrow tumbled down the side of the hill, spewing its contents along the way.

I looked up to see Nancy and the guys laughing. She called

out to see if I was OK, but I was so pissed, I couldn't even answer. I started to climb down to fetch the wheelbarrow. She yelled to me to let the guys help me get it after lunch. I hollered back that I didn't need any help as I half stumbled down the hill and retrieved the wheelbarrow.

My anger kept festering as I pushed the wheelbarrow back up the hill. By the time I reached the top, it was all I could do to look at them. I picked up the water bottle, chugged down a long gulp, and then poured the rest over my head. I wanted to go inside the *rustico*, curl up in some dark little corner, and lose myself in the smell of cool, wet stones and cobwebs.

But I didn't want the guys to think I was upset, so I plunked down next to Nancy under the dappled shade of an ancient olive tree. I was hungry but the sandwich she handed me felt heavier than a shotput. I held it in my hands, trying to muster the strength to bring it to my mouth as Nancy and the guys ribbed me about the wheelbarrow. They were chattering in that high-speed, back-street Italian that I always have trouble following, but I did manage to hear that my wife had anointed me with a new nickname, Goffo, 'clumsy'.

I wanted to crack some kind of self-deprecating joke to let them know I was being a good sport, but my brain felt spongy and my tongue lay in my mouth like a cinder block. Plus, my stomach had started to reel as the fumes from Umberto's lunch engulfed me. In spite of the heat he was eating *zambone*, a heavily spiced pork sausage encased in the skin of a pig's foot.

Nancy was on a roll, as if inspired by this incident to recount every klutzy thing I had ever done in my life. The guys were howling with laughter as she continued her monologue. The comedy writer's wife. Years of living with me and she could certainly hit a punchline. I just smiled and nodded, trying to mask my seething rage. I knew the guys couldn't wait to repeat her stories to all their friends until the whole town was laughing at me.

How dare they laugh at me? Here I was, a fifty-something guy, a lifetime office worker, busting my hump in this heat to keep up with guys in their thirties who did this every day. And they were laughing at me.

I spent the rest of the day sulking. Nancy knew I was upset and made a special effort to be loving, but I didn't respond. I just pretended to be busy and answered her questions with one-word answers. As soon as the guys left and we were alone, she cornered me and tried to apologise.

I heard her say that she had just been kidding around and that she had only done it to amuse the guys and take their minds off the heat, and what was the matter with me anyway? I used to have such a good sense of humour.

That did it. As difficult as it is for me to express my anger, I exploded. The gall of her accusing me of not having a sense of humour! It was that very sense of humour that had gotten us almost everything we had in life. Why, because I wasn't making any money at it now, did that suddenly mean I no longer had a sense of humour?

As is so often the case when you get mad at somebody, they get mad at you for getting mad, so the argument escalated. She glared at me in a way that instantly trivialised everything I was saying. Then she accused me of secretly wanting us to fail so we could go back to L.A. and I could resume killing myself trying to worm my way back into show business. I told her I didn't have to go all the way back to L.A. to kill myself, because this house was doing a pretty good job of it right here. We started screaming at each other and I wound up saying some things I really didn't mean, like how she dragged me here so she could finally be in control of everything.

Her cheeks went crimson, and she told me that if I really felt that way maybe I should go back! I told her that maybe I would, and if there was one thing I was grateful for, it was that I hadn't let her talk me into selling our house in Brentwood, because that's exactly where I wanted to be right now!

22. FIESOLE

Nancy was already in the shower by the time I staggered into the bedroom and stripped off my muddy clothes. I was in the process of kicking the whole sweaty mess into a corner when I noticed a pair of tickets sitting on our nightstand.

A few weeks before, when we were getting along much better, I had seen a billboard for a concert in Fiesole, a dramatic little hill town on the outskirts of Florence. It was an evening of love songs performed by a cast of popular Italian singers in an outdoor amphitheatre originally built by the Romans. It had all the makings of a wonderfully romantic evening, except that tonight we happened to hate each other's guts.

Nancy was just coming out of the shower when I walked into the bathroom holding up the tickets.

'That's not tonight?' she said, wrinkling her nose.

'Uh-huh.'

'I'm in no mood. You go.'

'Oh, like I'm going to drive two hours to sit there by myself and listen to an evening of love songs.'

'I don't care, do whatever you want.'

She reached up and began towel-drying her hair. I sighed in full knowledge that it's hard for a man to be angry at a woman when she's standing in front of him naked.

'I'll call Rudolfo and see if he wants to take Pia.' I went back into the bedroom and picked up the cellphone. 'Maybe it'll light a fire.'

She popped her head out of the bathroom door. 'How much were they?'

'Forty euros apiece.'

She clucked at the waste of money.

'I'm not going to give 'em away,' I said as I dialled. 'I'll sell them to him.'

'You can't call up somebody last minute and sell them tickets.'

'They're great seats.'

'Whatever.' She withdrew into the bathroom.

'He's not answering,' I called out as I redialled. 'I'll try him at his parents'.'

'While you're at it, tell Dino we're out of hot water.'

'Again?' I stormed into the bathroom, stuck my head in the stall, and turned the tap. Icy cold water splashed on my hand, and as I waited and waited it didn't get any warmer. 'Aw, man . . .'

'I had just finished rinsing off when –'

'Oh, thank you.'

'Think I did it on purpose?'

'Obviously, you weren't going to mention it until I got in there, all set for a nice hot shower, only to –'

'Oh, shut up!' she screamed.

'You shut up!!' I bellowed.

And on that convivial note we threw on some clothes, piled into the car, and roared off for an evening of love songs in Fiesole.

Even though it was over a hundred kilometres away, and there was lots of traffic, we weren't overly concerned about being late. The concert, like most operas and theatricals in Italy, was scheduled to begin at 9.15 p.m. This odd starting time is due to the fact that Italians must eat before a performance, and of course, the only time they can possibly have dinner is at eight o'clock. Now, there's no way that any restaurant in Italy is actually ready to seat you at eight, since the waiters have just finished their dinner and they're still enjoying an espresso and a cigarette.

You're finally shown to your table at about eight-twenty, where you sit sipping bottled water and sucking on a breadstick until somebody deigns to take your order, so realistically, it's coming up hard on nine bells before any food ever arrives. Given time for your *primo*, your *secondo*, and your *dolci*, washed down with a glass of grappa of course, it's now well after nine-thirty by the time you've signalled your waiter a half-dozen times for the cheque. Then there's the driving to the theatre, the nightmare of parking, the confusion of finding your seats, and the meeting and greeting of all your friends and neighbours in the audience. This explains why if any curtain in Italy ever goes up before ten o'clock, it's a miracle on the magnitude of changing water into wine.

Fiesole was founded by the Etruscans seven hundred years before the birth of Christ, making it far older than its larger and more celebrated neighbour, Florence. From the beginning the famous and the affluent have flocked there to seek comfort in its cool, steady breezes and sweeping views of the countryside. So renowned are the vistas that if you look closely at many of the masterpieces of Renaissance painting, you will recognise Fiesole's lily-speckled meadows in the background.

Kings, bishops, popes and pop stars have all owned villas in Fiesole, which has been especially receptive to the creative community, housing everyone from Boccaccio and Marcel Proust to Gertrude Stein and Frank Lloyd Wright.

Architecturally, there is nothing spectacular about its cathedrals, museums, monasteries or civic buildings, save for how they are clustered upon a series of hilltops so that the entire *centro storico* (historic centre) of the city has views to burn. There is, however, one edifice in Fiesole worth writing home about, and that is the Teatro Romano, the Roman Amphitheatre. Actually, it's a complex of structures built at the beginning of the Imperial Period in the first century AD and featuring, in addition to the outdoor theatre, one of the earliest Roman baths ever built.

Originally ordered by Augustus, the baths were remodelled two hundred years later by Hadrian. In its expanded version you can look at the skeletal walls and easily imagine fleshy patricians steaming in the *caldarium*, then cooling off in the *frigidarium*, before oiling up and donning their togas for the Saturday-night orgy at Octavius's pad.

Luck was with us when we pulled into the Piazza Mino in the heart of Fiesole, as we found both a parking space and a table for two at a restaurant called Il Lordo, which means 'the filthy person'. Apparently, giving something an unsavoury name doesn't diminish the commercial appeal of a place in Italy, because I've eaten at a restaurant called Puzzadolce (Sweet Stink), which that day was serving sformati di verdure, or, as we would translate it, 'deformed quiche'. I've gotten a haircut at a unisex salon called I Piccati (The Losers) and spent the night at a popular hotel in Florence called Malaspina, which means 'bad back', causing me to wonder if anyone has ever said, 'say, how are the beds at the Malaspina Hotel?'

After dinner, we crossed the cobblestoned piazza, passing the Bandini Museum, which does not showcase the history of fertiliser, but rather a fine collection of thirteenth-to-fifteenth-century religious art and a splendid sampling of Byzantine miniatures.

We entered the amphitheatre as it was filling up with the three thousand people it holds. Most were season ticket holders who each year purchase seats for the annual Estate Fiesolana (Fiesolian Summer), a series of musical performances featuring everything from Sicilian folk dance to a stageful of Italians phonetically belting out a selection of Broadway showstoppers.

But tonight it was Italian love songs. And, oh, what love songs. '*Nessun dorma*,' trilled the lyric soprano, her eyes closed in rapture. '*Che bella cosa 'na giornata è sole*,' sang the baritone, his powerful voice caressing the opening stanza of the famous 'O Sole Mio'. Romance was in the jasmine-scented air as men put their arms around their women, and a plump white moon rose over the hilltop that Leonardo da Vinci had once used to try and launch one of his flying machines.

'*Caro mio ben, credimi almen, senza di te languisce il cor,*' the tenor crooned.

> My dearest one,
> Believe me,
> Without you,
> My heart languishes.

I looked over to Nancy, who seemed lost in the dream of love. I felt bad that I was somehow less than she wanted me to be. After all these years together it was sad how little we understood each other's needs. She wanted me to be committed to our life in Italy, heart and soul, while I longed for her to understand how hard it was for me to feel intensely about anything now that I no longer had my career.

But it seemed the more we talked, the less we knew each other. I kept trying to tell her how I felt, and she kept saying that she understood, but how can anybody really get it unless they've been as fervently committed to their work as I have? How can you make another person comprehend that when your whole being has been defined in a certain way for twenty-five years, you can't suddenly say, 'OK, I used to be powerful and important, but now I'll just tootle off to the shed and build a birdhouse'?

I wished I could be different, but how much do people really change at their core? And how much can the person they live with expect them to change? Where did her right to have her dream end and mine begin?

By the time we got on the Autostrada outside of Florence, it was almost two in the morning. We drove in groggy silence, mesmerised by the hum of the tyres, and squinting at the occasional oncoming headlights.

I was numb with exhaustion, but unbidden thoughts kept

flapping around inside my head because I needed to figure out what I was going to do. Nancy and I were not getting along. It wasn't anybody's fault, just the old familiar case of two people wanting or needing different things. And as much as I hated to face it, perhaps some time apart might do us some good.

Maybe I needed go back to L.A. and chill for a while. Let her stay here and deal with the problems. I knew that I was running away, which I was good at, but what was the point of being together when we were at each other's throats all day?

And what was the point of keeping the house in Brentwood if I was going to be the only one living there? So maybe we should sell it. Take the money and split it. She could spend hers on the *rustico*, and I could get myself a little place in the Hollywood Hills. Nothing fancy, just your basic little bachelor pad . . .

Is that what I'd be . . . a bachelor? And is that what I wanted? To be alone? With no one by my side as I got old? And died? A wave of despair swept over me. I started to panic at the thought of how radically different my life was about to become, and I suddenly needed air. I rolled down my window and a rush of cold wind roared in.

'I'm freezing,' Nancy said.

'Sorry.' I rolled the window up. 'I didn't want us to get drowsy.'

'I'm fine.'

'Sure you don't want to pull over? Get some coffee?'

'You have to go to the bathroom, don't you?'

Why was she always doing that? Treating me like I was three. And why did I keep getting mad at everything she said? How did it go so wrong so fast? Jesus, you hear about this kind of thing all the time. A couple's been together for years, then suddenly he retires or the kids move out, and the next thing you know, they're splitting up, because without all the distractions they've got nothing to say to each other. *non come noi eh!*

I started to get depressed, because even though we still loved each other, Nancy and I might become one of those stories. And as comforting as it would have been to wallow in self-pity, I couldn't afford that indulgence right now. I had lost my career and I was losing my wife. Life was throwing me a gutter ball, so it was time to suck it up and bowl for the spare. I wasn't dead yet, and as bad as Hollywood had treated me, they couldn't take away my pen. I could still keep writing and ... well, if things didn't work out between Nancy and me, who says I had to die alone? Last time I checked, there were still lots of women in southern California. Beautiful women. Actresses, models, spokespersons. Yeah, maybe this wouldn't be so bad.

But did I really want to be with another woman? Listen to her life story and tell her mine, while both of us pretended to be interested? Go through that weird, awkward stage that lasts for months until you feel comfortable enough to burp (or worse) in front of each other? Put up with a whole new set of annoying little habits, like her running to floss after every meal or punctuating everything she says with inappropriate laughter? It seemed like so much work and effort, unless, of course, she happened to be a really great-looking young chick in her twenties. I thought for a moment about my agent's assistant, Greta, lingering on those inevitable tan lines.

Hmm, that definitely made it more interesting. But people in their twenties can be so crazy and needy. And they listen to that God-awful headbanger music. I have a friend my age who loves younger women because, as he likes to say, 'They have shorter stories.' But every time I see him with a twenty-something on his arm, I want to laugh because he looks old enough to be her ancestor. Besides, how could I keep up with a girl that age? She'd want to go out clubbing, and I'm dozing off by nine-thirty. And what about performing sexually? I'd have to walk around with a Viagra drip in my arm.

OK, so maybe she didn't have to be so young. There were

plenty of great women in their forties and fifties out there. I could think of two or three right off the bat. Most were ex-wives of friends of ours, and they were smart, attractive and interesting. But if they had all been divorced, what was wrong with them? What did their ex-husbands know that I had yet to discover? Maybe they were crazy, and needy, and listened to that God-awful headbanger music. And what if one of their ex-husbands started hitting on Nancy? How would I feel about that?

Maybe I was thinking about this all wrong. Instead of instinctively looking to pair up with some hapless woman, perhaps I should use this period of my life to learn and grow. Devote this time to just me. Really get to know myself and understand my deepest underlying motives. Develop as a person by reaching out in bold new directions and, for the first time in my life, begin to honour the strength and power buried deep inside me.

Nah, that'd never work.

Our headlights brushed across the exit sign to Cambione in Collina, and as Nancy steered us towards the off-ramp, I noticed that her eyes were noticeably drooping.

'Let's not go in to work tomorrow,' I said, trying to make a joke.

'Uh huh,' she replied, in a voice that was tired and faraway.

I was glad we were so close to home, and as the car entered that familiar Y-shaped intersection that led us into Cambione, I opened the CD case. I flipped through it until I came across something that was lively enough to keep us awake. I was just about to take it out of its sleeve when I looked up.

There was a blur of colours behind a blinding flash of headlights heading straight at us. Nancy slammed on the brakes, but the oncoming car ate up the distance in a nanosecond, and all I could do was widen my eyes in disbelief as the BMW crashed into us head-on.

23. CARABINIERI

The BMW was a big one. A 500 Series sedan that outweighed our Volkswagen by a thousand pounds. We were halfway through the Y of the intersection when the Beemer blew the red light and slammed into us at forty miles an hour. The point of impact was just to the left of dead centre, puncturing the radiator and driving it into the engine so hard, our motor was sheared clear off its mounts.

We were whipped back hard against our seats and then hurled forwards just as the air bags inflated. The car filled with what I thought was smoke but was really propellant from the air bags. That ghostly white vapour, coupled with steam shooting out of the radiator, made me think the car was on fire.

I screamed for Nancy to get out, but the pop of the air bags had so deafened me, I couldn't even hear the sound of my own voice. I reached out for her, but she was all blurry. I touched my face and realised that the air bag had knocked off my glasses. I was looking around for them when I saw blood on my shirt and realised my nose was bleeding.

My door was wrenched open and a cluster of Italians peered in. I undid my seat belt as a set of hands helped me out of the car. Somebody tried to unbuckle Nancy's seat belt, but when they touched her shoulder, she bellowed in pain.

A good Samaritan had set off a highway flare and was using it to guide the stalled traffic trying to get around us. The flare made the night reek of sulphur as it bathed the scene in an eerie smoke, tinted red from the taillights.

I got to my feet and started wandering through the debris field. Even though I could feel my shoes crunching on crystals of shattered glass, I felt as if I were floating above this surrealistic landscape. I took a wobbly step and a young guy latched on to my arm to steady me while his girlfriend handed me a handkerchief for my nose.

They led me over to where Nancy was sitting on the curb with her head between her knees, as a couple of people stood over her, excitedly reliving the details of the accident. I laid my hand on Nancy's shoulder and she looked up at me. Her eyes were glassy, her breathing was shallow, and I got very frightened.

'She tell me she got a big headache,' a young Italian woman said to me in English.

'Huh?' I pointed to my ears and moved in closer so I could at least read her lips if she was, indeed, speaking English.

'My husband he call for an ambulance,' she hollered. 'They come here right away.'

'Thank you,' I said with profound gratitude. '*Grazie mille.*'

I went back to survey the damage and search for my glasses. The two cars were still locked together, but while the BMW had suffered only sheet-metal damage, the entire front end of our Polo was crunched up like a cheap accordion. I pried open a door, and after feeling around in the dark, I found my glasses in the crack between the seat and the console. They were twisted and bent, but I managed to rest them on my face. I still couldn't hear, but at least I could now see.

An elderly man in a white linen suit came over and started hollering at me. I realised that he was the other driver and his aggressive attitude was somehow meant to make this our fault. I distinctly remembered our light being green as we came through the intersection, but who knows? Perhaps it would come down to his word against ours . . . he was Italian and we were *stranieri.*

I tried to respond to his accusations, but my attention was drawn to the arrival of the ambulance. The paramedics jumped out and huddled around Nancy, checking her eye movements with a flashlight and taking her pulse. I worked my way into the knot of people surrounding her, and found myself next to the lady who had spoken to me in English. She explained that the paramedics were concerned about a concussion, so they were taking her to the hospital. I watched helplessly as they loaded Nancy on a gurney and wheeled her towards the ambulance. Walking alongside it, I told her that I would stay and deal with the police and the car, and that I would get to where they were taking her, although I had no idea how. I stopped talking when I realised how disoriented she looked, as if she couldn't understand what had happened to us. I smiled at her and squeezed her hand, and she smiled back as they loaded her in the ambulance, slammed the door, and drove off into the night.

I felt alone, dazed, and confused. For some odd reason, even though I still couldn't hear anything, my ears filled with music. The tenor's voice from the concert was saying just what I was feeling.

'*Caro mio ben, credimi almen, senza di te languisce il cor.*'

> My dearest one,
> Believe me,
> Without you,
> My heart languishes.

Just then, the *carabinieri* pulled up. There was only one, actually, and as he got out of his patrol car, I recognised him as the tall, skinny Barney Fife who had left his Uzi in our trunk. He seemed overwhelmed as he took out his notepad and began asking questions. The other driver got to him first and, pointing at me, launched into an invective-filled rant. I tried to object, but when the skinny *carabieniere* turned his questioning to me, I was scarcely able to hear what he was saying, or even understand the words if I could.

The guy in the linen suit took this as proof of our guilt, but the wonderful lady who spoke English cut him off. Speaking alternately to the cop in Italian and to me in English, she testified that she and her husband had been in the car directly behind us, and that we had had the green light. Moreover, she pointed to another man in the crowd who had been in his car sitting at the red light when the other driver roared past him and smashed into us. Besides, the lady said with no small amount of disdain, she could tell from his licence plates that the other driver was from Massa, and we all know how badly they drive!

But the other driver wouldn't give up, adamantly hurling the blame back at us. As he steamed through this tirade, I noticed that he was leaning against the patrol car for support and that his eyes were bloodshot. Calling upon my limited, but sometimes appropriate, Italian vocabulary, I pointed to him and shouted, '*Lui è ubriaco!*' He's drunk!

I didn't know the word for 'Breathalyser', so I pantomimed for the cop to test him. The cop paused, looked into the other driver's eyes, and then, with a flap of his hand, declared that the guy looked OK to him. How differently, I thought, this would have played out if it had happened on the Pacific Coast Highway instead of the Via Aurelia.

Now came the filling out of the accident report. I went back to the car and fetched the registration and our insurance information, and when I got back, the *carabiniere* was taking down the other driver's statement. As the guy in the linen suit described the incident, he repeatedly referred to his own car as a Bee-Em-Voo, which is how Italians pronounce the letter W. The *carabiniere* would then repeat 'Bee-Em-Voo' as he wrote down what the other driver had said. And, oddly enough, each time one of them said 'Bee-Em-Voo,' I started to giggle, until they were both looking at me like I was the one who was *ubriaco*.

With the help of the lady who spoke English, I was able to give the cop our version of what had happened. He was impressed with the accuracy and the sincerity of her corroborating testimony, and she went to great pains to make sure I had both her phone number and the numbers of other drivers who had also witnessed the accident.

The way these people rallied around me, not only a stranger

but a foreigner, made me feel guilty about all the unflattering things I may have thought about them. Here it was three-thirty in the morning, and nobody left until they were sure I was OK.

Even the *carabiniere* was sympathetic, getting on his radio and ordering the ambulance driver to come back for me and take me to the hospital so I could be with my wife. And when the tow truck arrived, a bunch of people helped me collect all the personal items in our car.

'*Che è questa cosa?*' an elderly gentleman asked. What's this? He handed me the half a copper heart that Signor Mazzetti had made for us.

I took it and thanked him. It had gotten bent in the impact, and I very carefully straightened it. It seemed like such a long time ago when Nancy and I had laughed and loved each other so much that a man – another total stranger – made us this copper heart I was now holding.

I suddenly felt empty and exhausted. I felt my knees buckle and a set of hands latch on to my arm, as the elderly gentleman caught me. He called out for help. The *carabiniere* came running over and grabbed me. I was barely able to put one foot in front of the other while he guided me over to his patrol car and helped me into the passenger side. I thanked him, and as I collapsed into the seat, I felt something hard and metallic under my butt. I looked down and realised that he had sat me down on his machine gun.

24. OSPEDALE

I dozed off during the ambulance ride and dreamed of rain. A hard rain, hot and torrential, that beat down with such fury, it whipped the cypress trees around as if they were feathers and turned the unplanted farmland into vast fields of shoe-sucking ooze. Umberto suddenly appeared. He was talking to a man who looked like my grandfather and somebody asked me if I wanted soup.

I felt my shoulder being shaken and I woke up to see us pulling up the driveway of the Ospedale Generale di Versillia. As if triggered by being near a hospital, my various body parts started reporting in. My nose was no longer bleeding, but I couldn't turn my head more than fifteen degrees without a sharp pain that didn't feel like it was going away anytime soon. That, coupled with a soreness in my back that made me wince as I got out of the ambulance, seemed like the classic symptoms of whiplash, which I had always thought was some fake malady invented by an evil cabal of chiropractors and personal-injury lawyers. My hearing had started to return, but I was still a little deaf, for as I thanked the paramedics for the ride, I could tell that my voice was coming out a lot louder than I intended.

I trudged up the stairs of the hospital under a cloudless sky that was starting to brighten by the first rays of dawn. The lobby was empty and I looked around for either a person or a sign that could tell me where to go. Finding neither, I wandered down a series of long, dimly lit corridors that smelled of stale cigarettes, Mercurochrome, and accumulated layers of disinfectant.

The personal items I had taken out of the car, CD case, flashlight, sunglasses and the half a copper heart, kept slipping out of my hands, and whenever I tried to rearrange how I was holding them, I managed to drop one or more of them. I had no idea where I was going, or even what ward I was passing through, since the only indications that I was moving from one unit to another were the small carved-out altars dedicated to the saint of that particular sickness or malady.

It felt as if I had been walking for miles when a small, dark-skinned Moroccan man in hospital greens found me. He seemed to know who I was, and without a word he led me through another maze of corridors until we reached a waiting room holding a few scattered people, some bandaged and some waiting to be. He guided me past an examining room where an indifferent nurse was wiping dried blood off the head of a semiconscious man. He asked her where the Americana was and she pointed.

We continued down the corridor until we got to the only room with a light on. I peeked in and saw Nancy lying on a cranked-up hospital bed. She was wearing a dressing gown and her arm, held out to her side by an elaborate brace, was encased in a formidable plaster cast.

'Oh, my God,' I said as I entered.

'It's broken,' she said, sitting up with great difficulty. 'I'm not going to be able to sculpt.'

'It's OK.'

Her lips started trembling. 'I don't know how I'm going to finish that piece.'

'Let's not worry about that.' I held her as delicately as I could, grateful that she no longer seemed disoriented. 'How's your head?'

'I'm still a little dizzy. And I'm so nauseous.'

'Did they give you anything?'

'Just something for the pain.'

'Where's the damn doctor? What'd he –'

'I just saw him. He wants to keep me here tonight.'

'OK.'

'You go home.'

'No. No way.' I spotted an easy chair and dragged it over to her bedside. 'I'm staying.'

'How's your nose?'

'It's not broken, but I'll probably be sounding like Elmer Fudd for a while,' I said in an exaggerated cartoon voice.

She smiled and I smiled back, even though the change of expression hurt my face.

'Go home,' she said. 'You'll be a lot more –'

'I'm not going anywhere, OK?'

'OK.'

'Try and get some rest,' I said. 'I'll be fine.'

She laid her head back down and closed her eyes. I listened to the rhythm of her breathing, and after a few minutes I sensed she was falling asleep. I was about to do the same, when I spotted a figure in hospital greens passing by our door. I quietly rose and rushed after him.

'*Scusi*, *Dottore*, *scusi*,' I stage-whispered, stopping him in his tracks.

I caught up with him and asked if he was the one who had examined Nancy. When he told me he was, I asked him about her condition. He blew a blizzard of Italian at me until I was able to implore, '*Lentamente*, *per favore*, *lentamente*,' 'Slowly, please, slowly.' Speaking to me as if I were a refugee from special ed, he explained that her X rays showed a fracture in the upper arm. Her body had been twisted by the impact of the collision, and when the air bag burst, it slammed her shoulder into the car's window post. A more serious problem, he went on, was the indication of a shoulder separation in that arm. He had scheduled an orthopaedic surgeon to come in and look at her tomorrow. I asked him about her headache, and he said that that, along with her nausea and dizziness, were the usual symptoms of a grade-one concussion. They were going to monitor her overnight and give her an MRI first thing in the morning.

I rigged up a little bed on the easy chair, using a folding chair for my feet and Nancy's balled-up sweater for a pillow. I turned off the light and tried to fall asleep, but as exhausted as I was, I couldn't doze off.

I couldn't find anything to read, so I sat up, crossed my legs, and thought I'd try to meditate, since that stupid bird that went Hoo-hoo-hoo-hoo-hoo every minute of the day wasn't around to distract me. I took in some deep breaths and felt my heart rate slow. The room was quiet and my inhalations fell into lockstep with Nancy's soft breathing and the steady pull of a respirator from somewhere down the hall.

But I was still so revved up from the accident, my mind kept chattering away and no amount of ujjâya breathing would settle it down. After a few more futile attempts I decided that maybe the problem was my mantra. I had been using Om, which was what Meditation for Morons had suggested. But Om is just so been there/done that. I mean, it's so five minutes ago, it's like a cliché, so no wonder I couldn't take it seriously.

I decided that this might be a good time to search for a new mantra. So I began experimenting with some different sounds. I closed my eyes, and in a quiet voice not to disturb Nancy, I chanted such soothing sounds as 'Reeeee . . .' 'Baaaaa. . .' and 'Neeee.' But my voice kept coming out like Elmer Fudd, and it was making me laugh. I was just about to concede that some people, like me, were just too immature for the world of metaphysics, when I suddenly came up with 'Laaaaaaa.'

Even through my pinched nose, chanting 'Laaaaaa' seemed fraught with promise. I said it over and over, hoping the power of 'Laaaaa' would carry me off to a spiritual nirvana so serene that for once in my life my brain would stop jumping around like a circus monkey on angel dust.

'Laaaa.'

'Laaaaaa.'

'Laaaaaa–aaaahhhh . . .'

I started playing with it, finding variations. I saw colours as I pictured the letters: EL and AY.

Then I realised my new mantra was L.A.

All tranquillity was shattered as my mind flooded with images of agents and managers and personal trainers and stretch limos. My eyes popped open and I felt like screaming, when I heard a voice.

'Yo, Dog, whassup?'

I looked up and Charylie was standing in the doorway.

'What are you doing here?' I said. 'I'm not writing about you.'

'Well, you should be,' she said, sashaying into the room. 'I seen what you was writing and, man, it sucks.'

'Oh, thanks.'

Charylie struck a heroic pose and pointed an imaginary pistol at me. '"He ripped back the trigger of his Glock and emptied the whole clip into the serial killer's face." Yo, that is pure shit!'

'I'm just trying to sell a script, OK?'

'Oh, yeah, you're all that and a bag of chips.'

'Don't you have someplace else to be? Aren't you, like, late for a drive-by shooting or something?

'Have you ever fired a Glock?' she said, sitting on the edge of Nancy's bed. 'Do you even know what a Glock is?'

'Hemingway never fought a bull, but it didn't keep him from writing about it.'

'Well, you ain't no Hemingway, sucka, so you better stick to writin' what you know.'

'Any other pearls of wisdom?'

'Yeah, G, word up. This lady here loves you, and if she ever walks out on you, you're life's goin' straight down the crapper.'

'OK, on that we agree.' I nodded. 'Nancy and I love each other, that's a given. . .'

'That's a given?' She made a face. 'Listen to you, man, you sound like some science teacher. Where's your feelings? Where's your passion?'

'I got passion.'

'Oh, yeah, I seen how you was slobbering over that little

hottie that works for your agent,' she said, giving me that side-to-side chicken neck thing black girls do. 'I'll bet that bitch got tan lines –'

'All right, that's it! Get outta my head, will ya!' I turned away. 'Go!'

'Oh, save the drama for your mama, chump, and listen up. I'm tryin' to tell you what you better do before it's too late!'

That got my attention.

'You got to take a clue from these here Italians. Now, these motherfuckers really know how to open up their hearts and let their feelings out.'

'I know. These people'll cry over the opening of an envelope. Well, I can't do that, it's not me.'

'That's 'cause you're too busy trying to be cool, fool. Or you're too scared you're gonna make a mistake. Well, that's messed up, man. You got to try to be more Italian, 'cause when they feel something, they go for it!'

'Go for it. Just that simple.'

'I ain't sayin' it's simple, Dog. We all afraid of some shit or another and it's that fear that chases away our feelings.'

Charylie was right. The moment she said those words, I instantly understood why I felt such hostility towards the Italians. I had lived my whole life within a narrow band of emotions. I never cried, I rarely screamed, and I didn't even laugh that loud. Whenever I came up against the vast range of their feelings and the unfiltered intensity of their emotions, it made me squirm. All the while, I wasn't even aware of how much I envied their ability to participate in their own lives. It took a near-death experience for me to feel even a tiny fraction of what the average Italian experiences every time he hugs his mamma, gazes at a sunset, or tickles a baby.

Her words were the single stone that started the avalanche. My chin began to tremble and there was a pinprick of tears behind my eyes. I was connecting with my inner Italian, that deeply buried part of each of us that craves to savour life to its fullest.

'You got to be showin' her how you feel, boo,' she said. 'And not just with talk and promises. You got to do something big! And if that don't work, do something bigger, until she knows she's the most important thing in your life. You do that and you'll be together forever!'

'You're right,' I said. What she was telling me was so simple and obvious, it made me gasp that I hadn't already known it. 'You're absolutely right.'

'Who are you talking to?' Nancy said in a voice thick with sleep.

'Uh, I was . . . hey, how're you feeling?'

'Thirsty.'

'Hang on.' I reached over to the nightstand and filled a glass with water from the carafe. She took it with her good hand and gulped it down, taking big gasps of breath between swallows.

'I love you!' I emphatically declared. 'I really, really love you!'

'Oh – kay,' she said looking at me, slightly frightened, as she put her glass down.

'And I don't want to ever be apart from you anymore.' My words were just tumbling out and I had no idea what I was going to say. 'I've been stupid and selfish and immature, and I'm so sorry. Please forgive me. I want to sell our house in Brentwood and live here in Italy with you. Forever!'

'You mean that?'

'I want us to start over. With a clean slate. Have a whole new beginning with a brand-new life!'

'I want that too.'

'Yeah?'

'Of course! What do you think I've been talking about?'

I went to hug her, as best as I could with her arm in a cast. She grimaced and clutched her stomach.

'You OK?'

'I drank that water too fast,' she said. 'I'm queasy.'

'Should I call . . .?'

'No, I'm OK.' She straightened up and blew out a breath. 'It's getting a little better.'

We sat for a moment in silence. My nerve endings were electrified and my skin felt transparent. I was intoxicated by the smell of my own burning bridges. Strange and radical thoughts were bubbling up inside of me, and they all seemed right.

'Let's get married.'

'What?'

'I'm proposing to you. Let's get married again.'

She stared at me. 'You're serious.'

'Yeah! You know how we're always joking about what a farce our wedding was.'

'OK, the boat was my idea, but you're the one who found Reverend Elvis.'

'Let's do it right this time. Here in Italy. Maybe the house'll be ready and we can do it there.'

'I was the one who got hit on the head, wasn't I?' she said.

'Look, coming this close to death or whatever made me see how I'm wasting my life obsessing over all the wrong things. The only important thing I've got is you.'

'Oh, God, I can't believe you're saying this!'

'So what's your answer? Will you marry me? Again?'

'I'll think about it,' she said, as her voice broke and she hugged me.

I started to cry as I blubbered over and over that I loved her. My nose was running, tears were streaming down my face, and my shoulders were heaving with each sob.

I felt her heaving, too, and I thought we were both crying. I didn't realise it at the time, but she was heaving from nausea, and when I squeezed her, she threw up all over me.

Love is a many splendoured thing, isn't it?

25. MISERICORDIA

Italians have so much empathy for suffering that instead of saying 'Emergency', their ambulances and hospitals are usually printed with the word *misericordia*, which, if not by dictionary definition, then at least by common usage, means 'mercy for the miserable'. And that certainly described us as we took a taxi home from the hospital the following day.

After examining her, the orthopaedic surgeon saw evidence of a separation in Nancy's shoulder, and even though her MRI was clear, the neurologist who was brought in for consultation felt she had suffered a slight concussion. Her doctor wanted her to stay longer, but she wanted to go home. So, he agreed to discharge her if she promised to get plenty of rest. Above all she needed peace and quiet.

And that was precisely our intention until our taxi pulled up in front of the house we were renting from Dino and we discovered that there was a party going on. The living room was filled with flowers and baskets of food from our neighbours and the many well-wishers in the town we didn't know we had. The kitchen was gridlocked with women who included Dino's wife, Flavia, Mrs Cipollini from next door, Mina (whom we had heartlessly dubbed Mean Girl, from the hardware store), and those ancient aunts: Nina, Nona and Nana. All of them were jockeying for position around the stove as they clashed over how best to make *polenta con gorgonzola* and *zitti alla pinzimonio*.

We heard hammering and cursing coming from the bathroom where Dino and his cousin, the fabled plumber Turrido, were tearing up our shower to finally determine why we weren't getting a sufficient supply of hot water. Additional ruckus was being raised by the pack of dogs and the flock of chickens scattered inside and out who, for our sake, had struck an edgy détente where no blood was shed, but they continually growled and clucked as they spent the afternoon circling each other.

Added to that, our phone was constantly ringing with an endless succession of callers. Signor Tito Tughi called to tell us that our car had been towed to his lot and he was working up an estimate of the damages. As he told me this, I pictured him holding the phone with one hand as he stuck out the thumb and pinky of his other hand, making *le corne*, that horn-shaped gesture meant to keep our misfortune from spilling over onto him.

Umberto called to inform us that the lady he had hired to help his wife with the housework while her broken foot was mending would be coming over this afternoon to do our laundry. Father Fabrizio called to praise God that our lives had been spared, thanks to all the holy work our little VW had been involved in.

Next came a call from the mayor's office. Over the jangling of African jewellery, his assistant informed us that even though His Honour was tied up all day in a conference (presumably with a particularly irascible jigsaw puzzle), he wanted to express his concern for our well-being and offer anything he could to help. That was followed by a call from the mayor's wife, who whispered into her cellphone that she was just about to light a candle for us at the side altar of Santa Ursula, the Patron Saint of The Miraculously Not Killed.

One of the unexpected consequences of our crash was to swing public opinion in our favour. Many Cambionese felt that our accident had been caused by Vesuvia Pingatore's casting an overzealous *malocchio* on us. And whatever her grievance, the town felt that this was much too harsh. In fact, it was gratifying to learn from Dino that the official odds, as posted by the patrons of Lucca's Barbershop, had dramatically shifted to where we were now slightly better than even money to hold on to our *rustico*.

Much of this largesse was due to the general kindness of the Italian nature, but a good deal must also be attributed to their deep affection for the people of the United States. I know this seems odd in the wake of so much anti-American feeling throughout Europe – and the world, for that matter – but many Italians really do like us. And not just our movies, our music or our leggy supermodels.

Just as there are parts of the American South where the Civil War is very much alive, people living in this corner of Tuscany still have a tremendous sense of gratitude for how we saved them from the ravages of Fascism. And at no time of year were those feelings stronger than at the time of our accident. By sheer coincidence we were coming up on the Festa della Liberazione (the Festival of the Liberation), a holiday celebrated every year by the Cambionese, and marking the day the American army liberated their town. Each year a few of the surviving GIs from that detachment of soldiers came to Cambione to make speeches, drink wine and reminisce with the grandmothers they once tried to seduce with chocolate bars and nylons.

I was helping Nancy towards the bedroom, thanking everyone I encountered for their kindness, but gently imploring them to leave because of how badly she needed to rest. They, of course, insisted on staying, promising to make the others, who were thoughtlessly making so much noise, be quiet. Besides, there was no way we were going to get past Flavia without eating first, since she was implacably blocking our path like the Praetorian guard protecting Caesar. So we sat down to an eleven-course lunch containing the 26,000 calories Flavia felt every human body needed to maintain good health.

Somewhere between a warmly comforting *timbalo di riso* and a nutty-tasting *agnello al rosmarino*, the doorbell rang. I went to the front door and opened it to the *signora* from the news kiosk. She had come on her lunch hour to make sure I got today's *Herald Tribune*. I felt guilty that she had walked all the way over here in the heat just so I could check the ball scores and read 'Doonesbury'. so I thanked her profusely, and in my clumsy Italian, I pointed out a number of articles on the front page alone that could well change my life.

When I dug out some coins she told me that it was *un regalo*, a gift. I invited her to join us for lunch, but she insisted she couldn't stay, so I handed her a couple of sweet potatoes from a box of fruits and vegetables given to us by our friends from the Alimentari Brutti. She thanked me for the potatoes and left, being far too polite to mention that the produce I had handed her was crawling with aphids.

I had just gotten back to the table when, once again, the doorbell rang. I turned my head too fast and I had to clutch my neck in pain. The bell kept ringing, so I pulled myself up and trudged back to the door, opening it to the self-satisfied visage of Dottore Spotto. Even though I hadn't seen him since that dinner at Dino's some months ago, he embraced me and firmly kissed me on both cheeks, as if we were on the verge of picking out furniture together.

He had rushed over as soon as he had heard about our accident, he said as Nancy translated. He had come to offer his professional services, but Nancy told him that we had already been examined by just about every kind of doctor one could think of, and as kind as his offer was, we were OK.

But what about psychologically? It turned out that Dottore Spotto was an eminent psychologist and he had come to treat us for post-traumatic stress disorder. This was an insidious malady, he explained, as he sat down at our table and helped himself to a heaping portion of *baccalà fritta*. Between mouthfuls of fried cod, *il dottore* cautioned that we could be cruising along months after such a collision, thinking that everything was fine, when suddenly we could start experiencing night sweats, heart palpitations, sexual dysfunction, and even regressive bedwetting. I saw his point, and as Mrs Cipollini brought out a chicken *cacciatore* that looked suspiciously like it had been sacrificed from one of her brood, I began sharing with Dottore Spotto how I had sucked my thumb until the age of six because I was improperly breast-fed.

If I live here forever I'll never get used to how Italians will come over to your house at any time of the day or night. In L.A., the last person to drop in on anybody unannounced was the Hillside Strangler. And from practices such as these I have come to understand how much a sense of place can shape a person. How the 'where you are' ultimately becomes the 'who you are'. And from what I have so far observed, there is no greater difference between Italy and America than our relationship to our natural surroundings.

One of the more enduring axioms in literature is the idea that life in an American suburb is sterile and emotionally desolate. This is a theme that has been well explored by writers and poets from T. S. Eliot to John Updike, and in popular films from *The Graduate* to *American Beauty*. And I must admit that before I lived in Tuscany, I never really understood what they were talking about other than venting some Bohemian contempt for middle-class values.

But I now understand that in creating our man-made environments, we have distanced ourselves from the primary experience of reality. Tuscany is far older than America, but ironically, it is more unspoiled. Tuscany is the reality, where our suburbia is the re-creation of that reality.

Think about it ... our neighbourhood park is really a re-creation of a meadow. A mall is a re-creation of a village and a swimming pool a re-creation of a pond. The net effect is to make one's experiences a step removed from the immediate impact of life. Our lives in the 'burbs are clean, efficient, well organised and essentially soulless. And I never would have understood that if I hadn't come to live in Italy.

Most of our well-wishers had gone home and I was helping Nancy on with her nightgown when we heard a tapping on the bedroom window. I peeked through the shutters and spotted Mario Pingatore.

'I say, old trout, hope I'm not knocking you up too late,' he said to my eyeball.

'No, no, not at all,' I said.

Nancy threw a robe over her shoulders and I opened the window.

'I was gobsmacked when I heard the news. Frightful business, eh what?' He held up a cardboard-boxful of vegetables and started hoisting it through our window.

'Please, *signore*,' I pleaded. 'We have so much food.'

'But they're fresh from my garden,' he insisted.

'Thank you, that's very kind.' I took hold of a box filled with fat carrots, dewy tomatoes and shiny scallions. Mario was paying us the highest compliment one Tuscan can give another ... vegetables from one's garden so newly picked, the dirt was still on them.

'This is very generous of you,' I said, shooing one of Signora Cipollini's chickens off the bed so I could put the box down.

'Coo, look at you with the wonky arm,' Mario said as he regarded Nancy's cast.

'It's just a slight fracture,' she said. 'But the doctor didn't want to take any chances.'

'And how are you feeling, dear boy?' he said to me, his face a cameo of concern.

'Well, I got a little banged up,' I said. 'But, thank God, it turned out to be nothing serious.'

'Ave Maria,' he said, momentarily forgetting his English affectations and crossing himself like a real Italian.

'We just need rest. Lots of rest,' Nancy said, hoping he'd get the hint.

'What a terrible thing to happen here,' he said ruefully. 'Our hospitals are so *primitivi*. Nothing like you have in America.'

'I thought the hospital was excellent,' Nancy said. 'And I was very pleased with my doctor.'

'Well, the beastly way these cheeky buggers around here drive, you'll need him,' he said.

'Yes, well, we'll just try to be real careful from now on,' Nancy said, wondering where all this was going.

'And the red tape.' Mario slapped his forehead for emphasis. 'Wait till you try to settle your insurance claim! It's nothing short of a flippin' nightmare.'

'Whatever it is, we'll deal with it,' I said.

'Too bad we're not more like America,' Mario lamented, 'where everything is so –'

'I hope you're not thinking that we've soured on Italy because of this accident,' Nancy said.

'It was the furthest thing from my mind.'

'Because if that's what you came over here to find out, you can go home and take your mouldy vegetables with you!' I had to hold Nancy to keep her from grabbing the box with her bad shoulder and throwing it at him.

'My dear woman!' Mario exclaimed as he backed away from the window. 'Don't get your knickers in a twist.'

'We're staying, Mario,' Nancy proclaimed. 'And, no matter what it takes, we're going to get our house finished.'

'Bully for you.' He turned to go, and in his hurry he almost tripped over Tiberius, who was sniffing at whatever was stuck to Mario's heel.

'And here's something else,' she hollered after him as she squeezed my hand. 'We're going to get remarried in that house! And we're going to live there for a long, long time and be so damn happy, it'll make both you and your sister miserable!'

26. LA FESTA DELLA LIBERAZIONE

I learned the story of how the town was liberated from two of the men who were there that day. I had gone into the village to pick up one of Nancy's prescriptions at the *farmacia* when I heard voices that were distinctly American. Sitting at the café was an elderly black man in the company of a young couple with their nine-year-old son. They were being hosted by Uncle Carmuzzi, who had smuggled in a bottle of his home-brewed wine and was plying them with it.

I struck up a conversation and they invited me to join them. I had figured out they were here for the festa, because aside from Nancy and me, we didn't get many Americans in this neck of the woods.

The man's name was Robert Hilliard, from Louisville, Kentucky, and he had travelled here with his daughter, his son-in-law, and his grandson to show them the town he had helped liberate during World War II. After a few glasses of wine, we got around to what had happened that day as former sergeant Robert Hilliard and former partisan guerrilla Uncle Carmuzzi each told me their side of the story.

Angelino Carmuzzi caught the squirrel with his bare hands. After skinning it, he and his sister, Mariella, shared slices of raw meat in the grainy darkness of a ditch that ran alongside the Via Apua. In the distance they heard the constant rumbling of heavy artillery and an occasional staccato burst from a machine gun as it pointed its long finger of tracer shells across the landscape. But their ears disregarded those sounds, straining to listen only for the tread of marching boots or the diesel whine of a tank.

Suddenly there was a short, nervous bird whistle, followed by the stumbling footsteps of Pietro Pingatore tumbling into the ditch.

'*Sono venuti!*' he whispered, his face glazed with sweat. 'They're coming!'

The three of them clambered out of the ditch and proceeded down the road. Eyes darting from side to side, they silently stepped around shell holes filled with pools of oil-stained rainwater from yesterday's downpour. Twice they had to jump back into the ditch when fighter planes roared overhead at treetop level. The planes were American, the Luftwaffe having been blasted out of the skies weeks ago, but they had still had to dash for cover because the fighters were strafing anything that moved.

When they approached the junction where the road branched off towards the marble quarries, they readied their machine guns. Since the fall of Livorno three days earlier, elements of the 29th Panzer Brigade had been spotted retreating on this road, and they well understood the German army's policy of shooting partisans on sight.

They were walking slowly when Mariella stopped them by silently putting out both arms. She was sniffing the air when she detected something. Something good. Then, out of the mist, they saw the outline of six soldiers coming towards them. By the shape of their helmets and silhouettes of their rifles, they instantly knew.

'Americani!' Angelino yelled.

'Halt!' Sergeant Hilliard hollered. Weapons were levelled as both groups cautiously approached.

'Viva America!' Pietro Pingatore called out. 'Viva Franklin Roosevelt!!'

'*Siamo partigiani!*' Mariella squealed, hoping they would understand that they were all on the same side.

'OK.' Sergeant Hilliard waved at them to come forward. 'Slowly.'

The partisans approached each of them, thinking that the first light of dawn was playing tricks on their eyes by making the faces and hands of all the soldiers look black. The Italians looked at each other in confusion. Was this some new kind of camouflage invented by those ingenious Yanks?

'We-are-try-in'-to-get-to-Pietra-santa,' Hilliard said pronouncing each syllable as he pulled a map out of his shirt pocket.

But the partisans could not look at the map because their eyes were riveted on the soldiers' skin. Surely this wasn't the colours of Americans, they wondered. These faces were not like those of Jimmy Cagney or Gary Cooper, whom they had seen in the few Hollywood movies that had managed to play there.

'Pietrasanta?' Sergeant Hilliard repeated, pointing up the road.

'Sì, sì, Pietrasanta,' Angelino Carmuzzi said. Then he tried to explain how they must first come to Cambione, which was on the way. For even though the Germans had pulled out two days ago, until the Americans occupied the town, there was always the chance the Nazis would come back.

The two groups proceeded down the road, each eyeing the other with curiosity. The GIs were not altogether convinced that these Italians weren't really pro-fascists leading them into a trap, and the partisans were unaware that they had stumbled into the advance units of the 92nd Infantry Division, an all-black fighting unit known as the Buffalo Soldiers.

After marching for the better part of an hour past the rusted hulks of burned-out armoured cars and an occasional dead horse lying in the road, the GIs and the *partigiani* reached the ancient Roman wall. There, in the full light of dawn, they saw that half the town had turned out to welcome them with flowers, bottles of wine and home-made American flags. Black faces split open with wide, toothy smiles as the Buffalo Soldiers passed out chocolate bars and packs of Lucky Strikes. While the crowd cheered, and an impromptu band played, the mayor looked at the partisans quizzically.

'*Loro sono Africani*?' he asked. 'They're Africans?'

'*Loro sono Americani*,' Angelino Carmuzzi replied. 'They're Americans.'

We decided that the Festa della Liberazione would be our first public appearance. We were hoping to marshal whatever sympathies we had accrued, by being both accident victims and Americans, into a way to get our house moving again. And like a complex military operation, Nancy and I drew up our plans to target Marco Mucchi, isolate him outside the fortress of his office, and soften him up until his bank unfroze our money.

Nancy would spearhead this operation, so she woke early to dress for battle. She chose black to properly frame the hospital whiteness of the plaster cast on her arm. Her dress was lacy, sheer, and clingy, yet respectful to the point of sombre, and all topped off with an antique wooden crucifix, designed to say that only through strong faith were we able to endure this catastrophe.

The holiday fell on the hottest day of the hottest month of the hottest summer anybody could remember. The sun had baked all the stone surfaces of the Piazza Maggiore until it felt like a kiln, and the only relief was a seat close to the fountain or the chance that a passing pigeon might flap its wings near your face.

We waited for the actual ceremony to begin before making our entrance. The mayor, select capos from the Comune, and several prominent local Poo Bahs were seated on the podium set up at the open end of the piazza. The United States of America was represented by an assistant undersecretary from the consular office in Florence and a lieutenant colonel from the NATO base at Camp Darby. We chose the moment when the makeshift marching band made up of volunteer firemen and local forestale (forest rangers) struck up the national anthem. As the opening strain of 'Oh, say can you see . . .' played on in a brassy, off-tempo way, we entered.

Nancy was on my arm and our steps were slow, but steady, in testament to our resolve to overcome any adversity. I could feel all eyes upon us, and when I looked over to Nancy, her chin was trembling, but her head was high. She looked like Greer Garson coming out of the bomb shelter after the blitz in Mrs Miniver. I could feel gratitude and affection pouring out of each one of our friends and neighbours as we passed. Italians love high drama, and we were giving it to 'em, baby, we were giving it to 'em.

Dino and Flavia had saved us two seats in front, and we got to them just as the mayor finished his speech and introduced Angelino Carmuzzi. The old man stood up and nodded to the applause, and I realised how differently I now saw him from that first time at Dino's party when Uncle Carmuzzi had fought with Dottore Spotto over my approval for their home-made wines. How different this gnarled old man was from the brave 22-year-old hiding in a ditch, waiting for the Americans to come free his village.

Uncle Carmuzzi paid tribute to the other members of his little band of partisans, reminding the audience that small groups such as theirs, operating all over Italy, managed to pin down twenty divisions of German soldiers and keep them from being used at Normandy. His voice wavered when he reminisced about Pietro Pingatore, father of Mario and Vesuvia, who were sitting two rows in front of us. Not to be outdone by our theatrics, Vesuvia clutched her heart and sobbed dramatically at the mention of her father's name, reminding the town how she had dutifully cared for him during that long and fatal illness that took his life in the bitter winter of 1986.

Any Italian in the crowd who was not crying already completely broke down when Angelino Carmuzzi offered up a prayer for his sister, Mariella. Small and frail as a baby bird, she had survived countless firefights and ambushes with the enemy, only to step on a German land mine two months after the war.

And just when you thought it couldn't get any more

emotional, the mayor introduced the last survivor of the American platoon that liberated their town. Former sergeant Robert Hilliard, 79 years old, stood up in a slightly bent military posture. The elderly black man walked stiff-legged to the microphone, saluted the mayor, and embraced Angelino Carmuzzi.

The crowd cheered, the band struck up 'The Stars and Stripes Forever', and I started crying.

'Nice touch,' Nancy whispered to me.

'I'm not faking,' I sniffled.

Oh, my God, what was happening to me? I'd turned into an Italian. An Italian woman!

After an Italian has a good cry, he has to eat. And then dance.

Long banquet tables had been set up ringing the piazza, and in spite of the heat, outdoor kitchens were churning out prodigious quantities of *penne alla carbonara* and *risotto con funghi*. People of all ages and walks of life sat together, laughing, shouting, eating and drinking toasts to everything and everybody.

We didn't sit, but circulated, thanking many of our fellow *cittadini* (citizens) for their kindness and reassuring them that, despite any rumours to the contrary, we still loved Italy and had no intention of leaving. We also spent some time chatting with the Hilliard family. Robert's wife had passed on some years ago, so he had been brought here by his daughter and son-in-law.

He told us how different it had been back then, when the armed services were segregated, and even the fabled 92nd Infantry was made up of black foot soldiers under the command of white officers. As we chatted, various people came up to shake his hand and thank him. I commented that the Italians seemed as glad to see him today as they had been back then, and he joked that if his rifle company had taken a different fork in the road, Cambione would have been liberated by soldiers from the

Brazilian Expeditionary Force, who were operating on their right flank. That made me smile to think about samba music and how different this party would have been.

As we were talking, Uncle Carmuzzi came over with another bottle of his home-made wine. He had been saving this bottle for this occasion and he assured us that more than mere vino, it was closer to being an elixir of the gods. He filled our glasses and we drank several toasts to the eternal friendship between the peoples of Italy and the United States.

Shade was now covering the centre of the piazza, so the folding chairs were cleared away and couples began to dance to the synthesised melodies of a local Bar Mitzvah band. For a country that seems to be organised along chaotic lines by a people with a deep-seated sense of anarchy in their souls, Italians dance in a highly structured way. The couples executed a rather intricate four-step fox-trot, where everybody moved at the same speed in the same counterclockwise direction, like many small wheels turning inside one gracefully turning pinwheel.

But we hadn't come to dance. We were here on business, and to that end we were surreptitiously stalking the vice president of our bank, Marco Mucchi. We waited until he got his wife and two small daughters seated at a table, and when he went to bring them food, we positioned ourselves at the end of the serving line so our backs were to him as he fell in behind us.

Just as he was about to greet us, Nancy's knees buckled and she started to swoon. A surprised Marco Mucchi caught her.

'Honey?' I said anxiously.

'It's OK,' she said, regaining her balance. 'It's just the heat and the excitement' – she clutched her broken arm and grimaced – 'and the pain. . . .'

'Please, come sit over here.' Marco Mucchi led her to a chair and helped her ease into it.

'Did you take your pills?' I asked.

'I guess I forgot,' she said.

I opened her purse and handed her the prescription bottle. 'I'll get you some water,' I said, disappearing into the crowd.

Later Nancy described to me how profusely Marco Mucchi was sweating as he hovered around her, fanning her face with a programme from the day's event. Nancy then sighed, took a deep breath and proceeded to sum up the status of our life by using the word *rotto*, broken. Her arm was broken, our car was broken, our house was broken . . . and with the mounting bills and no decent place to live, our spirits were broken. She told him that she had not even told her mother about the accident, because the poor woman was so frail. Besides, how could she call her mother with any news except to tell her to pack up and come back to Italy, where she could spend her last days in our *piccolo rustico*?

He was starting to weaken, so Nancy applied the coup de grâce. Her eyes glistening with tears, she talked about how her mother had been living alone since the death of her father – a man who, incidentally, had served his country with great distinction during World War II.

This was true, but Nancy managed to omit the part about her father having been assigned to the Army Corp of Engineers and having spent the entire war running a supply dump in Hawaii, from which he returned with a tattoo that said Leilani and an insatiable appetite for poi.

All this combination of patriotism and motherhood was just too much for Marco Mucchi, and he caved. A sheen of perspiration covered his round face and caused his normally plastered-down hair to splay across his forehead like spit curls as he offered a solution. By law he could not unfreeze our funds, but he could allow us to use that amount as collateral to secure a loan.

'*Un prestito*?' Nancy said with disappointment. 'What if it took years for the Comune to approve all the things they had to sign off on? We'd have to pay on that loan forever!'

'*Non preoccuparti*.' In hushed tones Marco Mucchi told her

not to worry. There was a vacancy on the Comune board and he was running for it. Everyone felt that he had an excellent chance, and the first thing he'd do when he got elected was to make sure our *rustico* was fast-tracked for approval.

I returned with a glass of water, and as Nancy took her pills she told me the good news. I wished him luck on running and told him if there was anything we could do to help, we would. He told me that as a professional writer, perhaps I could give him a little help with his campaign. He took out a folded-up sheet of paper and spread it out on the table, explaining that this was the mock-up for his poster and he'd like my opinion before it went to the printer.

The page featured a prominent posed photo of him in a dark suit and a yellow power tie. Under the picture was the caption that declared him to be:

Onesto, Competente, e Disponibile

That is to say, Honest, Competent, and Available. In my rudimentary Italian I told him that I was fine with the first two, but the last one made it sound like he'd been sitting around the house with nothing to do when he decided to run for office. He pursed his lips and nodded in agreement. I told him that if he gave me a chance to come up with some ideas, I'd get back to him. He told me that he didn't want to impose on my time, but I assured him that I was happy to do it for all he had done for us.

We then gave him our word of honour that we were not putting up a three-storey aluminum-and-glass California beach house and, in fact, our rebuilt *rustico* would become a great source of pride for the community. Marco Mucchi shook my hand with the same double-handed shake the mayor used, and I noted that, win or lose, Signor Mucchi did have a good learning curve. He kissed Nancy goodbye on both cheeks, wished her good health, and rejoined the food line.

'Well, this does call for a toast.' I raised my glass of Uncle Carmuzzi's wine and tipped it towards Nancy.

I was about to take a sip when I spotted Dottore Spotto coming towards me with an agitated look in his eyes. He took the glass I was holding, spilled out the contents as if it were so much swill, and proceeded to fill it with his own home-made wine.

'Have you seen where Carmuzzi gets his grapes?' he said to me in Italian while Nancy helped translate. 'The vines are held up by aluminum posts instead of branches! They use plastic sticks instead of bamboo, and clothesline instead of real twine. No wonder his wine tastes like cat piss!'

Wars may come and go, but here in Cambione, feuds last forever.

27. FERRAGOSTO

In the month of August the Italians celebrate something called Ferragosto, a national holiday on the magnitude of Thanksgiving or the Fourth of July. It's a celebration of the harvest that, like most things there, dates back to the Roman Empire. It was named for the emperor Augustus, who apparently liked the idea so much that he decided to name the whole damn month after himself as well.

Ferragosto marks the official end of summer, and it's somehow tied in with the Feast of the Assumption. But over and above its religious implications it is best known as the day in Italy when everything is closed and everybody goes to the beach. In a country that shuts down for the flimsiest excuse, it's hard to describe how totally and absolutely everything is locked up – so much so that pregnant women pray not to go into labour on that day out of fear that the hospitals will be *chiusi*, closed. It was therefore surprising when Nancy and I discovered that work was actually going on at our *rustico*, leading us to surmise that between the intensity of the heat and the importance of the holiday, the only ones working on that Ferragosto morning were the prostitutes on the Via Aurelia and Umberto and his crew.

Umberto was taking advantage of the holiday to tell Vesuvia Pingatore that his guys wouldn't be working on her wall that day. The fact that her jagged silhouette could be seen watching us didn't seem to bother him. Also, the issue of paying overtime for holidays was not relevant, for as we learned, Italian construction workers are not paid by the hour, but by the actual measurements of whatever it is they're constructing. They are literally paid by the metre, which explains why the workday will often drift into the evening with no one grousing about overtime, and also why walls seem to become mysteriously thicker and windows larger.

No one was particularly happy about it, of course, except for Va Bene, who didn't seem to have any problems with single-handedly laying the foundation of a patio, which would eventually become our *forno*, an outdoor pizza oven. Problema, on the other hand, unleashed a constant stream of complaints as he hammered the narrow wooden beams called *travicelli* into place on our bedroom ceiling.

I wasn't able to hear what Vagabondo was complaining about over the roar of a pair of duelling chain saws. He and Umberto were cutting tree trunks into squared-sided beams that would be used to hold up the roof of our *terrazzo*. Assisted by Umberto's father, an old man no bigger than a ten-year-old boy, they were using chain saws on logs they'd drape across their knees for support. No goggles, no gloves, and only measuring by eye. Wood chips were flying around like shrapnel.

While Nancy kept up a steady stream of bottled water, I contented myself with staying out of everyone's way by breaking large stones into small ones with a pickaxe, in an attempt to show everybody that I could use a dangerously pointed instrument without impaling myself on it.

The stones needed to be made smaller so we could use them for the reconstruction of our walls. It was brutal work, and I was only able to do it because the pain in my neck and shoulders from the accident had been dramatically lessened when I heeded our neighbour Annamaria's advice. She advocated the application of an ice pack followed by raw heat, as hot as I could stand it. The idea of ice sounded refreshing, but I balked at the prospect of laying a water bottle, hot enough to iron a shirt, on my neck on the hottest day in the history of the universe. But it felt better almost immediately and that, in concert with a little made-in-the-USA Advil, enabled me to swing a pick like I had spent my last twenty years on a chain gang.

In fact, the steady motion of swinging the pick and the rhythmic clanging of forged steel on stone seemed to do for me what no amount of meditation or vino could.

I felt my mind disengage and a soft, peaceful feeling ease over me. My muscles were on some kind of autopilot, moving free and easy as if lubricated by the flow of my own sweat, and the only mantra I needed was the panting of my own breath, which was coming out hot as a blowtorch.

Clang.

This is the way of a man.

Clang.

This is the way of the warrior.

Clang.

I am a samurai.

Clang.

I am a Jedi Knight.

Clang.

I am an idiot! I just hit myself in the ankle!

Pain shot up my leg like a jolt of electricity. I bent over in agony and checked to make sure I hadn't shattered it. Mercifully, I had just grazed my anklebone with the side of the tool as it careened off the rock. I rubbed my ankle and could feel it swelling up in my hand. I looked around to see if anyone had noticed and saw Nancy staring at me.

'I'm OK,' I called out with the aplomb of somebody with an arrow sticking out of his eye.

She shook her head in disbelief as she came towards me. 'Let me see it.'

'Honest to God, I'm fine.'

'It's not bad enough my arm's broken, you've got to –'

'Look, I'm fine,' I said taking a few steps without limping. 'Really.'

She stared at me for a long beat, then blew out her breath. 'Dino just called. They've taken a place at the beach and they're inviting us to join them for lunch.'

'Great. What about the guys?'

'They're going to knock off soon, so I want to go back to the house and jump in the shower.'

'Can I scrub the parts you can't reach?' I suavely suggested, trying not to grit my teeth in pain.

'Before we leave, why don't you go water the *orto*?' She pointed me towards the garden as if to say, Think you can handle that without drowning yourself?

I watched her walk away and reached down to tie my shoe, but really to check my ankle, which was now the size of a slo-pitch softball. I just needed ice, heat and Advil and I'd be OK, I vowed as I hobbled towards our vegetable patch, with but one thought burning across my mind ... how much I loathed gardening.

There, I had said the unthinkable. Especially for one living in this heavily agricultural area, where the locals are fond of saying that if a man has a woman he's happy for a day, if he has a cow he's happy for a week, but if he has a garden he's happy for a lifetime. That may work for them, but, except for one psychedelic summer back in the seventies when I grew some pretty lethal marijuana, I absolutely despise the idea of growing things.

I know ... millions and millions of seemingly normal people ascend into absolute rapture at the prospect of mucking around in the dirt and coaxing some form of vegetation out of the soil. But I hate it. Never mind the running to the store every five minutes to lug back hundred-pound bags of what was essentially dirt, and all manner of arcane planting implements, there was the daily weeding, tilling, hoeing and watering that had become the bane of my existence.

You see, our land was terraced in such a way that our garden, small as it was, meandered onto three different elevations. And as hard as I tried, with all the climbing up and down, I could never seem to water it without getting the hose all twisted and tangled. I'd get frustrated and start cursing and yanking on the hose until I had managed to tear out half the things we'd planted, making myself sopping wet in the process, and coming home at the end of this adventure looking like a nine-year-old boy who had been out playing in the mud.

Additionally, I discovered that, although we like to think we own this land, our garden is the rightful property of a species of housefly the Italians call *il tafano*. I think they're referred to as houseflies because they're big enough to live in one. These flies are not just annoying, they're downright aggressive. And until they start selling insect repellent whose active ingredient is Ebola virus, nothing can stop them. They fly right up into your face and try to bite you at the worst time, like when you have the hose wrapped around your knees and you're trying to bunny-hop away from them, landing in puddles of muddy water with each hop. These bugs are big enough to carry off a baby goat and not leave a scrap of meat on its bones. I'm telling you, these little bastards are nothing but two hundred milligrams of bad intentions.

And so I hobbled over to our garden, unravelled the Gordian knot that each night our hose mysteriously twisted itself into, and began the ritual hunting for my favourite nozzle. For some odd reason Nancy liked to stand farther back and use a nozzle that shot the water out with such force, it looked as if it had once been used to break up a civil rights demonstration in Birmingham, Alabama. But even though I detested gardening, I kind of liked the way my nozzle, which got hidden by the same unseen forces that kinked up our hose, diffused the water into a wide, gentle stream. It sprinkled each plant with a cooling mist that coalesced into fat silvery drops that reminded me of morning dew in the Alps.

I also liked it because when some bloodthirsty *tafano* tried to bite me on the cheek I could drive it away by turning the hose on myself with a delicate cooling spray instead of a blast of water powerful enough to rip off my eyebrows.

I had also convinced myself that my favourite nozzle was more economical than the other. With two straight months of temperatures in the nineties (thirties, Centigrade) and no rain for weeks, we were forced each night to soak the garden down till it was as flooded as a rice paddy. By midmorning, as the water evaporated, the ground was caked hard enough to dribble a basketball on.

The Comune hadn't sent us our first water bill yet, but judging by how people complained about theirs, I was figuring that each tomato we grew was costing us at least thirteen dollars.

By the time we got to the beach at the Lido di Cambione, traffic was backed up all the way to Sicily. I dropped Nancy off in the shade of a tall umbrella pine and left her sitting on our cooler as I drove around in our rented Fiat Punto looking for a parking space. I considered myself luckier than had I been born Ringo Starr when I found a spot a mere two and half miles from the Bagni Veronica, where each year Dino and his family celebrate the holiday.

This is a routine of Ferragosto that Italians slavishly follow. Unlike in America, where we are accustomed to public beaches, here, they are few and far between. Instead, the entire coastline, it seems, is lined with private *bagni*, which is the plural of *bagno*, meaning 'bath' or 'bathhouse'. In layout they're all pretty much the same. The fancier ones have swimming pools and video machines for the kids, but they all have a restaurant/snack bar, rows of small changing rooms, and walkways that lead you to a fenced-off area of the beach. These walkways are lined with clusters of beach chairs and chaise longues, each under the cover of either *un ombrello* or *una tenda*, a tent.

Dino had rented one of the largest *tende* they had, and it was barely sufficient to shade him; his wife, Flavia; their son,

Rudolfo, and his girlfriend, Pia Tughi; cousins Faustino, Spartaco, Turrido and Aldo; along with Aldo's mamma, plus the 'pious' Cousin Monica, with her 'mythically gifted' children, Leonardo, Rafael and *la bimba* Artemisia. And, of course, no family gathering would be complete without aunts Nina, Nona and Nana, who were covered in so much black they looked like they were dating a Muslim cleric.

Mercifully, Dino had not brought along all twelve of his dogs, selecting only two – Torpedo and Luna – to take up space on the blanket, their tongues hanging out and their furry bodies casting off more heat than a pair of Franklin stoves.

The population density under the tent was no worse than that on the rest of the beach, since the month of August signals the time when all the large Italian cities empty out and everyone with the time, the money or a relative living anywhere near the Med comes to the coast. This is also the time of year that the fair-skinned people of Northern and Eastern Europe begin their annual invasion of Italy. This onslaught was first begun by Attila the Hun, but has now been continued by the Swedes, the Danes, the Brits and, more recently, the Russians, the Hungarians and the Poles.

It was, in fact, this collection of long-legged blonde women in bikinis that distracted Cousin Spartaco, who had been sent out to find us. As a result, Nancy and I had to wander up and down a crowded beach looking for Dino and his brood. This was not easily negotiated, since Nancy's arm was in a cast and I was limping across the scalding hot sand as I struggled to carry a cooler full of victuals. In contrast to all the robust sun-worshippers, we looked like a pair of refugees from an orthopaedic ward who had been taken to the seaside to air out.

'Hey, hey, over here!' somebody yelled.

I heard English over the babble of a United Nations' worth of voices, and I turned to see Rudolfo waving his arms at us.

We slogged off in their direction as Dino, Flavia and an

assortment of cousins and dogs came out from under their shade to hug us, kiss us and lick our hands. Our cooler was taken and combined with an already belly-bursting collection of edibles, and space was somehow found for us under the tent, which was now as hot and crowded as any back alley in Calcutta.

And like any back alley in Calcutta, it was also teeming with intrigue. Cousin Aldo was fretting with his mamma over his bathing attire. Though I'm all for self-expression, I could well understand her aggravation over a 260-pound man with a huge gut wearing a skimpy red Speedo that barely covered his butt and showed his penis sticking out like one of those little pencils they give you when you play miniature golf.

At the same time Nina, Nona and Nana were berating Cousin Fausto for leaving the family for long stretches of time to sit in the snack bar listening to a motorcycle race on the radio; Cousin Turrido was hollering at Leonardo and Rafael for kicking sand on his *insalata con funghi* while they played Marco Polo; and Flavia was accusing Monica of being a negligent mother because she was too involved in her trashy novel to notice that *la bimba* Artemisia had crawled over to Torpedo, stuck the dog's tail in her mouth, and was sucking on it like a pacifier.

But the main event was what was going on between Rudolfo and Pia. More accurately, what was not going on between them. They sat on the blanket with their backs to each other, hardly like boyfriend–girlfriend. Dino cast me a sharply pointed look urging me to intervene. When I blankly stared back at him, he resorted to a hand gesture, putting his flattened hand, palm down, in his mouth and biting down on it, to let me know how much he hated what was going on.

'Yo, dude, let's go check out the water,' I said to Rudolfo, more to get away from Leonardo and Rafael, who had managed to step on my swollen ankle three times already.

Rudolfo needed no more coaxing than that to spring to his feet. '*L'acqua fa male*,' Flavia scolded, reminding him that he had just eaten and any contact with the water would bring about his instant death.

Rudolfo kissed his mamma and assured her that we were just going to look at the sea and maybe stick in a toe.

But Flavia wasn't convinced. She urged Pia to go along and make sure we two boys didn't do anything foolish. I was happy to note that no one had referred to me as a boy for twenty years, but Pia looked peeved. She flashed an angry look at Rudolfo and commented that he was old enough to take care of himself . . . or at least, he should be.

Rudolfo's eyes went hard and he stormed off. I caught up with him, and as we threaded our way through the throng, I tried to engage him in conversation, even though it was difficult to hear over the clamour of a beachful of Italians laughing and talking with their usual exuberance.

'Everything OK with you guys?' I said.

He shrugged.

'Seems like Pia's on your case.'

He flicked three fingers under his chin, which means 'I could care less.'

'Yeah, women,' I clucked, allowing my focus to settle on a magnificent Italian girl who was sunbathing topless.

'Why is she never happy with the way I am?' he finally said. 'If she loves me, why is she always trying to change me into something else?'

'Beats me.'

'They're so complicated. They say one thing and do another.'

As if to underscore the mixed messages we get from them, the girl I had been watching raised her arm to reveal an unshaved armpit that looked like it belonged to Charles Bronson.

'Why is it I can be with a man and he's OK with me just how I am, but every time I'm with her we get into a fight?'

'I don't know,' I said. 'Sometimes it feels like we're from two different tribes.'

'And yet, we're expected to pick one and live with them for the rest of our lives.'

'Crazy, isn't it?'

'I can't do it,' he said, stopping an errant soccer ball with his foot and kicking it back to the players. 'I can't marry her.'

'OK . . .'

'I mean, I love her. But more like a friend and – and, look, I met somebody.'

'Oh, man, you got to tell her.'

'Telling her is not the problem,' he said. 'My father's going to freak. And Mamma . . .'

'You know what? They're going to scream and holler and it may get ugly for a while, but eventually they'll get used to it.'

He started to say something, but whatever he was about to tell me got swept away by the sudden uproar of electrified cheering, hooting and laughing. And as loud as that was, it was all but drowned out by the commanding sound of a thunderous drumbeat. The source of this raucous euphoria was a vast army of young men, maybe two or three hundred, marching down the beach in lockstep, each holding a red plastic bucket upside down under one arm as they pounded out a beat on it with the flat of their hands. The actual moving mass of humanity was almost double that size when you included the giggling young girls and excited little kids cheering them on.

I was witnessing the spectacle the Italians call *gavettone*, and for reasons no one's quite sure of, it's only played out on this day, on beaches and piazzas, *maggiore* and *minore*, all over the country.

This particular army proceeded up the beach until it encountered another army heading in the opposite direction. Then, the two opposing legions broke into a furious water fight, hurling buckets of seawater at each other in a pitched battle that lasted over an hour. After everyone was sopping wet and laughing, the armies disengaged, reassembled, and continued their drumbeat march in opposite directions.

As this was going on, people all over the beach were also deploying their buckets, either individually or in small groups. There is particular pleasure in sneaking up on someone reading a book or taking a nap and dousing him. Some more aggressive males have perfected the art of dashing their bucket of water with sufficient force and at the proper angle to take down the bottom of a girl's two-piece bathing suit.

But that's about as aggressive as it gets. As I witnessed this, and got hit by more than one bucket of cold water, I couldn't help marvelling at what a joyous, fun-loving way this was to channel natural male aggression in a ritualised mockery of how, for centuries, rival city-states and religious factions had slaughtered each other with pike and musket.

Rudolfo and I borrowed some buckets, and while we were joining in on the madness, Nancy was getting Pia's thoughts on their relationship. When their conversation became the interest of too many ears, they left the *tenda* and took a walk to the snack bar. Pia confided that she loved Rudolfo but she wasn't sure about marrying him. He could be sweet, but he was such a *mammaiolo*, a mamma's boy. In a society of 40-year-old men who routinely live with their mothers, it's a sad indictment of anybody who can earn such a distinction as being singled out as a *mammaiolo*.

But Nancy's advice was to try and be more understanding. Men are immature by nature, she counselled, citing numerous examples of my *behaviour* for the record. But the good news was, with the right woman, a guy can sometimes learn to get it right. They talked like this for a long while, and as they headed back to the *tenda*, Pia was beginning to feel that with enough patience and love, Rudolfo could possibly become a stable, responsible adult.

Needless to say, Rudolfo chose that exact moment to sneak up from behind and dump a bucket of water on her head.

28. RITORNO SUBITO

If you're ever going to spend any amount of time in Italy, there is an expression you should know that comes up with greater frequency than *grazie* and *arrivederci*. The phrase *ritorno subito* is not usually spoken but is more commonly rendered on a home-made sign hanging on the door of a store or an office. It means 'be back soon', and the chances of that sign appearing will be in direct proportion to how urgently you need to get inside the establishment. It is also relevant to consider how the Italians define the concept of soon. Long before Einstein, the Italians proved not only that time was curved, but in the right hands it could be bent into more shapes than elbow macaroni.

And so it was that we found ourselves staring at yet another *Ritorno Subito* sign, this one hanging on the door of the office of Avvocato Bonetti. We hadn't started the day by planning to be tapping our feet in front of our lawyer's office, but this is how events unfolded.

Earlier that morning we had driven over to Tito Tughi's Auto Mundo Repair Shop to see what was going on with our VW. There wasn't much to see, since it was in the exact same state as it had been on the night that gentleman from Massa T-boned our car and turned it into so much scrap iron. Signor Tughi was not around, and the Tughi brothers didn't seem to know anything about it, so I demanded to see Pia, getting so aggravated that my swollen ankle began to throb.

Pia came trotting over from the sales office and greeted us with double-cheeked kisses. Before we could get to the reason we were here, she had to tell Nancy about yet another example of Rudolfo's *mammaioloism*. Every night this week, he had dragged her over to Mamma's house for dinner. She finally convinced him to take her out to a restaurant so they could be alone. But instead of paying attention to her, he acted as if he really wanted to be at Mamma's. He sighed all through his *antipasti*, and when the waiter came over to ask him about his main course, Rudolfo ordered the *tortellini bolognese* because that's what Mamma was making that night.

We expressed our sympathy for her being in love with a man who was attached to his mother in a preternatural way, but we really needed to deal with the issue of our car. After all, we were confused. We thought Auto Mundo had received a cheque from the insurance company and we couldn't understand why, after three weeks, nothing had been repaired.

Pia explained that they had only received a cheque for a very small amount, hardly enough to cover the towing and the storage fees. How could the amount be so small? Any idiot could see that it would take thousands of euros to fix it. But any idiot didn't see that, because not one single idiot from the insurance company had even shown up to look at it.

Once again we learned that, surprise, surprise, they do things differently here. In America, you hit somebody and the two insurance companies sit down, haggle over the damages, and the hitter's company cuts the hittee a cheque. The Italian way is for the hitter's insurance company, without any admission of guilt whatsoever, to send the other party a cheque for a rather paltry amount. The aggrieved party is then free to cash that cheque, without any admission that they have agreed to settle. They can either keep the cash and go away . . . or they can use the cash to hire a lawyer and sue the other party's ass off.

Guess which one we chose.

I called Avvocato Bonetti, and even before I could explain the situation, he was way ahead of me, predicting that in the next few days we'd be receiving another small cheque for our medical expenses and the rental car. He suggested that we come down to his office immediately, plan our strategy, and prepare to file the court papers as soon as possible.

Of course, as I explained earlier, the word soon can encompass any length of time from right now to the twelfth of never. Which is why we found ourselves standing in front of his darkened office, wondering why we were being greeted by a *Ritorno Subito* sign instead of Avvocato Bonetti himself. When I tried to reach him on any one of his many cellphones, all I got was a recorded message saying it was not in service.

There wasn't even a decent café to duck inside and get away from the heat, so we passed time squinting into a windowful of clocks in the shop next door. When we got bored with that, we switched over to the shoemaker's, where we were entertained by his skill at putting a tiny bunch of nails in his mouth, plucking out one at a time using a small hammer with a magnetic end, and driving it into a heel in one smooth motion without ever knocking out his front teeth. We were content to watch this for a while, but when the shoemaker heard the clocks from the clock store chime, he put on his hat, turned off the lights and left, hanging out his own *Ritorno Subito* sign.

By now the midday heat was approaching the level of a blast furnace, so we decided to pack it in, go home, and soak our battered bodies in the pool. We had just gotten into our car when we heard a horn blasting and a frantic screeching of tyres. We flinched, fearing that lightning was about to strike us twice, but were relieved when an orange Alfa pulled up behind us and Avvocato Bonetti popped out.

He never bothered apologising for being late, but predictably, he launched into a monologue designed to elicit our sympathy for his misfortunes. Today's episode of the Bonetti family soap opera featured a frantic search for his teenage daughter, who had run away from her eating-disorder clinic, and a harrowing experience with his mother. They had finally convinced her that her Siamese cat was dead, only to have the elderly woman show up at their church and accuse the priest of poisoning it. Not to mention all the *ritardi* at Telecom Italia who had so screwed up his phone bill, he could no longer call anyone on any of his many cellphones.

So masterfully did he weave his *storia* that we wound up feeling bad for him, even though we were the ones who had been waiting for forty-five minutes in the blistering heat. But that didn't matter now. He was here. We wanted to get down to business.

Unfortunately, he didn't have time to meet with us, because he was late for a luncheon date at a restaurant up the street. He would cancel it, of course, but the man he was meeting was someone who could help his chronically unemployed brother-in-law get a job. And it was a government job, so secure that even a *cretino* like his brother-in-law couldn't get fired.

But he invited us to walk with him to the restaurant, and perhaps we could settle some of our business on the way. He said walk, but we were really doing a brisk trot as I cursed my bum ankle and tried to keep up with the one guy in Italy who was actually in a hurry to get somewhere.

'It is important we go on the offensive,' he said to us over his shoulder as we struggled to keep up with him. 'Attack them with a barrage of medical bills, X-rays, and sworn statements from doctors.'

'Well, I was examined by the staff surgeon at the hospital,' Nancy said.

'And the paramedics checked me out in the ambulance,' I added, limping at a pace that put a sheen of sweat on my brow.

'That's not enough,' he announced. 'We need specialists. People who are the best in their fields. In fact, there's an excellent clinic in Geneva where I . . .'

'Geneva?' I said. 'That's ridiculous.'

'Don't worry, we'll bill them for the trip,' he said in a voice as precise as a trial lawyer's. 'And you will go first class.'

'We don't want to rip anybody off,' I said.

'Who is ripping anybody off?' he said. 'We just want to be compensated for our suffering.'

'Well, I can't work.' Nancy cradled her broken arm. 'I guess there's loss of wages involved.'

'And they've got to cover the repair of our car, and pay for the one we're renting,' I said.

'Of course they will,' he said as we reached the restaurant. 'But it's the medical bills that will make this case. The higher the better.'

'Nancy was injured and they should pay for whatever surgery or therapy she's going to need,' I said. 'But I'm really OK and I don't need –'

'How can you say you're OK?' he said. 'Look how you are limping. You should be on crutches or in a wheelchair.'

I chuckled at myself as Avvocato Bonetti opened the door of the restaurant and peered inside.

'Look, *signore*,' I said. 'I'm limping because –'

'Uh-oh, he's angry I'm late. OK, I'll fax you a list of doctors and clinics and we'll talk. *Ciao*,' he said, with a nod in our direction, before he disappeared into the darkness of the restaurant.

We never went to Geneva, but for the next few months we did go to Lucca twice a week, so a team of physical therapists, under the supervision of Dottoressa Mancini, could care for our injuries. Nancy was guided through a series of exercises designed to repair her torn rotator cuff without surgery, and my neck was treated with muscle stimulation and chiropractic adjustments.

Every few weeks we had a consultation with the *dottoressa*. She was an attractive woman in her late thirties with hair and eyes the exact same colour brown. After she'd reviewed our X-rays and charts, her tawny brown eyes would twinkle and she would declare the progress we were making to be *squisito*, exquisite, even though both she and Avvocato Bonetti were somewhat disappointed when I held firm that my ankle injury was self-inflicted.

The waiting room of the clinic was constantly filled with people from all walks of Italian life, sporting all kinds of broken and misaligned pieces. Since there was a great deal of waiting around involved, I took the opportunity to practise my language skills, which were now at the point where I spoke Italian about as well as Desi Arnaz spoke English. I was usually in the wrong verb tense and I comically mispronounced a lot of words, but I was pretty much able to make myself understood.

I was also able to understand so much more that I could tell Nancy, when she came out of her therapy, how the housewife next to me had said to her mutinous three-year-old, '*Stai ammazzando il tuo papà*'. . . that his unruly behaviour was killing his father, even though daddy was back at his office.

One day I struck up a conversation with one of my fellow patients, and he gave me an idea on how to cut through the morass of insurance-company bureaucracy that had ensnared us. His name was Andrea, which is a girl's name for us but not for them. Andrea drove a bakery truck, and he spent his days delivering the most outrageously delicious pastries to an assortment of stores and markets.

Unfortunately, Andrea had a sweet tooth. So for every dozen *biscotti di nocciuoli* he delivered, he ate three. For every *tiramisù* he handed over, he kept one for himself. Eventually, Andrea had blossomed to three hundred pounds, and when the bakery discovered that a sizable portion of their production was winding up inside the person in charge of delivering it, they were righteously pissed. Naturally, they wanted to fire him, but the union prevented that.

Not only did he manage to keep his job, but Andrea was able to petition the Servizio Sanitario Statale (National Health Service), claiming that his obesity was work related. As a result Andrea was sent, all expenses paid, to a health clinic, meaning a fat farm, for a month and a half.

When I met him he had managed to lose about forty pounds, but the excess weight he had been carrying had caused him to suffer back pain. So he had petitioned the Servizio again, and they were now paying for him to be seen by the staff of Dottore Mancini's clinic. And it wasn't costing him a *centesimo*.

We began chatting about America's reputation for having the highest medical prices in the world, and how, in such a rich nation, many of our citizens have no health insurance at all. Andrea then told me that it was both our lack of a national health plan and the astronomical costs of medical care in America that kept many Italians from immigrating there. Thousands of Italians, he felt, would love to move to the United States. But the thought of having to pay a fortune for basic medical services and prescriptions keeps them right where they were. And what if they needed an operation? Mamma mia!

It was then that I realised we were sitting on the best weapon we had. Nancy and I did have health coverage back in the States, but the Italian insurance company didn't know that. I grabbed my cellphone and called Avvocato Bonetti, and after I explained my idea, he quickly agreed. He got on his cellphone and called the insurance company, telling them that I was so frustrated by the lack of movement on our claim, I had decided to take Nancy back to America and have her surgery done in the best hospital in Los Angeles . . . on their dime.

Two days later a claims adjuster came out to look at our car and wrote Signor Tughi a cheque for the entire amount of the repair. And when we finally finished our physical therapy, it was paid in full without a squawk.

God bless America.

29. CINGHIALE

As summer sputtered to a close, each day became distinctly cooler and the very fragrance of the air changed. Summer smelled heavy, and soggy with humidity and perspiration, but the aroma of *autunno* was light, crisp and laden with the scent of burning leaves in a thousand backyards. The pearl-grey mist of the *sfumato* that had greeted us every summer morning was scattered by the winds, so the surrounding hills were sharp and no longer looked as if they were dissolving into the sky.

Umberto and his guys had finally finished Vesuvia's wall, and we now had all four of them working full time on our house. Pyramids of sand and gravel became concrete, which turned into staircases and archways under the pounding of jackhammers and the screaming of power saws. Progress was steady, and each day we'd cheer some small accomplishment, like the glazing of a window or the installation of a toilet. Knowing that it was always dicey to make plans for the future in this society, we cautiously hoped to move in around Thanksgiving, God willing and the creek don't rise.

Ironically, it was God, or a manifestation of Him or Her, who accelerated this plan. We were taking the back road into town one day, when we came upon our neighbour Annamaria and her goats. She looked distressed and, in halting, nervous fragments, she told us that for the last three nights she had seen visions of Santa Fabiola in her dreams.

We nodded, not knowing what to say, as she went on to tell us that in last night's dream, she'd seen Santa Fabiola hovering over our *rustico*, warning us that we must move in before the harvest. When we tried to suggest that perhaps it was only a dream, Annamaria spat on her fingers and quickly made a cross between her eyes.

To ask what would happen if we didn't move in before the harvest would be to beg the very question of Santa Fabiola's existence. She was the patron saint of Cambione, born here in 1866, and performing at least four of her eleven certified miracles within the city limits. Santa Fabiola grew up in abject poverty and endured one of those childhoods straight out of a Dickens novel. The eleventh of twenty-six children, she was blind, crippled, epileptic and covered with grotesque open sores. But her simple faith and pious soul soon earned her a following, and as Annamaria pointed out, Fabiola was canonised at a time when it was a lot harder for a woman, alluding to the existence of a glass ceiling even in the saint business.

Nancy and I left her with the assurance that we would do our best to comply, even though we had little intention of taking this seriously. To a pair of natural-born cynics like us, the idea of apparitions and miracles seemed like a lot of hooey.

And yet, I couldn't help thinking that perhaps it would be best not to tempt the fates, now that things were going well. After all, if one of Vesuvia's *malocchi* could cause our car accident, what would happen if we flaunted the words of a saint? I'm not religious, and despite my best intentions, I'm not even very spiritual. But I am highly suggestible. I can't even watch TV for any length of time without ordering a set of Ginsu knives.

So I found myself trying to convince Nancy that maybe we should urge Umberto to pick up the pace so we could move in sooner rather than later. Not for any of Annamaria's superstitions, of course, but if we were going to get remarried in the house, wouldn't it be great to do it as part of the festa for the olive harvest?

Nancy looked at me as if I had just told her that I was running off with the Moonies, but for reasons more secular she also felt that it was a good idea. We were both anxious to move out of the place we were renting from Dino, and it would be good to be in the *rustico* before winter set in. With us living there, we could better pressure Umberto to finish before the rain and cold weather halted all work and we'd have to live in a half-built house until the spring thaw.

When we approached Umberto with the idea, he was noncommittal. There was no way, he felt, that the house would be completed, but it might be habitable enough for us to move in, if we didn't mind them continuing the work while we lived there. Nancy and I had lived in houses that were under construction and found it to be a particularly unpleasant circle of hell. It's a life lived with the constant noise of power tools, clouds of plaster dust in your eyes and hair, and workers staring at you at six in the morning while you're having an argument with your wife in your underwear.

But the prime reason for moving in as quickly as possible would be that by legally taking occupancy, we would force the Comune to make their final inspection and sign off, which would unfreeze our bank account. So we told Umberto that we wanted to get in as soon as possible. When he passed the word down to his guys, they reacted along predictable lines. Va Bene thought it would be no problem for the house to be ready, Problema thought there was no way this was going to happen in time, and Vagabondo was frankly disappointed to learn that we were not going back to California for the winter, where he had hoped to come visit us so we could introduce him to some rich American women.

The last obstacle to our move was the installation of our electricity. This had to be done by a professional *elettricista*. Remarkably, Dino did not have a cousin who served in this capacity, so we had to rely on the recommendation of our crew, and even though they agreed on little else, they were all in accord that the best person for the job was Riccardo.

So Riccardo came up to the house and surveyed the job. He presented us with his bid, which seemed reasonable, so we agreed to engage him. Then, we timed our move to coincide with the completion of his work. This was all fine and dandy until the actual day he was to do the work arrived, and he didn't. When we called around and finally got his wife on the phone, she offered up the mother of all excuses, namely that Riccardo's mother had died and today was the funeral.

We were of course sorry, we explained, but we had made arrangements to move in. No problem, she said, giving us the phone number of the only other good electrician in town, Alessio. When we finally got Alessio on the phone he told us that he would be pleased to do the job, but he couldn't start today because he was digging the grave for Riccardo's mother.

Faced with funeral arrangements that were tying up every *elettricista* in the region, we now understood that we needed to wait until the proper period of mourning was over. Riccardo finally did show up. When he started the work, he was quick, efficient, and gave me an object lesson in yet another difference between their culture and ours.

It has been my experience that every Italian house I have ever been in is chronically short on electrical sockets. So when we were walking Riccardo through the room that would serve as my office, I made sure that Nancy accurately translated the idea that we would be running a full array of electronic equipment here. Computer, printer, stereo, TV, VCR, DVD, PDA, phone/fax/answering machine, and so on down the list of every gizmo and gadget one needs to survive nowadays, at least in the States.

We wanted a lot of plugs, I stressed, and I thought he understood. But when he finished, there was only one socket in the room. I tried to keep from getting angry as I asked why he hadn't put in more. He patiently explained that I should start with one socket, then, using a surge protector that has six outlets, I should see if that worked before spending any more money. If it didn't, he would come back and put in another socket.

I felt like a typically wasteful American, oblivious to how expensive electricity was here. In fact, throughout Western Europe there is a marked scarcity of such energy wasters as electric clothes dryers and hand blowers in public bathrooms. I tried to apologise and he told me not to feel bad. The number of sockets I wanted really didn't matter because Italy has its own system of guaranteeing no one uses too much power. As soon as you plug in more than three things, all the lights in your neighbourhood go out and all your neighbours start screaming at you.

We moved in on Election Day, piling up the car with load after load of our stuff amid the hoopla and chaos that Italians always manage to manufacture on occasions like this. The town was plastered with posters and draped with banners, but their preferred manner of electioneering were the sound trucks that drove up and down the narrow streets of the village, blaring out a candidate's name and extolling his virtues. Though we obviously couldn't vote, I did manage to make myself a player by getting involved in Marco Mucchi's campaign for the Comune board.

I came up with the slogan 'Marco Mucchi, il Magnifico!' Besides the alliteration it had a resoundingly regal, if not imperial, tone, designed to overcome what a mild-mannered little bean counter he was. Marco loved it, so it was headlined on all his campaign material and screamed relentlessly by sound trucks all over town, with the result that he won in a walk. He probably would have won anyway, but my contribution did give us a bargaining chip to play when we needed a friend at the Comune to get our paperwork processed sometime before the coming of the next Ice Age.

To our delight, the *rustico* was up and running, with a fully functioning bathroom, a kitchen where almost everything was operational and, thanks to Riccardo, electricity that worked at least as often as it did in the homes of people who had been living in them for years. Most of the outside construction had been completed at this point, so what the guys were focusing on now were those indoor jobs that kicked up more dust than a sandstorm and created enough noise to drown out a Hell's Angels convention.

One particular nasty piece of work was the reconstruction of our fireplace, which began with the ripping out of a section of wall and all the dust, rock and debris that went with it. Each morning we rose at dawn, gobbled down breakfast and covered the kitchen with a thick plastic tarp. Then we proceeded about our usual business, trying not to be distracted by a chorus of power tools loud enough that we half expected calls from the Pisa airport complaining about the noise.

As their daily work began, I realised that all the other times we had lived in a house while it was under construction, I hadn't thought it was so bad because I could go to work and hide out in my office until it was safe to go home. Now, there was nowhere to run and nowhere to hide.

But somehow we found ways to get through the ordeal. Nancy strapped on a Walkman and donned earphones to escape into the ethereal world of Enya and Tangerine Dream, as she painted in watercolours with her one good arm. I packed up my laptop and left every morning for the village, where I sat in a café, presumably to write but more accurately to sip cappuccino, schmooze with my fellow Cambionese and check my e-mail.

I was doing just that when I saw that there was yet another message from my agent. He was writing me regularly now, but unfortunately not a word was about selling my script. This particular e-mail was for one of his clients who wanted to rent a villa in Chianti. Of course, this villa had to have an Olympic-sized swimming pool and a fully stocked wine cellar. And, oh, yes, was there a way to arrange for a couple of mountain bikes? I could see now that in his eyes, I had descended from being a working writer-producer to his own personal concierge.

I had to remind myself that this relationship, as demeaning as it was, was better than that enjoyed by many of my peers, who had reached the age where their agents either no longer called them back, or had outright released them. And on the plus side, I could tell that my e-mails were making him laugh because he occasionally commented on some of the things I had said, like how in Italy nobody ever uses the address of anything, so when you ask for directions you get something like 'Turn left at the house with the three grey cats until you come to the café with the ugly waitress.'

I wrote him back promising that I'd make some calls, and before I sent it off, I made sure my e-mail had a few new jokes in it, because in Hollywood you're always auditioning. It may look personal, but everything is always about business. A classic Hollywood joke best makes this point.

An actor was in his car when he heard sirens and saw smoke coming from the direction of his neighbourhood. He rushed home, and sure enough, there was a cordon of police cars, fire engines and ambulances surrounding his house. He jumped out of his car, screaming, 'Oh, my God, what happened?!' After the cops managed to calm him down, they told him that apparently his agent came to his house, murdered his wife and family, and then set fire to the whole block.

The actor shook his head in disbelief. 'My agent came to my house?'

The weekend finally arrived, and the timing couldn't have been better. The fireplace had been finished earlier in the week, giving the mortar ample time to cure so that it was now ready for our first fire. We went to bed that Saturday night aglow in the expectation of spending Sunday curled up in front of a roaring fire, listening to nothing louder than the crackle of burning logs.

But Sunday dawned to a racket that all but jolted us out of bed. It was the first day of the hunting season, and the hills were alive with the sound of gunfire. There was so much shooting going on, it sounded like the Tet Offensive was raging in our backyard. From all over the area, it seemed, hunters had gathered in the woods behind our house to gun down songbirds and bunny rabbits.

But this was not just thrill killing for the sake of sport. This was the serious business of putting food on their families' tables. Ammunition was expensive, and if these hunters were going to shoot something, they were damn well going to eat it, which explains why the aroma of a gamy concoction that was euphemistically referred to as *stufato alla cacciatora* would soon be wafting from the hearths of our neighbours' homes. This stew was allegedly made with rabbit, but I strongly suspected its ingredients were any furry critter unlucky enough to have wandered into the cross hairs. Another delicacy I would never get used to during hunting season was that plate of tiny dead birds served as *antipasti* with wine. You're supposed to just pop them in your mouth, beak, feather and all, and crunch down on them as if you were snacking on some form of rustic popcorn with eyes, once again reminding me that it's not all one world.

But the prize catch of the hunting season was *cinghiale*, the wild boar that Tuscans love either as roasted meat or in a thousand varieties of sauces and sausages. From this day on I would never be able to pass our local butcher shop, where they proudly hang a leg so fresh the cinghiale's fur is still on it, without thinking of the carnage it took to get it there.

Anyway, it was far too noisy to enjoy our fireplace, so we spent the day trying not to flinch every time a shotgun discharged and crouching low whenever we passed a window. Our only hope was that the poor pigs would soon give themselves up so all this racket would stop.

Then suddenly it did. Just like that. Around four o'clock it grew silent as a tomb. Not even the chirping of a bird, most of whom either had been driven off or now resided at the bottom of a hunter's sack. We wasted no time taking advantage of this respite, lighting our fireplace, uncorking the wine, and plopping slabs of bread on our Tuscan oven to toast for *bruschetta*. The wine had scarcely had a moment to breathe when we heard a knocking on our door. It must be a neighbour, we figured, because we hadn't heard a car pull up. Perhaps Annamaria had come to tell us how pleased Santa Fabiola was that we had moved in before the harvest?

Nancy opened the door and there was Rudolfo, accompanied by a tall, pale-skinned young man with sandy brown hair. They were both carrying suitcases and overstuffed backpacks. Rudolfo looked dishevelled, bleary eyed, and his normally well-groomed beard was scruffy and overgrown. Nancy greeted them, and there was a long moment of awkward silence as Rudolfo stood there, blinking in adolescent confusion.

'Rudolfo?' I called out from the living room.

'I'm sorry to bother you, but . . .' He dropped his suitcase and his chin began to tremble.

'What's the matter? Are you OK?' Nancy said, putting her arm around his shoulder.

'We got the big troubles,' the other young man said in a thick Italian accent.

'Please come in,' Nancy said as the boys picked up their bags and she led them inside.

They came into the living room, and as they parked their luggage by the fireplace, the young man introduced himself in Italian as Stefano.

'*Piacere*, Stefano,' I said, shaking his hand. Then I turned to Rudolfo. 'So what's going on, bro?'

'I did like you said,' Rudolfo announced. 'I told them everything.'

'Everything?' Nancy said. 'What's everything?'

'That I can't marry Pia,' Rudolfo said looking over at his companion. 'Because Stefano and I are in love.'

Stefano gave Rudolfo a smile for support as Nancy and I glanced at each other to mask our shock.

'Oh. I didn't know that part,' I said. 'But it's cool. Maybe not with your parents, of course, but –'

'Oh, they went nuts! My father screamed like a madman and Mamma tried to throw herself out the window.'

Stefano nodded and told us in Italian that it hadn't gone that much easier with his family. His father and two uncles kidnapped him and took him to the local priest to have an exorcism performed.

'Well, at least the truth's out,' Nancy said, filling their wineglasses. 'And so are you.'

We shared an uneasy laugh.

'But now I don't know what to do,' Rudolfo said as he stared with elaborate absorption at a piece of cork floating in his wine. 'My father threatened to throw me out of the house, but before he could, I said, 'Hey, no way, I'm out of here.' So . . . I've run away from home.'

'Look, Rudolfo,' I said as gently as I could, 'a thirty-four-year-old man doesn't run away from home. You leave and you go live somewhere else with whomever you want, and that's that.'

'How can I go anywhere?' Rudolfo said. 'My father took away my car . . . excuse me, his car!'

'I'm so sorry,' Nancy said. 'You want to borrow ours?'

'He even took my motorcycle.'

'Those are just things,' I said. 'What's important is to be with the person you love, and if you've got that, everything else will fall into place.'

Then Stefano spoke while he studied Rudolfo for his reaction. In barely understandable English, Stefano said, 'I tell to him we go to live at Milano, he and me.'

'You know, that's a great idea,' I said. 'I grew up in a town not much bigger than this, and I couldn't believe how free I felt after I moved to Los Angeles.'

'I don't know. Maybe we'll go to the city someday,' Rudolfo said. 'But right now we need a place to stay.'

'We'd love to have you here,' Nancy said, 'but look how we're living. The workers are here every day and there's barely room for us.'

'Can anybody take you in for a few days?' I asked. 'A friend, a relative?'

Rudolfo shrugged. 'Well, my best friend was Pia's brother. . . .'

Stefano whispered something to Rudolfo and he nodded. 'Yeah, that could work out, I guess.'

'What?' Nancy asked.

'We could go stay with my aunts Nina, Nona and Nana up at Montemetato,' Rudolfo said.

'There you go,' I said. 'Get away for a couple of days and let all the dust settle. And then figure out what you want to do.'

'But we have no car,' Rudolfo said. 'Can you drive us?'

'Sure.' Nancy glanced at her watch. 'Only, it's getting dark and I hate that road at night.'

'Why don't you guys bunk here and we'll drive you up in the morning?' I offered.

They looked at each other and nodded.

'Great,' Nancy said. 'I'll make up the couch and we'll push these two chairs together for a second bed.'

'Are you hungry?' I asked, heading for the kitchen. 'All that gunfire was turning me into a vegetarian. I better have a steak before I turn into a complete tree-hugger.'

As I was seasoning the meat, I began to hear the baying of a truckload of dogs that sounded like they were heading up our driveway. We all knew what was coming, and braced for it as best we could. Rudolfo's face went ashen and his legs started quivering, as if he was trying to decide whether to stand or run.

From outside our house we heard Dino bellowing, 'Rudolfo! I know you're in there!'

I peered out the window and spotted Dino and Cousin Aldo

in full hunting gear. Shotguns were slung over their shoulders and their thick, quilted jackets were weighed down with cartridge belts and the carcasses of small dead animals.

'You come out here right now!'

I opened the door and poked my head out. 'All right, Dino, stop hollering. He's here and he's fine.'

'What did he tell you?' he demanded, his eyes narrowing into slits.

'Nothing. We were just talking.'

'If he told you he is a *frocio*, he's wrong! No one in our family has ever been that way!'

'You got to calm down,' I said. 'Nothing's going to get settled like this.'

'I show you how this will get settled.' Dino stepped in front of our door. '*Permesso*,' he said, asking me for permission to enter in the customary Tuscan way.

'You're not coming in here with those guns,' I said, feeling like Wyatt Earp.

Dino and Aldo unhitched their shotguns and propped them against the wall. I stepped aside as they knocked mud off their rubber boots and entered. By the time I came in behind them, the screaming had already started.

'Get in the truck, you're coming home!' Then Dino pointed at Stefano. 'And you . . .'

Rudolfo stepped in front of his boyfriend. 'Leave him alone!'

'How could you do this to your mamma?' Cousin Aldo shouted. 'You are her only chance to produce an heir!'

As if incensed by this thought Dino screamed, 'How are we going to have a grandson to carry on the family name?'

'Who cares?' Rudolfo came back at the same volume.

'Your mamma cares!' Dino said. 'She will die without a grandson!'

'Well, they could always adopt,' I said, trying to be helpful.

'And you!' Dino turned to me, but all I could see was the little dead animal draped over his shoulder staring at me with glassy eyes.

'What?'

'How could you do this to me?'

'What'd I do?'

'I asked you to talk to my son and you turned him into a Hollywood homosexual!'

'Oh, come on.'

'OK, I know, you didn't do it. This is all his mamma's fault . . . and those goddamn Buddhists. And I will deal with them later, but right now you are coming home. Get in the truck!'

'No!' Stefano cried.

'Yes!'

'No!!'

'Yes!!'

'No!!!'

And so it went like this, back and forth, a soaring aria of baritone bellowing and tenor hysteria. Raging accusations and tearful denials. All the dirty laundry of a family fluffed and folded in front of our very eyes. Nancy and I tried to stay out of the way, but it seemed as if everywhere we went, it followed us like a running gun battle. In the midst of all this turmoil the front door cracked open and Annamaria peeked in.

'*Permesso*,' she whispered.

Nancy noticed her and invited her in. Annamaria apologised, saying that she had knocked but apparently nobody had heard her. She didn't want to be a bother, now that we had company, but she had brought us over some things for the house. Nancy told her to please join us, and she entered, carrying a large basket covered with a red gingham cloth. She put it down on the table and the small white head of a baby goat popped out and started going 'Baa-baa.'

'What's that?' I said.

'I call him Pepe,' Annamaria said. 'But you call him whatever you want.'

'Oh, my God, he's so adorable,' Nancy said. She gently cupped her hand and started petting Pepe's head as the little goat baaed indignantly.

Annamaria took a baby bottle out of the basket and handed it to Nancy. 'This is from the mamma.'

Nancy put the nipple in Pepe's mouth. 'Oh, you are so hungry.'

The delicate frailty of the animal drew everyone's attention. The hollering stopped and Dino, Aldo, Rudolfo and Stefano gathered around the basket.

Annamaria explained that she had brought us the customary offerings of bread, salt and a crucifix, but once again Santa Fabiola had appeared in a dream and told her that our house needed a living symbol of the land. So Annamaria knew that this must be her gift to us.

'Gee, thanks,' I said, trying to think of the last time anybody had given me a baby goat.

'*La capra* is a good sign,' Dino said as Cousin Aldo nodded in agreement. 'Symbol of strength and virility.'

'What about peace and love?' Nancy said, catching the eyes of both Dino and Stefano.

'I think the symbol for that is a baby lamb, but she makes a good point.' I put my arm around Dino. 'This is not worth losing a son over, you know?'

Dino nodded and let loose a deep sigh. Then, ignoring Stefano, he turned to me. 'You are a good friend.'

'Thanks.'

'And you, Nancy, have a good heart and you love animals just like me.'

'Yeah,' she said.

'I tell you what, I shot a *cinghiale* sow this morning and I give you half. You got a chain saw?'

30. CITTAPAZZA

So now we owned a baby goat. Neither of us had a clue what to do. Nancy brought him into bed and cuddled him so fervently, I feared that if I left the room she might start breastfeeding him. I dragged him outside and tried to teach him how to fetch. But Pepe seemed not to care what either of us did, making himself content to eat grass and poop, often at the same time.

But the small inconveniences we suffered with our goat paled in comparison to how we were put upon by our two other kids. Being the sons of Italian families, it never occurred to Rudolfo or Stefano to prepare their own meals, wash out a dish, or even pick up the clothes they seemed to drop wherever they were standing. We could have tolerated this for a day, but they showed absolutely no interest in going up to Montemetato. They claimed to have appointments and activities that necessitated their borrowing our car and being gone most of the day. They did manage to make it back to our house in time for dinner, however, only to tell us that they needed the car that evening. This pattern continued for the next few days, until one night they staggered home from a disco at four in the morning, making so much noise that it frightened poor Pepe and he pooped in our bed.

We were sympathetic over the rejection they had suffered at the hands of their families, of course, but they just couldn't stay with us any longer. So the following morning we woke them up early and as I handed them steaming mugs of coffee, Nancy struck the edges of her hands together in the shape of an X, which is how one Italian tells another that it's time to hit the road. As the boys packed up their belongings, we arranged for Annamaria to goat-sit Pepe, and we soon found ourselves on our way up the mountain to Montemetato.

The distance between Cambione and Montemetato is only about eighteen kilometres, so the fact that it took thirty-seven kilometres of paved road to connect the two gives you some idea of just how many hairpin turns one needs to navigate. If the road weren't problematic enough, it fell on me to do the driving because Nancy's broken arm kept her from working a manual transmission. But with me driving it left her completely free to shudder with fear at every bump, suck in her breath at every turn, and dig her nails into my leg whenever I tried to pass a slower-moving vehicle.

Other than a few puncture wounds on my thigh, the drive itself was magnificent. The road dipped and heaved like a roller coaster as we glided past a seamless wall of forest made up of evergreens, puffy young poplars, dense thickets of *corbezzoli* shrubs, and hoary *leccio* trees laden with acorns.

We passed through many small villages along the way, and there was a comforting sameness to the inevitability of the church bell tower and the faded war memorial in the piazza. But just when they've lulled you into feeling it's all the same, Italy manages to pull a surprise on you, like the café we came upon that was sitting out in the middle of nowhere.

There was no sign, nor any advertisement whatsoever, except for a mannequin missing an arm standing by the side of the road in a rain-drenched waitress uniform. Her glazed expression met the oncoming traffic head-on. Perhaps her arm had fallen off beckoning people to pull in and patronise the café.

With an inducement like that, naturally we had to stop, even though we were only a few miles from our destination. We entered the café to find it pleasantly crowded, which is always a good indication of a place's quality. But upon closer inspection we discovered that many of the patrons of this café were also mannequins. A pair of dummies dressed as Italian peasants were seated at a table with a bottle of Chianti and two dusty wineglasses, while another, inexplicably dressed in a Mexican serape and sombrero, was propped up on a barstool next to a jukebox that was playing an old Barry Manilow song.

The actual human patrons of the café turned out to be a rather surrealistic lot. There was a woman of indeterminate age wearing a multicoloured wig, smoking a pipe, and talking to herself. Every so often she would stop, look in our direction, and give us a spooky little smile.

A middle-aged man in a serge suit that had seen better days was sitting at the counter with a cup of coffee. All the time we were there, he never once took a sip because he was too busy cleaning his spoon with the end of his necktie. Rounding out the scene was a pair of twin teenage boys of about fifteen, wordlessly playing a pinball machine. They had big eyes and shaved heads with a low cephalic index, and they looked like something out of a Diane Arbus photo shoot.

The four of us stood at the bar, staring at the decrepit espresso machine, wondering if there was anyone around to operate it. We were about to leave when a small man with a pinched face and a body shaped like a potato came out from the back. We told him what we wanted, and his response to everything we said was to give us back a short but distinct bird whistle. When Stefano asked him where the bathroom was, the man pointed with a fluttering hand that looked like a sparrow taking off. Stefano said, 'Grazie,' and the man bird whistled, 'Per niente.'

I looked over at Rudolfo and bounced my eyebrows for an explanation of this Tuscan version of the bar from Star Wars.

He uttered one word. 'Cittapazza.'

Rudolfo went on to explain that, like many towns high up in the remote hills, Montemetato was isolated from the rest of the world. The very road we had driven up on had not even been put in until the 1950s. As a result, there was so much inbreeding, the village became well known for the odd behaviour of its citizens and it was dubbed Cittapazza . . . Crazy Town.

'I never heard that expression,' I marvelled.

'Well, they like to keep it a secret,' Rudolfo said. 'But some of the most important families of Cambione came from up here.'

'Really?' Nancy said.

'Oh, yeah, the Tughis, the Rinaldis, the –'

'The mayor's family?'

'Uh-huh.'

'What about the Pingatores?' I asked.

'Absolutely. We'll drive right past the farmhouse where they all came from.'

'This is quite interesting,' I said as the lady with the spooky grin took out her teeth, making her grin even spookier. 'Any other secrets we should know about?'

'Oh, there are stories galore, *multi sussuroventi*,' he said using the archaic expression that means 'whispers in the wind'.

'And what are they?'

'Who remembers?' he said. 'But my aunts know all that stuff.'

'And what about your folks?' Nancy asked. 'Are they from up here?'

'No, our branch of the family moved away years ago,' Rudolfo answered. 'We're all crazy for reasons of our own.'

The house that Nina, Nona and Nana lived in was even more ancient than they were. There was some stonework to it, but it was mostly built of rough-hewn logs and done in such a way that the three-storey structure stood as crooked as a witch's hat.

Our arrival was heralded with shrieks of joy and barrages of kisses on our cheeks. From the overwhelming affection of their greeting I assumed that perhaps Rudolfo's aunts hadn't heard the reason for his expulsion. I soon discovered that, not only did they know all about it, they were remarkably accepting of the situation. Nina felt that this was a stage most boys go through and he would soon grow out of it. Nona believed that many men who like other men eventually marry and sire families, and Nana wondered what the big deal was about having grandchildren anyway, since it just meant more mouths to feed and more diapers to change.

Almost as remarkable as their degree of tolerance was the lunch they laid out before us. In spite of the fact that Nina, Nona and Nana were over eighty years old and had five bad legs between them, they had prepared a meal that, even for Italians, was of gargantuan proportions.

It began with a vast selection of *legumi al sotto*, which are freshly dug-up vegetables marinated in olive oil and white wine vinegar. This was accompanied by *crostini di polenta* (corn fritters on toast), and *carpaccio*, lean raw beef pounded tissue thin and adorned with *parmigiano* cheese and olive oil. We were all pretty hungry when we arrived, so we made the mistake of devouring the appetisers with such ferocity, you'd think the Visigoths were at the very gates of Cittapazza.

Next came the soup. Since they couldn't decide on one, they made two: a *zuppa di zucca* made from the small, sweet pumpkins they grew in their garden, and *pasta e fagioli*, classic Tuscan pasta and bean soup.

We were stuffed, but Nina, Nona and Nana were just getting warmed up. For our *primi* they brought out platters of *fettucini carbonara* made with bacon and eggs, broad *pappardelle* noodles with roasted red potatoes in a pesto sauce, and a heart-stopping lasagna made with alternating layers of spinach and ricotta cheese.

At this point all of us could have stopped eating and lived on our body fat for a month, but that would have meant missing out on the main course, *trota*. These grilled trout had been caught that morning by their neighbour from the little stream that ran behind their house, and if any of you who are reading this happen to be sitting on Death Row awaiting your execution, I would beg you to consider this for your last meal. The taste of these fish grilled in their skin on an iron skillet with lemon, olive oil and sage was the culinary equivalent of making love to Marilyn Monroe. Something you could look back on in your old age and savour.

After all that food, topped off by a scrumptious *torta di cioccolata* and assorted roasted figs, Nancy and I decided that we needed either a long walk or a stomach pump. So while the boys got settled in the guest bedroom, we followed the gurgling little trout stream as it led us deep into the woods.

We walked without speaking, our path a spongy bed of pine needles that quieted our footsteps so as not to disturb the cathedral silence of the tall trees. Eventually we came to where the stream emptied into a small pond. The water was incredibly still and held the shimmering reflection of the clouds overhead as well as the upside-down image of an ancient, abandoned mill. The mill was completely encased in moss and overgrown vines, its water-wheel frozen in time and decomposing in soundless splendour.

We sat on a fallen tree trunk, staring at the mill, only occasionally distracted by the silvery flash of a trout in the icy blueness of the pond.

'It's so beautiful here,' Nancy murmured amid the buzzing of insects and the soft rustling of the grass.

I loosened my belt and unbuttoned my shirt where it was tight across my belly. 'I don't think I'll ever eat again.'

'Until dinner.'

'We got to stop.'

'I know,' she said. 'I'm out of control.'

'My problem is I still feel like I'm on vacation here,' I said, 'so every day I'm partying with the *gelato* and the cheese.'

'The cheese is killing me,' Nancy said.

'We got to get serious about a diet, and this time I mean it.'

'We'll help each other,' she vowed. 'If one person starts to weaken, the other one stops me.'

'We're only talking about eight or nine pounds here. You know the drill: fruits, vegetables, fish.'

'Exercise every day,' she said. 'And keep each other away from the cream sauces.'

'It'll go quick,' I said. 'Say we lose a pound a week –'

'Which isn't much.'

'In two months we'll have taken off so much, we could really pig out at our Christmas banquet.'

'We're having a Christmas banquet?'

'Yeah, we're inviting the neighbours over for roasted goat.'

'Shut up.'

'It's a tradition around here.'

'Don't even joke about it!'

'What? You thought we were keeping him? I thought you knew we were just fattening him up for –'

She put her hand over my mouth and tried to wrestle me to the ground as she yelled, 'I hate you, I hate you.'

'Mmm, I can smell that sauce now.' I laughed as we rolled around on the small apron of grass. '*Pomodoro alla Pepe*.'

'Why do you keep teasing me about him?'

'I'm just trying to get your goat.'

We were anxious to get on the road before dark, but Nina, Nona and Nana wouldn't let us leave until they had packed us up with enough food to provision an Arctic expedition. We sat in the kitchen as they bustled about, and I took this opportunity to ask them about some of the 'whispers in the wind'. I was especially interested in the ones that involved the Pingatores. After weaving me a convoluted narrative about people who had been dead for a hundred and fifty years, they finally got up to the present time, and then they proceeded to tell me the most astonishing story I had ever heard.

31. FARE UNA BELLA FIGURA

The two Italian words most firmly embedded in the English language are *graffiti* and *paparazzi*. Interestingly, both involve a public display. This tells us much about their national psyche, for the average Italian is motivated by two powerful forces: *fare una bella figura* (looking good to his friends and neighbours) and *non fare una brutta figura* (not looking bad to his friends and neighbours).

With this in mind I was trying to figure out how we could most benefit from the story Rudolfo's aunts had told us. First I had to make sure it was more or less true. Having spent my entire career as a professional sitcom wordbag, I realised that I didn't know very much about journalism. But I had seen *All the President's Men* a couple of times, so I understood that if you wanted people to believe your story, you needed independent corroboration. And to get that I had to talk to the one person I had been avoiding. The mayor.

Every Wednesday the mayor had lunch at Trattoria Toscana, where the special of the day was always *saltimbocca*, a veal dish so named because it literally 'jumps into your mouth'. Then, after a leisurely meal, he would go see his mistress. Interestingly, a popular Italian expression for mistress is *contorno*, which means side dish. Italians love those polite little euphemisms. They commonly refer to a public toilet as a *vespasiano*, from vespa, the word for wasp, presumably for the buzzing noise inside, and their discreet way of describing the streetwalkers on the boulevard is to refer to them as *le lucciole* ... the fireflies, because they only come out at night.

I had positioned myself between the *trattoria* and his girlfriend's apartment, directly in the path of his booty call, and it wasn't long before I spotted the mayor coming down the street with the jaunty air of a man who had just satisfied one appetite and was about to satisfy another.

'*Scusami*, Signor Sindaco, *buon giorno*,' I said, greeting him in my best Italian. My language skills had developed to the point where I could carry on a reasonable conversation without Nancy's help, which was good, because a lady's presence might have further embarrassed him.

He seemed pleased to see me and eager to find out whatever had happened to that article I was writing about him. And he was not shy about reminding me how quickly our *denuncia* had disappeared because of his intervention. I told him that I was glad he'd mentioned the article, because I had just come upon some new information that I needed to confirm. As I laid out the parameters of the story, he stared at me with growing unease.

He started to back away, denying the story by chalking it up to the ramblings of the uneducated peasant mind with nothing better to think about. But from the jittery edge in his voice and the way he was trying to get away from me, I knew it was true. I took out my notebook and followed him down the street, calling out questions as if I were a member of the Washington press corps trying to engage the President before he could get to his helicopter.

He was just about to reach the sanctuary of his girlfriend's apartment when Horn Dog appeared. As if incensed that somebody was going to get some nookie and he wasn't, the little mutt starting growling at the mayor and yipping at his ankles. The commotion of my questions and Horn Dog's yapping caused windows to open and curious heads to look out. All this attention was too much for a man on his way to visit his mistress, so he doffed his hat in my direction and bolted up the street, having to settle for a lunch without his favourite side dish.

Now that I'd field-tested our story on the mayor, I knew it was ready for prime time, so we set about trying to come upon the key players when they were both together. Fortunately, they were also creatures of habit. So, the following Sunday we parked our car under the shade of the lead-coloured dome of the church and sat waiting for the noon Mass to let out. When we spotted Vesuvia Pingatore in the crowd exiting the chapel, we were somewhat surprised to see her walking arm in arm with Marco Mucchi, the pair of them chattering away like old friends. They stopped in front of the eroded saints on the façade of the church doors, and Vesuvia took out a sheaf of papers. She handed them to Marco Mucchi and waited while he looked them over.

What fiendish plot were they hatching against us now? With Marco's new position on the Comune board he could cause us no end of fresh grief. I simmered with rage at how I had come up with his campaign slogan, only to have that smiling little Judas turn against us.

Their conversation continued as they crossed the street and ambled towards the little café with the green awning. We got out of our car and followed them at a distance discreet enough to see Marco Mucchi, still holding on to the papers, bid her goodbye. Marco then sat down with his wife and two small daughters, who had been to the earlier Mass, while Vesuvia continued over to another table where her brother, Mario, was waiting. No sooner had she sat down and ordered herself an espresso than we approached and greeted them.

'Sorry to bother you,' I said, as Nancy translated so nothing would be missed, 'but I was wondering if you could spare me a moment.'

Mario cocked his head at us like a spaniel.

'I've been working on this article on Cambione. . . .'

'Bully for you,' Mario said with hollow cheer. 'Not even a car accident or the Holy Sabbath can keep you Yanks from making a buck.'

I gave him an accommodating smile as I took out my notepad and flipped it open. 'It's going to feature some of the town's most prominent citizens, which, of course, must include the Pingatores.'

Mario translated for Vesuvia, who responded with a suspicious smile.

'So I need you to help verify a story I heard about you . . . and your zia Teresa.'

The mention of their aunt, who had gone off to live in America, caught them both short. They turned to us with expressions that ranged from guarded to contemptuous.

'Apparently, when you were kids – during the hard years after the war – your family was pretty much kept alive by regular shipments of food from your zia Teresa.'

'We received a leg up from many relatives,' Mario said, nervously glancing around to see who was in hearing distance.

'Seems these shipments from America continued for a number of years,' I said, as Nancy and I sat down at their table. 'Every month she'd send you a packageful of Hershey bars, Spam –'

'Eh, it was so long ago, who remembers?' Vesuvia suddenly said in Italian, her jaw clenched in anger.

'Even after Zia Teresa died, her son kept on sending you packages like clockwork. Then, one day, a box arrived like no other. When your mamma opened it, it was filled with a strange, dry powder.'

'Who told you this?' Mario signalled the waiter for their check. 'They don't know bugger-all!'

'There was a note inside, but since it was in English, nobody could read it. After much discussion your parents decided that it was powdered milk. So they mixed it with water, and you kids drank it.'

'You don't know what you're talking about!' Mario said.

'Well, other people think I do. See, your parents generously shared it with some of the other kids in the village . . . like the mayor.'

'Bollocks!' Mario hissed. 'We knew what it was and we didn't eat it!'

'According to my source, which I can't reveal, you didn't find out what it was until years later when Zia Teresa's son showed up, wanting to see where you were keeping his mother's ashes.'

'This is utter rubbish!' Mario started to rise, but I put my hand on his arm.

'So you're saying that a box of strange-looking powder arrived with a note that you couldn't read, and you instantly knew what it was?'

'OK, maybe at first mamma thought it was some kind of yeast.'

'Too bad she didn't bake it up in a loaf of bread,' I said. 'Because then the dead could have risen again.'

'Why are you spreading lies about us?' Vesuvia said to Nancy in Italian.

'Why were you spreading lies about us?' Nancy fired back. 'Telling the Comune we were putting up a three-storey aluminum-and-glass California beach house!'

'We did no such thing!' Vesuvia said, her voice biting like a rusty saw.

Nancy cupped her hands to the heavens, making the Italian gesture that implores the other person to be honest.

'If we did say anything,' Vesuvia muttered, 'we were only repeating what somebody told us.'

'That's exactly what I'm doing,' I said waving my notebook in their face.

'How dare you!' Mario's voice strained as he struggled to keep it to a whisper. 'Don't you know my sister already feels bad that the whole town is blaming her for your accident?'

'Well, let's see how bad she feels when the whole world reads that you're a pack of ghouls who eat their own dead.'

'If anybody has the right to feel bad, it's us,' Nancy said. 'After I made you that bas relief, and you never even acknowledged it!'

Vesuvia's face twisted into a sardonic expression. Her left eye bulged out so far, her eye shadow cracked. Just then, Marco Mucchi approached our table, beaming at the sight of the four of us sitting together.

'*Un miracolo*,' he declared. A miracle. '*Il leone e l'agnello*.' The lion lying down with the lamb.

But his delight was short lived. Mario shot out of his chair so abruptly that he momentarily lost his balance and wheeled like a spooked horse. He regained his composure and signalled to his sister that they were leaving. Thinking he might have caused the problem, Marco lavishly apologised. Vesuvia ignored him as she rose and gathered up her purse, but Marco kept explaining that he had only come over because she had forgotten to initial one of the pages.

'*Criminale!*' Vesuvia screamed, grabbing the pages out of Marco's hand and ripping them up. '*Farabutti!*'

'We'll take you scoundrels to court and sue your pants off!' Mario echoed as they steamed towards the door.

Marco looked at us dumbfounded. When we explained what happened, his face turned as ashen as Zia Teresa's remains.

'How could you do this?' he said. 'You've ruined everything.'

'Look, I really wasn't going to write the story,' I explained. 'We were just trying to scare them into dropping all claims on the house and accepting us as the rightful owners.'

'And to make them stop harassing us.'

Marco picked up the ripped pages and handed them to us. 'See this? It's a document she asked me to file with the Comune. It transfers the ownership of the property at the top of the hill to you.'

'What?'

'She felt so bad the town was blaming her, she wanted to give you the land as a peace offering.'

Nancy and I looked at the shredded document and then at each other in stunned silence.

'But why didn't she just respond to our offer?' Nancy said. 'That was months ago.'

'She told me that when she was opening the package, your bas-relief fell on the floor and broke. She was so embarrassed, she didn't know how to tell you.'

'Oh, that's crazy,' Nancy said. 'I probably could have fixed it, or made her a new one. I wish she would have said something.'

'I think she wanted to surprise you,' Marco Mucchi said, looking mournfully at the ripped pages. 'This was going to be your wedding present.'

32. IL RACCOLTO

The only thing worse than feeling bad is feeling bad on a day when everybody else is feeling so damn good. And the source of such universal good cheer was the time of year known as *il raccolto*, the harvest.

By late October the grapes and olives had ripened. From all over the area, vineyards and olive groves were reverberating with the collective joy of gathering in the land's bounty. It was the time of year when one could safely say that the only places on earth where Communism was still practised were North Korea, Cuba and this little corner of Tuscany. Friends, neighbours, in-laws, passing acquaintances and occasionally even a pair of *stranieri*, all pulled together to help bring in the harvest.

We had spent the past few days recoiling from the fiasco we had created with the Pingatores. Nancy and I moved around the house like a pair of ghosts, as if dazed by the hurt we had caused. Even the sight of Pepe frolicking in the heather or eating one of my brand-new Nike running shoes failed to cheer us.

The weather outside matched our mood. The all-powerful sun had faded into a pale white ball that was constantly obscured by grey skies until it looked like just another feature of the landscape. Cold, wet winds howled through hairline cracks in the walls, as people packed up the citrus-coloured linens of summer and donned thick wools and heavy cottons in sombre shades of navy and brown.

I think no country on earth benefits from the sunshine more than Italy. When it's overcast and dreary, the grey seems to accentuate how everything is slightly threadbare and the villages have an almost shabby, Eastern European feel. But when the sun shines, the ordinary becomes remarkable and the remarkable becomes transcendent.

We might have stayed in this wintry funk forever if the ham-sized fist of Gigi hadn't pounded on our door one morning, rousing us out of our malaise. What were we doing lying around the house? he demanded. Hadn't we seen the gathering storm clouds? We needed to harvest our olives right now before it started to pour. A hard, cold rain like this could decimate our crop.

We had been so preoccupied with construction problems and the internecine warfare with the Pingatores that we had neglected to notice that our olives had, in the last week or so, grown much fatter. Had we been more attentive, we would have seen how the hard, dark-green berries had morphed through a hundred shades of purple as they swelled into jellybean-shaped pods so saturated, they were almost sweating oil.

There was no time to waste, Gigi proclaimed, pointing to a swirl of leaves caught in the jaws of a cold wind, a sure augury of a big storm. We craned our necks to look around his shoulders and saw a flatbed truck jammed with many familiar faces. Climbing out of the truck were Va Bene and Problema, cousins Spartaco and Faustino, Signora Cipollini and Annamaria, along with a collection of grandmothers, wives, children, chickens and dogs. They had been going from house to house harvesting, and we were next.

We threw on our grubbiest jeans, grabbed some gloves, and reported for duty, only to be scolded for not having put up our nets. We were supposed to have hung sheets of netting, as fine as cheesecloth, between our trees by securing them to the trunks so that they didn't touch the ground but gently sagged like a safety net under a trapeze artist.

Our netting should have been hung days ago, and here we were clearly negligent. Cousin Faustino reminded us that he had kept offering to do it for us, but we never got back to him. Nancy and I looked at each other sheepishly. We remembered him explaining that the nets needed to be in place early because, as the olives ripened, they became so heavy that gravity began the harvest far ahead of the first human hand.

Nancy and I were now ready to make up for lost time and pick olives, but the first thing we had to learn was that olives are not picked. The actual harvesting is done by shaking and beating on the trees. Nothing subtle or romantic about it, the big guys shake the trunk while the others stand on ladders and beat on the branches with bamboo sticks until the olives come raining down. This is a method that's remained essentially unchanged in over two thousand years, and back then it was probably the best show in town when they couldn't find a martyr to burn or an adulterer to stone.

The only concession to modernity was Va Bene kicking on his gas-powered leaf blower to separate the leaves and twigs that got mixed in with the olives. That done, the olives were gathered up and gently poured into baskets with a loose enough weave to allow them to breath. Everybody exercised great care not to let a single olive touch the ground, or it would be declared damaged and be quickly discarded before it could spoil the whole batch.

Like everyone else we didn't have enough to process individually at the *frantoio* (olive mill), but by combining our crop with our neighbours', we would all come away with more than enough oil to last until the next harvest.

The truck was loaded, everybody hopped on board, and we chugged away like something out of *The Grapes of Wrath*, itinerant farm workers bouncing down a bumpy road in a junky old truck. Any minute I feared we might break into a Woody Guthrie song. But it was not all merriment. The black clouds churning on the horizon gave a real urgency to our mission. If a big storm washed out the roads, we wouldn't be able to get to the mill. This delay could be fatal, because olives start to ferment the moment they're picked, and that would ruin the flavour.

Thunder boomed and lightning hissed across the sky. Those of us bouncing around in the back of the truck covered our heads with everything from newspapers to burlap sacks. Va Bene gave us a little horseshoe of a smile as he flipped up the hood of his sweatshirt, while Problema blew on his hands and cursed. Annamaria fished out a crucifix from under the five sweaters she was wearing and Mrs Cipollini threw on a raincoat that looked like something she had made out of a shower curtain.

On both sides of the road lay sombre evidence that everything of value had been harvested. Fields of earth glistened where ploughs had freshly turned dirt so it could breathe over the winter. Vineyards were plucked clean and cornfields were levelled bare, but nothing was more desolate than the sunflowers.

The Italians call them *girasole*, which means 'turns to the sun'. In summer they burst into an eye-blinding yellow so brilliant that the very sun they turn to must burn with envy. But in the fall the seeds are gathered, leaving the dead sunflowers standing parched brown, their heads eerily bowed in the same direction like an army of mendicant monks.

Our truck lurched up a steep mountain road. Nancy and I had to hold on tight to keep from flying out. The flatbed was so overloaded and top heavy, it felt as if we were on a boat threatening to capsize at every turn. Fast cars whipped around us, blasting horns and shaking fists as we cheered their bravado. We were laughing and squinting at the raindrops that were slanting sideways into our faces. It was scary and crazy and exhilarating beyond description.

We finally came to a narrow mud-and-gravel driveway that was overgrown with foliage to the point where we could have lived in Cambione in Collina for the rest of our lives and never have found it. We turned onto that road and the rain stopped pelting us, thanks to an arch of overhanging branches and leaves that formed a lush green tunnel dense enough to compel a driver to use his headlights on even the sunniest of days. This canopy began to thin as we approached a two-storey stucco villa that was painted a soft reddish pink. Our truck rolled to a stop under one of the low-hanging eaves and we climbed out, to be greeted by Roberto and Roberta, the owners of the *frantoio*.

Roberta was a tall, willowy woman with otter-black hair and the sheeny brown skin common to generations of Tuscan farmworkers. But Roberto was short and thick with red hair, milk-white skin, and eyes as blue as delft, living testament to somebody's great-great-great-grandmother being paid a nocturnal visit by a raiding party of Vikings.

As Roberto and Roberta greeted us, we could see how exhausted they were. During harvest time the *frantoio* operated twenty-four hours a day, and as we hauled our baskets out of the truck, there were quite a few growers ahead of us waiting to have their olives weighed. Most of them had sought shelter under the tin roof of a patio whose main attraction was a *forno* that was churning out a constant stream of baked bread.

Eventually our load was inspected and the bad or bruised olives were discarded. The rest were spread out and hosed down, then fed into a machine that looked as if it were hammered together from three other machines. This contraption fed the olives onto a conveyor belt that deposited them into a stone vat, where they were crushed by a large granite wheel that looked like a whetstone. This ancient wheel moved in a slow, steady circle, squashing the olives as well as their pits, for the Tuscans believe that the crushed pits act as a natural preservative.

The wheel smashed everything into a greenish-black paste that looked like a mixture of bread mould and beach tar. This paste was then spread out on circular wicker mats stacked one on top of the other to the height of about twenty feet. The tower of mats was hydraulically compressed and the raw oil started to flow. This is where the term 'cold press' comes from, and it can legally be used when the oil has been extracted using no heat or chemical interaction.

As far as the terms 'virgin' and 'extra virgin' go, there are strict definitions based on things like acidity levels and organoleptic properties, which gets pretty complicated. A simpler way to understand it is that when the oil is made from the very first pressing it can be called 'extra virgin'. The remaining pulp is then spun to separate out all the water, and the oil that's made from that second pressing is designated to be 'virgin'.

Incidentally, I have no idea why they use such religious and sexually loaded words to describe what is essentially cooking oil and salad dressing, other than to remind you that we're dealing with a people who are obsessed to the point of dementia about whatever they put in their mouths.

But I was curious, so I asked the group how these terms came into usage, and they replied as if in one voice. Olive oil is the essence of Italy, and like the Madonna herself, it is both pure and life bearing.

We raised glasses of beet-red Chianti and drank to that, as Roberta took a rack of freshly baked bread out of the *forno*. The rain was falling in earnest now, making a steady drumroll on the tin roof. Potholes overflowed and pathways became fast-moving streams. The leathery aroma of wet leaves and the scent of burning olive branches combined with the smell of the garlic cloves that Gigi was cracking open with his fingers.

We rubbed chunks of raw garlic on the hot, rough bread just as Roberto appeared with a clear glass bottleful of our oil. He held it up and we cheered. It was golden green, like congealed sunlight shining through a rain forest, and although Nancy and I were greatly impressed, people who knew far more about it than we reminded us that colour alone was not necessarily an indication of quality.

The only indication of quality was the taste, and as we drizzled our oil over the garlic-scented bread, we knew we had something special. It was sharp and fruity and peppery, and in an instant, it brought to mind how olive oil has been lubricating life for six thousand years around the Mediterranean. It has anointed the heads of kings, massaged the bodies of noble Romans, and is referred to copiously throughout the Testaments both Old and New, as well as the Koran.

We drank to that, toasting '*Al olio nuovo e vino vecchio.*' 'To new oil and old wine', and as is so often the case in Italy, what started out as serious business turned into a party. Food appeared, thanks to Roberto and Roberta's daughters, who were an eye-catching combination of walnut skin and ginger-coloured hair.

We ate and swapped stories well into the night. And as pleasing as this *festa piccola* was, it was only a prelude to the *festa grande* that was to follow.

33. CAVALLOMANIA

It rained for most of the following day and night. Nancy and I passed the time in front of our fireplace. I read a book I had been waiting for a day like this to read, while she petted Pepe, who was curled up on her lap making contented little goat noises. Despite the serenity of the scene, the problems we had stirred up with the Pingatores weighed on us. We needed to heal this rift, and although we didn't realise it at the time, that opportunity would come much sooner than we were expecting.

The following day, the rain stopped. The clouds rolled away and exposed a cornflower-blue sky and a dazzling sun. A magnificent double rainbow appeared, arcing over Cambione as if to herald the beginning of the Festa di Raccolto, Festival of the Harvest.

It was the biggest event of the season, and every street in the village was lined with multicoloured tents and stalls that suddenly popped up out of nowhere like a fairy ring of toadstools after a spring rain. There were food vendors, fortune-tellers, puppet shows, portrait painters, mimes, drummers, acrobats and flag twirlers in brilliant medieval garb. Rows and rows of kiosks selling costume jewellery, carved African masks, farm implements, bras, panties, scarves, neckties, bootleg DVDs, home-bottled bee honey . . . and a whole world of soaps, lotions and candles made from it. Huge throngs of milling people, bands playing different songs at the same time and packs of children laughing as they chased each other through the cross eddies of the crowd. Dogs barking, babies crying, lovers kissing. Just the kind of organised chaos the Italians love.

As soon as we left the *rustico* for the ten-minute walk into the village, we caught the scent of a thousand odours twisting and braiding together. Smoked *porchetta* still on the pig, aged pecorino cheese, cotton candy, exhaust fumes, backed-up Porta Pottis, night-blooming jasmine swollen to grotesque proportions by the rain and, above it all, the heady whiff of a hundred sweaty horses.

These horses, or *cavalli*, were here to take part in the centrepiece of the festival, a sublime piece of madness known as Cavallomania. A rodeo. That's right, a good, old-fashioned, down-home, Wild West rodeo smack dab in the middle of Tuscany.

When I first spotted people in Levi's, cowboy boots and ten-gallon hats, I thought that they might be from the area known as La Maremma in the southern part of Tuscany. This is Italy's beef-producing region, and although I had never seen it, I had no reason to believe that there weren't vast stretches of open grazing land covered with huge herds of cattle. But as I discovered, the concept of wide-open spaces is uniquely American. La Maremma is small. Grazing land is parcelled into lots no bigger than a suburban backyard, and a herd is often no more than a small cluster of highly prized cows.

What Cavallomania represented was a homage to a way of life as American as apple pan dowdy. These urbano cowboys were a product of our cultural juggernaut. Years of watching John Wayne and Gene Autry had not only spawned the spaghetti western, but also a thriving subculture of bronco busters from Bologna, saddle tramps from Siena, and cowpokes from Cortona. Maybe it is all one world after all, we mused as a rodeo rider trotted past us, dug his spurs into his horse, and cried out, '*Vai*, Bessie, Geeddy-yup!'

Interestingly, their spin on the rodeo comes out far more humane than ours. For starters there are no quick-draw contests, nor even a single cowboy walking around with a six-shooter strapped to his hip. No signs of weapons at all. Their treatment of their animals is also gentler. Thanks to the efforts of the Green party, such events as calf riding or steer roping are not practised.

In their place are barrel racing, rope twirling and a type of roundup where the cowboy and his horse execute balletlike manoeuvres in order to separate a specifically marked steer from the rest of the herd by nudging it along. They have so Italianised the rodeo, I can only assume that at the end of the day they all sit around the chuck wagon eating *pasta e fagioli* instead of chilli and beans.

Dolly Parton was warbling at us through a tinny loudspeaker as we wandered around the roping pen. We caught sight of Marco Mucchi, and instead of his usual banker's garb, he was wearing blue jeans with a big Mexican silver buckle, a white Stetson, and a gaudy Sons of the Pioneers shirt.

'Howdy, pardner,' I said, as if we were meeting on the streets of Tombstone.

He gave us back a howdy and touched the brim of his cowboy hat in Nancy's direction. We told him that we hadn't realised he was such an aficionado of the Old West, and he confessed that he really wasn't but that he had gotten interested when his daughter developed a love for horses. He pointed to a beautiful little ten-year-old girl mounted on a speckled pony. Marco swelled with pride as we watched her trot around the corral. The little girl had straight black hair pulled back into a ponytail, and her cheeks were peach coloured as if somebody had tinted a sepia portrait of her.

'*Che faccia bella*,' Nancy said, which is the expression one always gives a parent. It means 'What a beautiful face', and in this case it actually happened to be true.

While his older daughter continued to lead her pony through his paces, we moseyed over to where Marco's wife was standing with their younger daughter. We greeted them, and when Nancy smiled at the younger daughter, and told her that she, too, had *una faccia bella*, the little girl turned shy and disappeared into the folds of her mother's coat.

Just then, Vesuvia Pingatore appeared. She was carrying some cotton candy that she had just brought for the little girls, and when she approached, we were all equally startled by the presence of the other. There was a long, deadly silence that threatened to stretch on forever, until Nancy started talking.

She spoke quietly, yet directly to Vesuvia, telling her that we had never intended to create bad feelings between us. Vesuvia turned away, but Nancy would not let her disengage, reassuring her that no newspaper article would ever be written about them, and how sorry we were to have brought up such an unpleasant memory.

To our surprise Vesuvia responded, saying that she was also sorry she had made such a fuss when we first moved in, but the sight of their former land being devastated to make way for our road upset her. Nancy apologised for the inconvenience, but kept gently prodding until Vesuvia was forced to admit that what we had done with the *rustico* not only honoured the tradition of the stone, but also beautified the neighbourhood.

Then, reaching out and touching Vesuvia's arm, Nancy told her how much we wanted to get along with both her and her brother. We'd be having a big party soon, where we were going to renew our wedding vows, and not only did we want to invite them, but Nancy would be honoured if Vesuvia would agree to be one of her bridesmaids.

Vesuvia was flustered. She couldn't believe that Nancy would want her, but Nancy persevered until Vesuvia's hard crust cracked. Angry eyes that so recently had fired *malocchi* in our direction softened and filled with tears. Nancy's eyes welled up and the two hugged. I closed my eyes and felt tears sparkling under my lids. I joined their embrace, as did Marco, his wife, and their daughter, turning it into one large, sobbing group hug.

We were all talking at once. Apologies and regrets were flowing back and forth as we smoothed over a litany of hurt feelings. But being Italians, we were doing it at a volume and with such conviction that it looked as if we also might be at each other's throats. And that's exactly the impression Mario Pingatore got when he rounded the corner and spotted what looked like Nancy and me ganging up on his sister.

He came rushing over, jumped in front of Vesuvia, and tried to shield her from us. She pushed him away and screamed at him for being such an idiot. He yelled back that he was just trying to protect her as Nancy and I hollered that there was nothing to protect her from. Misunderstandings ascended, and when the shrieking reached the level where it started to frighten the horses, Marco stepped in. Like the sheriff of Dodge trying to break up a saloon fight, he separated the combatants and then calmly reviewed who had said what to whom. After a few sheepish apologies we all shook hands. And when that didn't feel fulfilling enough, we all reconnected into another group hug, this one prominently folding Mario into the mix. In the midst of all this serendipity I felt something strange around my ankle, and when I looked down I saw that, as a perfect complement to all the love in the air, Horn Dog was humping my leg.

34. LO SCIOPERO

No sooner had the last tent been folded and the last shovelful of horse manure dispatched than Nancy and I began the preparations for our remarriage. Even though it had been my idea, I was growing increasingly dubious, remembering my conviction that people avoided divorce not so much because of the alimony, but to keep them from ever having to endure another wedding ceremony.

That said, we went about planning the affair with the understanding that we were older and wiser now than at the time of our original wedding, so this one shouldn't degenerate into a bout of name calling and death threats. And it probably wouldn't have if we had been living in any place but Italy, where everything is run by the Italians.

The longer you live here, the more you fall in step with the idea that everything has a season. Not to get too biblical about it, but in the course of a year, you discover that there is a time to eat figs and a time to dig up porcini mushrooms. A time for the birth of your livestock and a time to visit the graves of your dead relatives. There is a season for hunting, a season for the opera, and a season to go on strike.

The word for strike is *sciopero* (she-OP-per-oh), and it's an important word to know for when you come to Italy and can't understand why something you vitally need is not open, running or serving. In times past Italian labour unions were fond of throwing a *sciopero* in the middle of tourist season, thereby paralysing the railroad system, the bus lines, and all the hotel chains without a moment's warning. Though these still go on, they are short, some lasting only a few hours, for the unions have learned that if they drive the tourists away, they'll be no need to go on strike because the whole country will be out of work.

In the fall, when the rest of the world leaves them alone, the Italians get down to the nasty business of going on strike in earnest. Aside from the basic human need to be paid more for working less, Italian labourers have been known to walk out because the walls were painted an irritating colour, they were being told what to do by someone who came from farther down the boot than they, or management had begun to insidiously brew the espresso with fewer beans.

Our own espresso beans had scarcely started to brew early on the morning of our second wedding when the phone rang. It was Nancy's mom calling from the Rome airport. She and Aunt Rose had just flown in from London, where they had started their trip, only to discover that the flight that was to shuttle them to Pisa had been cancelled by a strike. Moreover, no trains were running because the rail lines had already been on strike for three days.

This threw us into an immediate panic. One of us had to jump in the car and drive to Rome if there was any chance of getting back in time. We decided that Nancy would stay to make the house ready and await the arrival of the food, the flowers and the wine, while I threw my pants on and drove like a maniac down to Fiumicino Airport.

One of the first things you learn in Italy is that, although all roads lead to Rome, there are only two that matter. The major artery is the A1, which you pick up just west of Florence. You turn south and it's a straight shot all the way into the Eternal City. That, of course, was my plan, until I tried to get onto the autostrada that morning and found a line of cars backed up at the on-ramp.

A quick survey of my fellow drivers revealed the problem was an impromptu strike called by the toll collectors. No one knew how long it would last, so those without mothers-in-law stranded at the airports bided their time.

I peeled out of line and hauled ass towards the other route, the

Viale Mare. This is a lovely highway that runs from Pisa down the coast to a point west of Rome where the airport actually sits. The advantage here is that you don't have to go through or around Rome. The disadvantage is that it's slower and, on a pleasant Sunday morning like this, more apt to be clogged with pokey sedans full of families on their way to Mamma's for lunch.

I phoned Nancy to apprise her of my progress and she updated me on hers. The wine had arrived without incident, but Salvatore from Trattoria Toscana had called, and because of a trucker's strike, they had not received enough eggplant to make the *lasagna alla melanzana*. Would we be OK if he substituted a *fricand' di cavolfiore e guanciale*? I told her that would be fine because if I mentioned that I didn't know what the hell that was, she would have started to recite the recipe, and that's all I needed to listen to while I was stuck behind an enormous truck carrying such a wide load, it was labelled Trasporto Eccezionale.

I asked her if she had heard from my sister, and Nancy said that they had called from Genoa. My sister and her husband had flown in earlier in the week and spent a few days unwinding at Lake Como. Then they rented a car with the idea of driving down to us. But no one could have anticipated the toll collector's strike, and who knew how long that would go on? I told Nancy I'd call back when I picked up Mom, and not to worry because everything would work out. I then hung up and tried to convince myself of that as well.

Instead of dwelling over what would happen if I gave the truck ahead of me a NASCAR tap and tried to whip around it, I focused on relaxing the muscles behind my eyes. I took some deep inhalations to let my brain chemistry settle down as I sat back to enjoy the most beautiful part of the trip, even though that damn truck was blocking the best part of my view.

Sooner or later we'd get to a passing lane, but for now I let the hum of the car and gentle undulation of the highway calm me as the road curved around the ancient port city of Cecina. For the next hundred kilometres or so the highway presented a sublime diorama of the sea on one side and the mountains on the other. Fairy tale hill towns fought for my attention with the mist-shrouded loneliness of the island of Capraia. It was a rugged landscape, but not as savage as the Amalfi Coast, or even Big Sur. In fact, the assorted palm trees and orange groves I passed made me feel like I was tooling down the Pacific Coast Highway near Malibu. And in an odd twist of synchronicity, I passed a town, and I am not making this up, called La California.

I smiled at how different La California was from L.A., California. And that made me think about all the ways living in Italy had changed me. I hadn't been to a movie in seven months, but I'd seen five operas. I'd been well trained by an army of waiters never to sprinkle parmigiano cheese on pasta with seafood in it, and not to even think about getting a cup of coffee until after a meal had been eaten. I had discovered that there was life after the Dodgers because I'd started to follow our local soccer team, tooting my horn at every fellow *tifoso* (sports fan) I passed when we won, and sulking around the house, unable to speak, when we lost. Moreover, I'd begun to relish how everything closes down for three hours in the middle of the day so there's always time to eat lunch, drink wine and make love. When I first arrived, I thought the Italians were crazy, but now I know that they're sane – it's the rest of the world that's gone mad.

Something had happened to my body clock. It ran slower in Italy, for what was the point of rushing through life when all the Italians around you are busy enjoying the moment? There was less urgency to everything I did. I was more tranquil. Composed. Even serene.

'Va *fan culo*!' I screamed at the truck in front of me that had apparently decided to occupy both his lane and the passing lane at the same time.

Yes, I was more serene, except when I was driving, which I guess made me a genuine Italian.

By the time I pulled up in our driveway, our guests had started to arrive. Italians like to come early and stay late, so a social gathering tends to become a marathonlike test of a host's endurance. And this one promised to be quite an ordeal, judging by how frazzled Nancy looked as she came running out of the house to greet us.

'People started arriving as soon as you left,' Nancy hollered in my direction as she rushed over to hug her mom.

'Oh, my God, the house is magnificent,' her mom said. 'I'm so proud of you, honey.'

'Thanks, Ma, but this wedding is turning into a real disaster. Dino and Flavia invited even more cousins than I knew they had,' Nancy said, as she moved over to hug her aunt Rose. 'The flowers haven't arrived, I haven't even had a chance to change yet, and the wine sucks!'

'The flowers haven't arrived?' I said.

'You did a helluva remodelling job here, kiddo,' Aunt Rose said. 'It looks absolutely wonderful.'

'Unfortunately, Rose, so do you,' I said, out of breath from lugging their suitcases out of the car.

'Since when is that a problem?' Rose asked as we entered the *rustico*.

'Only when we've told everybody that you're my mom and that you've crawled out of your deathbed to be here,' Nancy said to her aunt.

It was true. Even though both women were in their seventies, Betty and Rose looked terrific. Despite a little bit of a hearing loss, Rose was a vibrant, cheerful woman with elegant silver hair. And Betty was slim and fashionable, like an older version of Nancy with a New Jersey accent.

'I don't know what to say,' Aunt Rose chirped. 'Tell everybody I'm so revitalised by just being here, I've come back to life.'

'Oh, la mamma has arrived!' Dino announced entering the kitchen in an ebullient mood.

'Mamma, this is our friend Dino,' Nancy said.

'*Piacere*, Mamma,' Dino said, swallowing Aunt Rose up in a hug.

'Pleased to meet you, Dino,' Aunt Rose said in a subdued tone of voice. 'My daughter has told me so much about you, but she never mentioned how *molto bello* you were.'

As Dino beamed, Nancy and I smiled at how clever we had been to pick an Italian to play an Italian.

'Thank you so much, dear lady. And how are you feeling?' he said with the voice one uses for the dying.

'I have good days and bad,' Aunt Rose said throwing in a little wheeze.

'And this is my aunt Rose,' Nancy said indicating her mother.

'*Benvenuta*,' Dino said, giving Nancy's mom a hug. 'I don't know why it is, but Nancy looks more like her aunt than her mamma.'

'Anybody hungry?' I said to change the subject.

'I'd kill for a glass of wine,' Aunt Rose said. Then, realising, 'My doctor thinks it's good for my blood.'

'I don't think this wine is good for anything,' Nancy said, picking up the bottle and making a face.

Dino looked at the bottle. 'Did you buy it from Enrico?'

'It tasted great at his store,' Nancy said. 'Think he switched on us?'

'Did he offer you anything to eat?' Dino said.

'Matter of fact, he did put out some snacks,' I recalled.

'Like what?' Dino asked.

'Sausages.'

'And what was in those sausages?' Dino said.

'Uh . . . meat?' I said.

'*Finocchio*?' Dino suggested.

'Yeah,' Nancy said turning to me. 'Remember how delicious that taste of fennel was?'

'Oldest trick in the book,' Dino said, shaking his head. 'Wine seller gives you a mouthful of *finocchio* and the next sip of wine you drink tastes fantastic.'

'*Che ladro*!' Nancy exclaimed. What a crook!

'Don't worry,' Dino said. 'I talk to him tomorrow and get you a full refund. Meantime, I send Cousin Turrido over to my house to bring over some good wine.'

Other guests started drifting into the kitchen. Avvocato Bonetti entered with a clock he had purchased at a discount from the shop next to his office, and when he put it on the table with the rest of our wedding gifts, it started chiming through its gift wrapping. Signor Tito Tughi caught my eye and took me aside to slip me an envelope as if this were the wedding scene out of *The Godfather*. But instead of containing a wad of blood money, it was the paperwork showing that the insurance company had sent him a cheque so the repair of our damaged car could begin. I thanked him, secretly wondering if he thought that he was going to get away with this being our present. Annamaria came in from outside, carrying Pepe and praising Santa Fabiola that the little guy was doing so well in our care. And Vagabondo strolled by to see if either of these American ladies was wealthy enough to afford a young Italian lover.

I peeled away and got on the phone to try and find out what had happened to our flowers. The florist shop was closed, but after some calling around, I was able to track down the owner. There had been a communication breakdown and it was my fault. When I placed the order I had meant to tell him *mandare fiori*, 'to deliver the flowers'. But because the words are so close, I mistakenly said *mandare fuori*, which means 'to put them outside'. Which is exactly what he did, so all our bouquets and floral arrangements were currently sitting on the sidewalk outside his shop.

'I got to go pick up our flowers,' I said to Nancy, grabbing my car keys and explaining on the run.

She followed me outside, begging me to calm down and drive carefully. We didn't need another accident today.

'You're right.' I slid behind the wheel and started the car in one motion. 'It'll be OK. Everything'll be just fine.'

I started to back out just as an ancient Lancia came chugging up our driveway, trailing a thick plume of exhaust. Through the dense blue smoke I was able to recognise the occupants as the lady and her daughter from the Alimentari Brutti.

'Tell them to park down the hill,' I called out to Nancy.

'Actually . . . they're delivering something,' Nancy said, biting her lip.

'Aw, no.'

'I couldn't help it. They dropped by when I was on the phone with Trattoria Toscana. She heard I was having trouble getting *lasagna alla melanzana*, so she said she they had tons of it.'

'Of course they do, it's been sitting in their store since 1974.'

'I know.' Nancy smiled and waved to the two ladies, who were approaching us with foil-covered chaffing dishes. 'What can we do about it?'

'Just tell everybody to have a good time but don't drink the wine or eat the food.'

I roared into town like I was holding pole position at the Daytona 500, screeching to a stop in front of the florist shop. To my relief no one had stolen our flowers, nor had any dogs irrigated them in the course of their morning ablutions. I gathered up our bouquets, corsages, boutonnieres, and assorted nosegays and tossed them in the backseat. I jumped back in the car, put her in gear, and popped the clutch. But the car died and when I tried to restart it, all I got was the sickening whine of the starter. I glanced at the dashboard and realised I had driven to Rome and back without ever checking the gas gauge. Empty.

I screamed enough obscenities to wilt the amaryllis in the backseat, pounding on the steering wheel with my fist until I almost broke it. Then I remembered having passed a gas station up the street and being surprised that somebody was there on a Sunday. Sunday is the worst day to gas up because almost all the filling stations are closed, leaving you with two choices: either try to deal with intricacies of an Italian self-service pump, or get on the autostrada and stop at one of the Autogrills.

I jumped out of the car and started sprinting towards the service station, praying that they'd have a gas can they'd let me use. If worse came to worst, I could always buy one. How much could they want for it? A couple of euros at the most. Maybe five tops.

But wait a minute . . . when they saw how bad I needed it they'd raise the price. Ten euros . . . no, twenty, that's what they'll want! Those greedy bastards, I fumed as I staggered into the gas station, ready to tell them what they could do with their damn can.

'Of course we have a can for you to borrow,' the mechanic told me. 'But we have no *benzina*.'

He had just come in to the station to work on his own car today because, thanks to the truckers' latest *sciopero*, they had not received their delivery of gas.

'How can they go on strike?' I fumed. 'What about the public safety?'

'*Ha ragione*,' he said, telling me that I was right. Then he explained that technically they don't go on strike but rather they call a big meeting to discuss going on strike, which has the same effect.

That was it! I was going on strike myself. I was going to lie down in the middle of the street and not move a muscle until I was either run over or this whole goddamn country came to its senses! And that's what I was thinking as I ran back to the car, scooped up all our stinking flowers, and started to jog home. Sweat was flying off my face and petals were flying off our flowers as I zigzagged my way through the line of cars that were creeping through the Piazza Maggiore. One car in particular started honking at me, and since I didn't have a free hand to give them the gesture the Italians call 'the fig', I kept running. Then I heard somebody call my name and when I looked back I recognised my sister and her husband as the ones who were honking at me.

I ran over to them, and there were hugs and kisses all around as I threw the flowers in the backseat and jumped in. By some miracle they had gotten all the way from Genoa without the use of the autostrada, and now they had to get me home in time to make my own wedding.

35. TANTI AUGURI

It was so crowded by the time we got back to the *rustico*, we had to park at the bottom of the hill. Every square inch of our property was covered with friends and neighbours, and friends and neighbours of friends and neighbours. New allegiances were formed and old animosities forgotten as our stereo boomed out a rousing tarantella and Dino's good wine flowed.

Maybe too much good wine, judging by how Cousin Aldo and Gigi got into an arm-wrestling contest that was fought to a red-faced draw. Then they laughed and started dancing with each other. Even Dino found himself in high enough spirits to tolerate Rudolfo showing up with Stefano. And while Dino was cool but cordial, Flavia was downright gracious, sitting down with Stefano and getting to know him, and delighted to learn that his family owned a fabric store in Massa that she shopped in all the time. This solved another problem, because the first thing an Italian woman worries about, with two men living together, is, who is going to do the sewing?

The mayor and his wife arrived and started circulating through the crowd. Perhaps he was still unnerved about having run into me on the way to visit his mistress, because he acted especially devoted to his wife in my presence. And since word had gotten around that I wasn't going to be revealing any dirty little secrets about the town, he didn't mention my article and I never brought it up.

More and more people kept coming. Pumping my hand and kissing me on both cheeks with repeated expressions of *tanti auguri* . . . a lot of good wishes. The *signora* from the news kiosk brought us a boxful of glossy fashion magazines; Gilberto from *la farmacia* gifted us with an elegant bottle of lemon-scented body lotion; and remember the tall, skinny *carabiniere* who was so helpful to me at the accident? The one who lost track of his machine gun? Twice? Well, wouldn't you know it . . . he left his present in his car and had to run back down the hill to get it.

I spotted cousins Spartaco and Faustino hanging out on the periphery of the party. Faustino was busying himself examining our olive trees for any reappearance of the fungus he had so efficiently exterminated, while Spartaco's attentions were focused on Pia Tughi and her shapely legs. Sadly, his gaze went unrequited because Ms 'Tughi was fully engaged in a conversation with Vagabondo.

Nancy's mom and her aunt Rose continued their masquerade of identities, greatly aided by the fact that they couldn't understand anyone, nor could anyone understand them. This language barrier, however, did not prevent them from enjoying a pantomime-augmented dialogue with Signora Cipollini over the tastiest things to do with the pope's nose, which ironically, is what both cultures call the chicken's ass.

At my request Dottore Spotto was using my camcorder to videotape the proceedings. In addition to the visuals *il dottore* provided us with a running narrative where he attached his own psychological analysis to those he photographed. Thus he informed us that Va Bene was a passive-dependent personality with poor coping skills and Problema's chronic melancholia stemmed from his plethora of self-esteem issues. And that they should both be in treatment and on medication.

Some weeks later, when Nancy and I sat down to look at the tape, we discovered that, although he had covered the main event, he had mostly left us with footage of his children, Leonardo, Rafael, and *la bimba* Artemisia. It did make us laugh, though, when he turned the camera over to his wife, Monica, so he could get in the shot, that while he was posing, Uncle Carmuzzi sneaked up from behind and put the horns on him.

I looked around for Nancy and was told that she was changing. I wanted to get cleaned up but there wasn't time. Father Fabrizio had finally arrived, with apologies for being late and a tale of woe over how poorly his new car was running, with the implication that he much regretted having given up the one we now own.

I told him that we needed to start because people were getting hungry, even if it was for the lasagna from the Alimentari Brutti. So while the priest took up his position at our makeshift pulpit, I rounded up my best man, Rudolfo, and made sure he had the rings. I then flashed a signal to Dottore Spotto's eldest son, Leonardo, to cue up the music. He clicked the remote and the sound of a pipe organ filled the air.

Taking their cue, our guests seated themselves on the rows of folding chairs with as much hushed anticipation as a crowd full of Italians can ever get. I got the high sign from Mina (from the hardware store, whom we no longer called Mean Girl) that the wedding party was ready. So I nodded to Leonardo, who flicked the CD to the next track, and the dulcet strains of the 'Wedding March' filled the air. Flash cameras popped as Marco Mucchi's younger daughter came down the aisle in a pink taffeta dress, spreading flower petals and drawing appreciative ooohs from the crowd

Next came the bridesmaids in their matching dresses. Pia Tughi, Avvocatessa Bonetti, and my sister, Debbie, looked beautiful, but Vesuvia Pingatore was absolutely radiant. As she glided down the aisle, her face was so luminous in its serenity that her brother, Mario, couldn't help but smile. My side of the wedding party then entered, consisting of my best man, Rudolfo, followed by Umberto, Marco Mucchi and my brother-in-law, Henry.

With everyone in place Leonardo clicked the remote and the music jumped to 'Here Comes the Bride'. All heads turned as Nancy started down the aisle. She was wearing a simple white linen dress that she had bought in the open-air *mercato* in Siena. Her blonde hair was sprinkled with tiny flowers, and she had made herself a veil out of a length of the white netting we had used to catch the falling olives. She looked like an angel, and I had never loved her more than I did at that moment.

She came to my side, and we turned to Father Fabrizio. He raised his hands and welcomed one and all to our ceremony. He spoke about the difficulties of keeping a marriage intact in this modern age of ours. How temptations and resentments were the potholes that threatened to break the axle of love between two people, and how much maintenance and servicing it took to keep a relationship running. It was a fine sermon, but at some point I felt as if he was referring more to his car than to our marriage.

He then told the audience that Nancy and I had prepared our own vows. And as I had prearranged with Rudolfo, I said mine in English, while he translated them for the audience.

'Hail to thee, blithe Spirit,' I said, taking both of Nancy's hands. 'That's the opening line of a poem by Percy Shelley, who knew quite a bit about what it was like to be a *straniero* living here. And like him, I came to Italy to make a new life, even though this was not my idea. If you remember, honey, I was perfectly happy in L.A. working on a show I hated, overpaid and underappreciated, coming home every night burned out, angry and exhausted.'

Rudolfo finished his translation and the audience chuckled at how only an Americano or a Milanese could live like that.

'But you kept working on me. Even though I was like the guy who sweeps up behind the elephant at the circus . . . I couldn't possibly imagine a life without the glamour of show business. We argued all the time, and I kept telling you that running off to Italy was crazy. *Pazza*! Well, it took months, and almost getting my brains splattered all over the Via Aurelia, but I finally came to see that hopelessly clinging to a way of life that was consuming me was the crazy part. It has been my lot in life to be dragged kicking and screaming into most of the really good things that have happened to me. And for that, my dear Nancy,

I give you the sole credit. And to tell you how much I love you for your bravery, your resourcefulness, and your determination. I love you for knowing me better than I knew myself . . . for loving me when I didn't even know what love was . . . and for showing me what joy there was in sometimes doing the craziest thing. Shelley was writing about a skylark, but he must have been thinking of you, when he ended that poem with:

> Teach me half the gladness
> That thy brain must know;
> Such harmonious madness
> From my lips would flow,
> The world should listen then, as I am listening now!

'Nancy, I vow to love you madly, treasure you deeply, and humbly offer you my undying devotion forever.'

Nancy stood facing me, her eyes glistening. She squeezed my hands and spoke.

'I want to express what you mean to me, but words fail me. You're the writer in the family, so if you will allow me, I'd like to show you what's in my heart.'

With that she nodded to Leonardo and he cued up another CD. The music started and Nancy lip-synced to an Italian version of 'You Light Up My Life'.

As everyone was laughing and applauding, Aunt Rose, who's a little hard of hearing, turned to Nancy's mom and said that she never knew that Nancy could sing.

'She can't,' Betty said. 'But that's never stopped her.'

36. LA LUNA DI MIELE

The party lasted all evening and well into the night. Our neighbours could scarcely complain about the noise, since they were the ones making it. Italians may never sweep all the gold medals at the Olympics or establish a permanent colony on the moon, but when it comes to having a good time, no people on earth can touch them.

Nancy and I wandered through the maze of people, clinking glasses and welcoming their congratulations and best wishes. There was so much good cheer in the air that, at least for the night, bitter grudges crumbled and new affections blossomed.

Although not approving of his lifestyle, Dino talked to Rudolfo about letting him use the house Nancy and I had once rented so the boys would have a decent place to live. After all, they were going to need to be close by, since Flavia and Stefano were seriously discussing opening a branch of his family's fabric store here in Cambione.

Pia Tughi and Vagabondo were sighted nuzzling each other before slipping out to a disco. Avvocato Bonetti's elderly mother latched on to Pepe and, after claiming that our goat was her missing Siamese cat, tried to take him home with her. Uncle Carmuzzi and Dottore Spotto took turns reciting verses of Dante from memory as they drank each other's wine and concluded that the great poet belonged to all the people of Italy.

Avvocatessa Bonetti enjoyed more than one dance in the arms of the *carabiniere* with the elusive machine gun, Cousin Spartaco tearfully confessed to Father Fabrizio about his obsession with girlie magazines, and nobody died of food poisoning from the lasagna from the Alimentari Brutti.

A tipsy Vesuvia Pingatore came up to us with a glass of wine that kept threatening to slosh on my shoes. She told us that this was the best time she had had in years, and she thanked us for inviting her. We thanked her for coming and for being in the wedding party, and she replied that she was honoured to have done it. I commented that now that we were all friends, there was no need for that high wall that she had put up. She blushed and confessed that she'd had the wall made taller because she liked to sunbathe in the nude.

I immediately took a swig of wine so as to not have that image permanently burned into my brain.

'I say, old duck.' Mario slapped me on the back. 'First-class wingding. Top drawer and all that rot.'

'Thank you,' I said. 'Glad you could come.'

'Yes, quite. But now I have to get the old girl home,' he said, helping his sister on with her wrap. 'And you two need to get rid of everybody so you can start *la luna di miele*.' He gave us a lascivious wink.

'Ah, yes, the honeymoon,' I said.

'Well, we've still got family visiting,' Nancy said. 'So after they leave, maybe we'll take a few days.'

'Splendid,' he said. Then he reached into his coat pocket. 'By the way, you're going to need this. Blasted Comune and all their bloody paperwork.'

He handed us a thick envelope. I opened it and took out two documents. Nancy read them over my shoulder, and then we both looked at Mario in astonishment.

'My sister is giving you the land at the top of the hill,' he explained. 'And I'm giving you the land at the bottom.'

'Oh, my God,' Nancy cried. 'This is so generous.'

'It almost doubles our size,' I said.

'Well, if you're going to grow olives, you need enough trees to make it worth the bloody trouble.'

'Thank you so much,' Nancy said hugging him.

'Yes, thank you both,' I said, hugging Vesuvia.

For the next few days we played tour guide, showing Nancy's

mom, Aunt Rose, and my sister and brother-in-law the glories of our little corner of Tuscany. We ushered them into secluded monasteries to see hidden masterpieces of medieval art, took them to a *trattoria* so *autentica* no tourist had ever set foot inside, and did all the haggling when they shopped at the outdoor *mercato* that's held every Friday morning in Cambione's Piazza Maggiore. At the end of the week my sister and her husband took off for France, and we dropped Nancy's mom and Aunt Rose off at Civitavecchia, where they caught a cruise ship for the Greek islands.

Alone at last, we drove up the coast, parked the car, and used the train to explore the Cinque Terra. These are five small, picture-perfect villages nestled into a series of ascending rocky coves that overlook the Gulf of Genoa. These villages are inaccessible by car, which does not prevent them from being totally overrun by tourists in the summer. But this late in the fall it was so quiet, we could almost hear the pine nuts falling out of the trees as they ripened.

We didn't do much for the first few days, preferring to lounge around in our room, gaze out at the sea and, well, do what people do on their honeymoons. Even their second ones. When we did venture out, it was to take long hikes on one of the fourteen walking trails that connect the five towns. Some of these paths are quite difficult, so we would stay on the easier ones, strolling leisurely through densely wooded forests richly permeated with the sweet decay of season melding into season for as far back as anyone can remember.

Sometimes we would stop for lunch at a cliff-side café that seemed to hang precariously over the sea. The cuisine was invariably seafood done in the Ligurian manner, plump *branzino* or shiny *orata* caught that morning and salt-roasted on a wood-burning stove. Or perhaps something more exotic, like *cozze ripiene*, stuffed mussels cooked in white wine and served in butter sauce.

It would be difficult to imagine a land where one could eat so well from just the bounty of the nearby forests, fields and sea. In addition to an amazing variety of edible mushrooms, there is oregano, sage and rosemary. Garlic and leeks, chestnuts and beets. Pine nuts for pesto sauce and an armada of fishing boats disgorging their daily yields of anchovy, mussels, squid and octopus. And it all gets washed down with a local wine called Sciacchetra, made from the Vermentino grapes that grow in the vineyards on the adjacent plains.

I have come to believe that the Italians should rule the world. Not that they'd want to. After all, they did it once, and despite their best efforts to civilise us, it still ended up in the hands of the barbarians. And then, what about the Renaissance? Just how many times do they have to show us?

I was thinking about things like this as I wandered around the village of Monterosso. Nancy was sleeping in that morning while I decided to go for a walk and explore the largest of the five towns. Monterosso is the hub of all tourist activities, but for that day at least, I seemed to be the only person around who hadn't been born there.

A grey drizzle was falling, leaving the cobblestone streets as shiny as polished glass. A group of schoolgirls in uniform rushed past me, giggling under a cluster of bright yellow umbrellas. I found myself wondering why my compulsion to be back in L.A., working in show business, had mysteriously vanished.

Where had it gone? And what had I replaced it with?

I heard somebody practising opera in a soprano voice, scales ascending out the window of her bedroom, and I felt so gloriously alive, I could sense the very blood rushing through my body. I was walking as if in a dream. I passed a *macelleria*, and through an opened door, I exchanged waves with a butcher in a bloody apron, a cigarette dangling out of his mouth as he hacked on a side of meat. I came upon a café whose frontage was bordered by fat terracotta planters bursting with riotous colours. I was particularly drawn to a patch of scandalously scarlet morning glories, and I bent over to admire how raindrops clung to the petals like silvery pearls.

These flowers were so beautiful, I thought, I should put them in our garden so it wouldn't look so desolate over the winter. I was in the midst of calculating how many flats we'd need when the supreme folly of all this struck me. I hated gardening, and here I was making plans to grovel around in the mud, planting something I couldn't even eat!

Living in Cambione had certainly changed me. The irony of it was, when you broke down the name of the town you got *cambiare*, 'to change', and *-one* (OH-nay), the suffix Italians use to say 'big'. That's right: Big Change.

I guess that I had had enough epiphanies for one morning, because I noticed that the café I was standing in front of was also an Internet spot. So I went inside, ordered an espresso, and bellied up to the computer. When my e-mails came up, I discovered that in addition to all the spam for low-interest bank loans and mail-order Viagra, there was something from my agent.

As I waited for his letter to open, I imagined that he was writing to tell me that another one of his big clients wanted to rent a villa, or needed opera tickets for La Scala, or perhaps they'd like me to meet them at the airport, holding up a little sign with their name on it like a limo driver.

His message began with congratulations on our wedding, and then, in the way of a gift, he told me that he had been showing my e-mails to some of the other agents in his office. And everybody really enjoyed them. One lady in particular got very excited and thought I had the makings of a terrific screenplay. Or even a book. She made a few calls and had gotten something lined up, and she needed to know how soon I could get back to L.A. to take some meetings.

I blew out a long, slow breath as I got up from the computer and went over to the window. I looked out at a pair of rowboats tied together at the fishing pier. One was fire-engine red and the other was painted as bright yellow as a banana. I stared at these two little boats bobbing in the grey-green water for a long moment as I wondered how I was going to tell Nancy about this.

INDEX

MEET THE DORANS
on a Dream Weekend for Two in Tuscany

Win a long weekend in beautiful Camaiore, including flights, accommodation and car hire for two people – courtesy of Virgin Books, Opodo and L'Oasi di Lombrici. Join Phil and Nancy Doran at their *piccolo rustico* for a tasting of their own 'Extra Virgin Nancy' olive oil, fine local wines and cheeses.

To enter the competition simply answer the following question:
What is the mayor's favourite pastime?

Send your answer on a postcard with your name, address and a daytime telephone number to:

THE RELUCTANT TUSCAN Holiday Competition
Marketing Department
Virgin Books
Thames Wharf Studios
Rainville Road
London, W6 9HA

Closing date for entries: 31 December 2005
See overleaf for terms and conditions

opodo.co.uk

Opodo addresses the real needs of today's traveller by offering an unbiased and competitively priced online travel service for world travel. With access to flights from nearly 500 airlines, over 45,000 hotel properties, 7,000 car hire locations, package holidays, city breaks, lifestyle holidays, ski deals, comprehensive travel insurance and value added services such as airport parking, with Opodo you really can 'Travel Your Way'.

www.opodo.co.uk

'Oasi' lies in Camaiore, a valley surrounded by the Apuan Alps and at a distance of only 8 km from the sea. The B&B encompasses two antique Frantoi (oil mills), renovated in traditional Tuscan style and surrounded by a large park with swimming pool. The owners, Roberto and Roberta, are present every day to offer their warm hospitality and to recommend places to visit and typical Tuscan dishes to try.

www.l-oasi-di-lombrici.it   E: loasidilombrici@tin.it

www.virgin.com/books

TERMS AND CONDITIONS

1. The competition is open to UK residents only, excluding employees of Virgin, Opodo, their families, agents and anyone connected with the promotion of the competition. Entrants must be aged 18 years or over and hold a valid 10-year passport.

2. Closing date for receipt of entries is 31 December 2005.

3. The first entry drawn on 9 January 2006 will be declared the winner and notified by Virgin Books. The winner will be required to confirm acceptance of the prize within 7 days of notification. If the winner does not confirm acceptance within 7 days he/she will automatically forego the rights to claim for the prize.

4. The decision of the judges is final. No correspondence will be entered into.

5. No purchase necessary. Entries restricted to one per household.

6. The prize will consist of a pair of free return economy class flight tickets from the UK to Pisa, courtesy of Opodo, three nights' accommodation at L'Oasi di Lombrici and car hire for the duration of the holiday. Not included in the prize: travel and other insurance, transfers to and from the airport, optional excursions, petrol, gratuities, food, drinks, laundry and any other items of a personal nature.

7. Flights are to depart on a Thursday, returning on the following Sunday, must be booked by 31 January 2006 and travel completed by 15th December 2006. Flights are subject to availability. Opodo reserve the right to refuse travel at peak travel times such as Easter, Christmas and school holidays. Opodo and the airline booking conditions apply. UK Air Passenger Duty and UK Departure Tax are included.

8. The winner must be one of the passengers flying. The winner may choose an accompanying travel partner and both travellers must fly on the same outbound and return flights. If the winner does not choose an accompanying travel partner, the other ticket is forfeited. No reservation changes are permitted after the ticket is issued.

9. If for any reason Opodo is unable to provide the prize, Opodo will endeavour to replace it with another prize of equal value.

10. L'Oasi di Lombrici will provide the best room available at the time of booking. The B&B is available from May – September with flats available during other months.

11. The opportunity to join Phil and Nancy Doran at their *rustico* for a tasting of their own 'Extra Virgin Nancy' olive oil and fine local wine and cheeses will be offered at their discretion, subject to their availability.

12. Car hire will be organised by Virgin Books, who will select both car hire company and vehicle type. The winner will be responsible for any costs outside the basic car hire and for ensuring the vehicle is returned on time.

13. The prize is non-transferable and non-refundable and no alternatives can be substituted.

14. Virgin Books reserves the right to amend or terminate any part of the promotion without prior notice.

15. Virgin Books cannot accept responsibility for the service provided by Opodo, the airline, L'Oasi di Lombrici and the car hire company.

16. No responsibility is accepted for fraudulent, damaged, illegible or incomplete entries. Proof of sending is not proof of receipt.

17. The winner's name will be available from the above address from 9 January 2006.

18. Winners may be required to participate in publicity events.